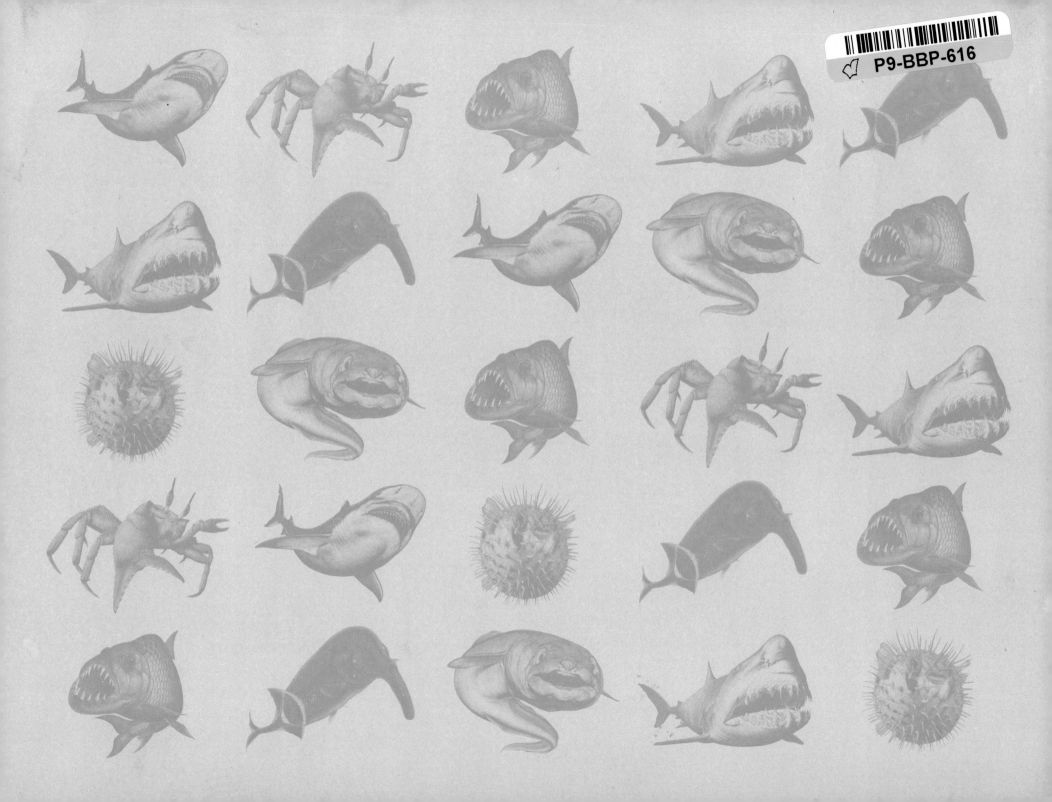

SHARKS & OTHER CREATURES OF THE DEEP

SHARKS & OTHER
CREATURES OF THE DEEP

General Editor: Susan Barraclough

Sandy Creek
NEW YORK

An Imprint of Sterling Publishing
387 Park Avenue South
New York, NY 10016

Project Editor: Sarah Uttridge
Designer: Brian Rust

ISBN: 978-0-7607-9143-1

Printed and bound in China
Manufactured 07 2012

Lot 5   7   9   10   8   6   4

Contents

Introduction

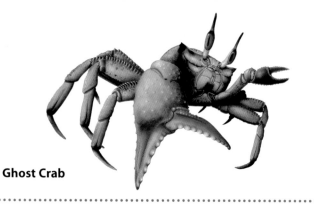

Ghost Crab

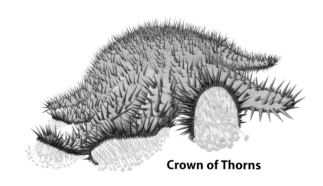

Crown of Thorns

Piranha

The seas, oceans, rivers, lakes, and other water environments of the world contain a vast variety of creatures. They come in all shapes and sizes. There are smooth-skinned, streamlined Sharks, built for speed and supple movement, or crustaceans with thick shells to shield them from attack. Other creatures grow warty hides for protection. The aptly named Crown of Thorns starfish has all-over spikes designed to keep predators away. Some sea creatures are long and slim, fat and round; some are equipped with spikes while others have suckers; and some can open their mouths to an enormous size in order to engulf their prey.

Several sea creatures provide intriguing material of the "curious facts" variety. The Saltwater Crocodile grows for as long as it lives. The Sea Snake sheds its skin by tying itself in knots and pushing through the loops, leaving the skin behind. Small cancer crabs sometimes stow

Sea Krait

Caribbean Reef Shark

Angel Shark

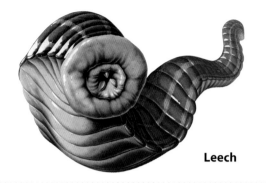

Leech

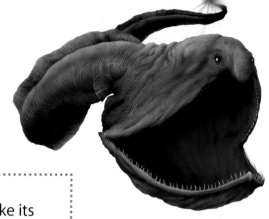

Gulper Eel

away inside Sea Nettles as a way of hitching a ride across the ocean.

Some inhabitants of the sea are beautiful while others are hideously ugly. There are few creatures prettier than the Sea Urchin, with its ornamental filigree of needles sprouting from a central core, making it resemble a brilliantly colored pin cushion. Equally, there are few more hideous than the Matamata. This odd-looking creature—whose name translates as "kill, kill"—has a piglike snout for a nose; horny, conical growths that make its back look like a mountain range in miniature; and flaps resembling stumpy feet on its underside.

But whatever their shape, size, or appearance, the denizens of the sea have one important thing in common: they all have their own methods of killing their food in order to live. For their habitat is a savage place where survival is the chief purpose of life, and the only rule is not just "kill or be killed", but "eat or be eaten."

Cone Shell

Sturgeon

Sharks

Thanks to the folklore of the sea, and, more recently, movies like Jaws, sharks have a very bad reputation as savage killers, terrorizing vacation makers.

They are not a pretty sight, with their huge mouths full of viciously sharp, often jagged teeth, which enable them to tear lumps of flesh from their victims.

Give sharks the slightest whiff of blood and they will be off at frightening speed, ready for a killing frenzy. They can pick up the slightest vibration that tells them a juicy prey is close by, and they also target their victims by means of electric sensors sited around their snouts. Some sharks adopt elaborate disguises to hide from their prey until the moment comes to strike out. The Wobbegong, for instance, has a blotchy skin and forked tassels around its mouth to make it resemble a rock encrusted with seaweed. Others, like the Tiger shark, have eyes with all-round vision for locating their prey.

Whatever method they use to catch their meals, sharks are among the most efficient as well as the most deadly hunters on Earth.

GRAY REEF SHARK

Latin name: *Carcharhinus amblyrhynchos*

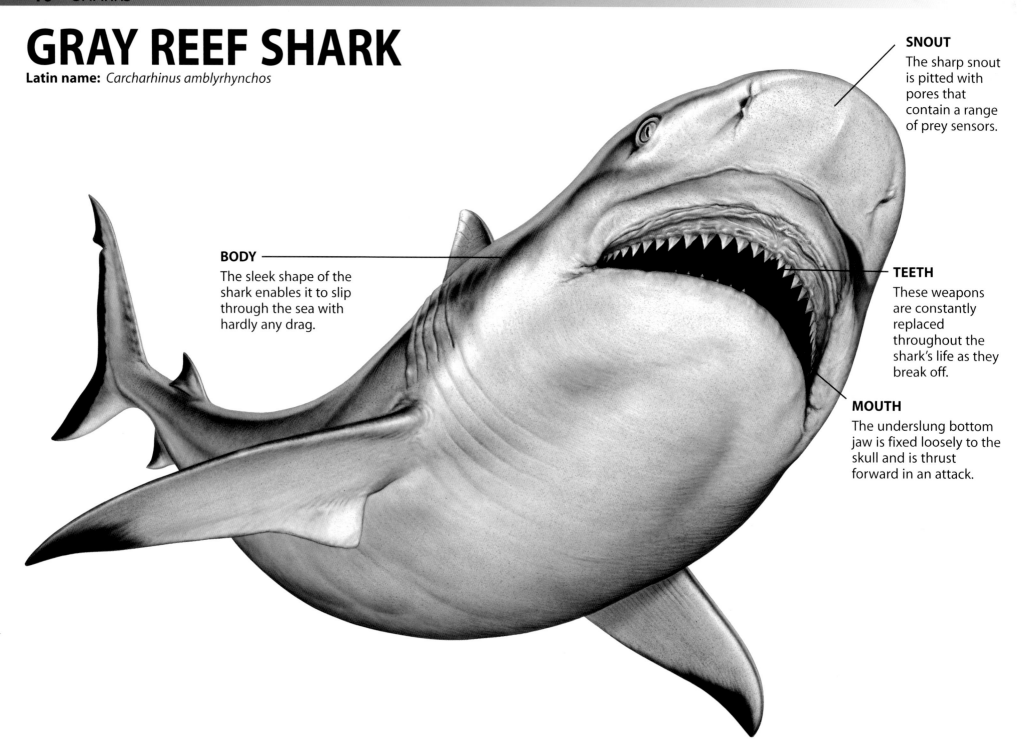

SNOUT
The sharp snout is pitted with pores that contain a range of prey sensors.

BODY
The sleek shape of the shark enables it to slip through the sea with hardly any drag.

TEETH
These weapons are constantly replaced throughout the shark's life as they break off.

MOUTH
The underslung bottom jaw is fixed loosely to the skull and is thrust forward in an attack.

ruising the waters of tropical coral reefs, the sinister shape of the gray reef shark haunts shadowy underwater cliffs and canyons, looking for prey to attack and devour. One whiff of blood and the shark goes on a killing spree. It has long, dagger-like teeth in its bottom jaw and slicing blades in the top. When it attacks, it thrusts its bottom jaw out to skewer its victim, then pushes its top jaw forward to chop out a great chunk of flesh.

Size

KEY DATA

LENGTH	Up to 8ft (2.5m)	
PREY	Mainly fish and squid; some crabs, seabirds, and carrion	
WEAPONS	Slicing and piercing teeth	The gray reef shark is one of the most common sharks in the Indian and Pacific oceans. It is found from the Red Sea in the west to Hawaii and Tahiti in the east. As it name suggests, it is most abundant around coral reefs.
ATTACK	Massive, crippling bite	
LIFESPAN	25 years or more	

1 A lurking gray reef shark watches warily as a curious diver swims toward the invisible boundary of its territory. Not knowing the shark's reputation, the diver incautiously moves in for a closer look.

2 The shark responds by arching its back, lifting its head, swinging its tail in broad sweeps, and corkscrewing through the sea toward the diver.

3 Suddenly the shark rushes at the diver and rips open his arm with its upper teeth, slicing deep into flesh and bone.

Did You Know?

● The gray reef shark's threat display is so effective that it can drive off a tiger shark, which at a length of up to 19ft 7in (6m) could kill a gray reef shark with a single bite.

● Once a year, female gray reef sharks gather in groups of ten or more individuals. A male dashes into the group, picks out a female and gives chase, repeatedly nipping her flanks. Eventually she slows down and lets him mate with her, but she is left scarred for life. A year later, she gives birth to up to six 19–24in (50–60cm) pups. They can breed after seven years, when about 4ft 5in (1.3m) long.

● A diver was once attacked and badly injured by a gray reef shark when he took its photograph and startled it with the camera flash.

● Scientists who fixed ultrasonic tracking devices to gray reef sharks discovered that they patrol an area of up to 12sq miles (30sq km) every day, visiting particular spots at regular times.

BULL SHARK

Latin name: *Carcharhinus leucas*

STREAMLINING

The body is rounded at both ends to reduce drag, enabling the shark to accelerate rapidly with the minimum of effort.

PECTORAL FINS

These act like wings, their curved forward edges creating lift, while the tail fin drives the shark forward and the dorsal (back) fin keeps it upright.

NOSTRILS

Scent plays a key role in helping the shark track prey. So, too, do a number of tiny electrical sensors around the snout.

CAMOUFLAGE

Viewed from below, the whitish belly blends into sunlit surface waters; seen from above, the dark back merges with the depths. This countershading makes it hard to spot the shark —until it's too late.

The bull shark is a supremely efficient predator, willing to attack almost any animal smaller than itself. It haunts the warm coastal waters of the world, and is the only shark known to swim up rivers as well. The bull shark targets its prey by picking up and trailing the slightest smell or vibration. Then it launches into a frighteningly fast assault of almost unbelievable ferocity.

Size

KEY DATA

LENGTH	Up to 11ft 6in (3.5m)
WEIGHT	Up to 505lb (230kg); female larger than male
PREY	Almost anything that swims, but especially large prey such as other sharks, rays, dolphins, porpoises, seals, and turtles
WEAPONS	Gaping jaws lined with rows of razor-sharp teeth
TYPICAL ATTACK	Charges victim to inflict a single, devastating bite
LIFESPAN	Probably about 14 years

The bull shark is common in the warm tropical and subtropical coastal waters of the Americas, Africa, Asia, and Australia. It rarely visits the open sea, but regularly swims up rivers, even entering large lakes.

1 A cruising bull shark detects the faint vibrations of a big animal swimming out of sight. It surges toward their source: sure enough, a sea lion comes into view.

2 The shark's open mouth hits the sea lion like a battering ram, sending it clear of the water in a spray of water and blood and killing it outright.

3 The blood flooding from the lifeless sea lion sends the shark into a frenzy. Sinking its upper teeth into the body, the killer thrashes about, using its powerful neck muscles to tear off chunks of flesh, which it gulps down whole.

Did You Know?

● The bull shark usually gives birth in estuaries, where its pups are safe from saltwater sharks. By the time the young reach the sea, they are larger and less vulnerable.

● In 1975, a crowded ferry sank in the delta of the River Ganges in India, hurling 190 people into the water. Bull sharks killed as many as 50 of them in the ensuing chaos.

● The bull shark is named after its extremely short, blunt snout, which is wider than it is long.

● Bull sharks in the River Ganges sometimes devour human corpses that have been floated down the river in Hindu funeral ceremonies.

CARIBBEAN REEF SHARK
Latin name: *Carcharhinus perezi*

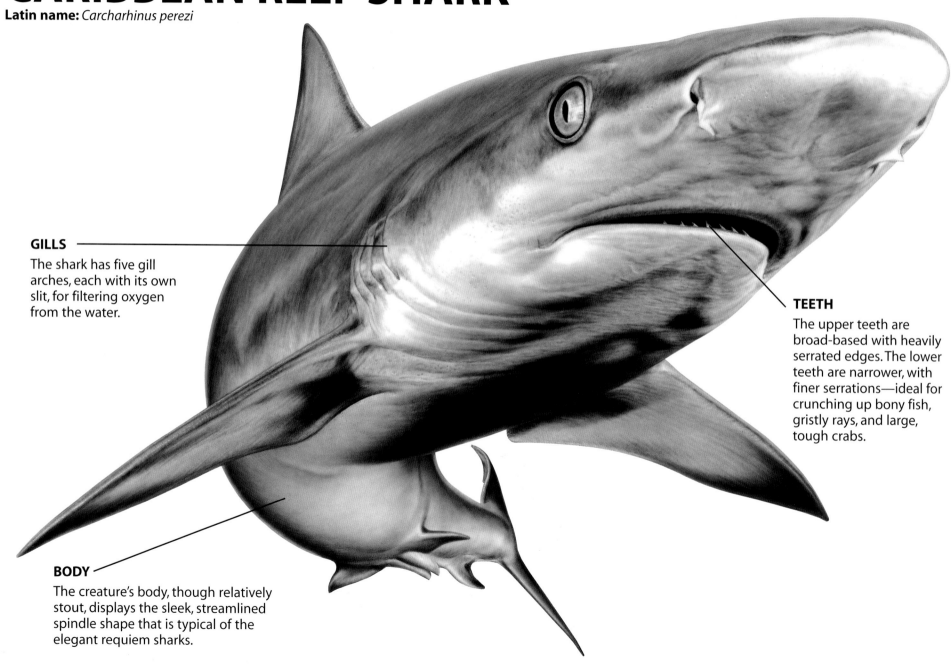

GILLS

The shark has five gill arches, each with its own slit, for filtering oxygen from the water.

TEETH

The upper teeth are broad-based with heavily serrated edges. The lower teeth are narrower, with finer serrations—ideal for crunching up bony fish, gristly rays, and large, tough crabs.

BODY

The creature's body, though relatively stout, displays the sleek, streamlined spindle shape that is typical of the elegant requiem sharks.

The majestic Caribbean reef shark may look peaceful as it glides through the colorful waters of balmy, sun-drenched coral reefs, but when it is attacking prey it is best to treat it with great respect. Like most sharks, it is often gripped by a fearsome feeding frenzy. The tourist activity of shark-feeding in the warm reef waters of the Caribbean rewards divers with an undeniable thrill. Occasionally, though, the sharks deliver "excitement" that is more dangerous than the holiday-makers hoped.

Size

KEY DATA

LENGTH	Up to 10ft (3m)
PREY	Smaller sharks and rays, bony fish, squid, large crabs
WEAPONS	Triangular, saw-edged teeth
TYPICAL ATTACK	Slashing attack on any creature that invades its personal space

The Caribbean reef shark is found in the tropical and subtropical inshore waters of the eastern American seaboard and the Bahamas, from Florida, south throughout the Caribbean, and Gulf of Mexico, as far as the coast of southern Brazil. As its name implies, it is common around reefs.

1 Out on a shark-feeding dive, a group of tourists sit calmly on the seabed, their arms folded to keep their limbs from tempting hungry sharks. The divemaster throws a canister of fish scraps on a line from his boat, and a cloud of blood stains the water. Pretty soon, numerous Caribbean reef sharks loom out of the gloom.

2 As the sharks begin to feed, one of the divers forgets the strict rules of the reef and points out a pair of sharks fighting over a piece of meat. He pays dearly for his overexcitement as a large reef shark bites at his arm, severing it raggedly at the elbow.

Did You Know?

● The Caribbean reef shark has enjoyed "bit-parts" in various James Bond movies. Some of its haunts off the Bahamas today include sunken, coral-encrusted movie sets from *Thunderball* (1965) and *Never Say Never Again* (1983)—although in this last film Bond really struggled with a tiger shark (*Galeocerdo cuvier*).

● Shark-dive tour operators in the Bahamas estimate that each Caribbean reef shark is worth up to US$100,000 in tourist revenue.

● Despite strict controls issued by the US Fish and Wildlife Service, the Caribbean reef shark is hunted for its meat, liver oil, and hide. It is also ground up for fishmeal.

● Unlike many sharks, which assist their breathing by swimming, thereby forcing water into the mouth and over the gills, the Caribbean reef shark can happily breathe while motionless, and is often found dozing in caves.

SAND TIGER SHARK
Latin name: *Carcharias taurus*

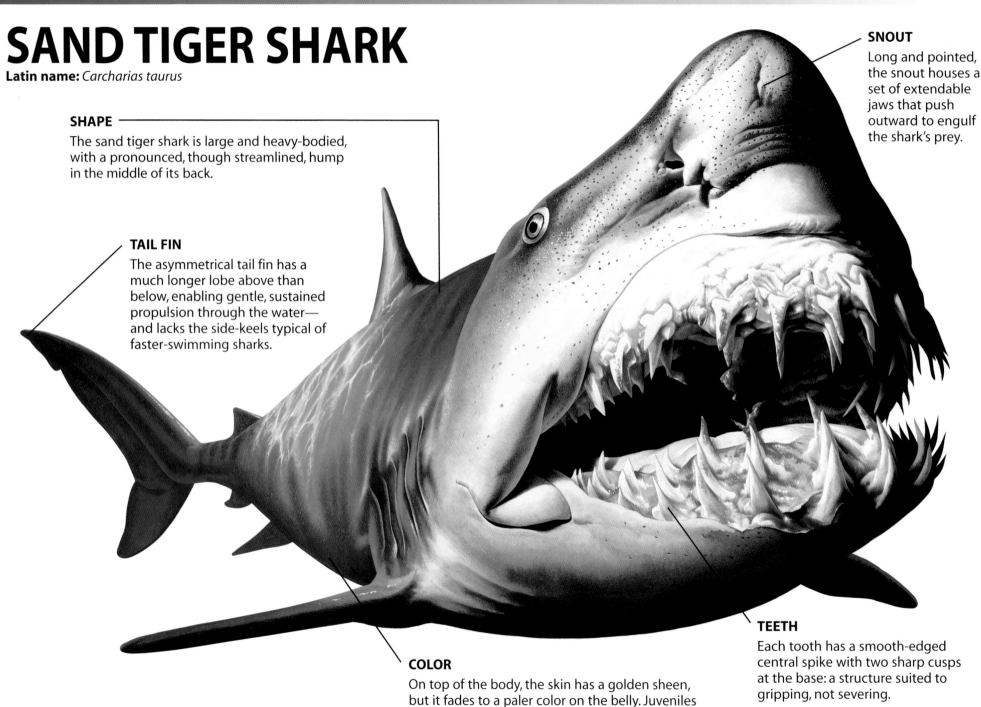

SNOUT
Long and pointed, the snout houses a set of extendable jaws that push outward to engulf the shark's prey.

SHAPE
The sand tiger shark is large and heavy-bodied, with a pronounced, though streamlined, hump in the middle of its back.

TAIL FIN
The asymmetrical tail fin has a much longer lobe above than below, enabling gentle, sustained propulsion through the water—and lacks the side-keels typical of faster-swimming sharks.

COLOR
On top of the body, the skin has a golden sheen, but it fades to a paler color on the belly. Juveniles are speckled with yellowish spots.

TEETH
Each tooth has a smooth-edged central spike with two sharp cusps at the base: a structure suited to gripping, not severing.

As the sand tiger shark glides through its watery hunting grounds, mouth agape, multiple jagged teeth seem to spill from its cone-shaped snout, earning it a villainous reputation. The sight of its menacing mouthful of fangs has struck terror into many a diver's heart. However, its disconcerting looks are misleading, for the sleek predator has no interest in human flesh and can be quite docile. Cocooned in their mother's womb, young tiger sharks lead a sinister, cannibalistic existence, preparing for their predatory lifestyle by gorging on any potential brothers and sisters that appear.

Size

KEY DATA

LENGTH	6ft 6in–11ft (2–3.5m)
PREY	Fish (including young sharks and rays), squid, and crustaceans
WEAPONS	Multiple rows of sharp, grasping teeth
TYPICAL BEHAVIOUR	Floats in caves, reef gullies, and wrecks by day, cruises in search of prey at night
LIFESPAN	Over 10 years in captivity

Sand tiger sharks are found in all tropical, subtropical, and warm temperate seas except the eastern Pacific, but they are most abundant in shallow coastal waters.

1 A female sand tiger shark can give birth to twins because she possesses not one uterus but two, each sheltering its own cannibalistic youngster (1 and 2). The young tear open their eggs and swim to the uteruses when about 2.5in (6cm) long, and initially feed on the contents of their egg sacs.

2 At first, each uterus holds several young, but soon the biggest exhausts the nourishment provided by its egg. Hunger prompts its predatory instincts into action, and it wiggles over to another pup and polishes off its sibling. The survivor will stay in its mother's womb for a year, feasting on a steady stream of eggs and embryos.

Did You Know?

● One researcher was dissecting a newly caught female sand tiger when her unborn young dramatically demonstrated its savagery. As he cut into her oviduct, he was shocked to receive a bite from the juvenile still alive within its mother's body.

● Fisherfolk sometimes call the sand tiger the "belching shark," for when it's caught on a line it burps out bubbles of air from its stomach.

● Some people claim to have seen sand tiger sharks working in large groups, herding together shoals of fish and driving them into shallow water, where they are easier to catch. If true, this is a rare example of cooperative hunting in sharks.

GREAT WHITE SHARK

Latin name: *Carcharodon carcharias*

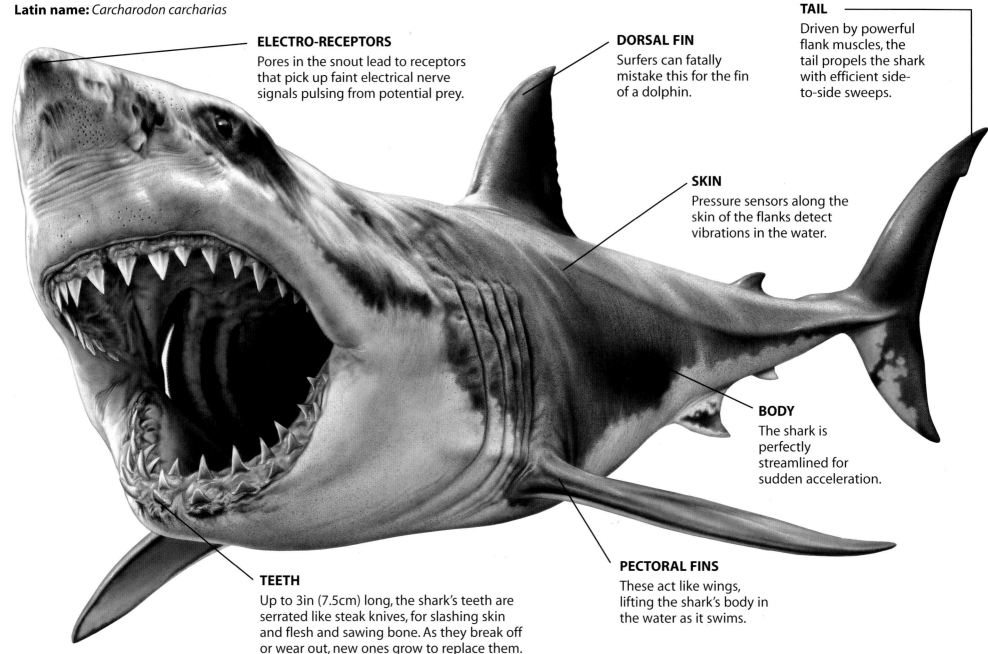

ELECTRO-RECEPTORS
Pores in the snout lead to receptors that pick up faint electrical nerve signals pulsing from potential prey.

DORSAL FIN
Surfers can fatally mistake this for the fin of a dolphin.

TAIL
Driven by powerful flank muscles, the tail propels the shark with efficient side-to-side sweeps.

SKIN
Pressure sensors along the skin of the flanks detect vibrations in the water.

BODY
The shark is perfectly streamlined for sudden acceleration.

TEETH
Up to 3in (7.5cm) long, the shark's teeth are serrated like steak knives, for slashing skin and flesh and sawing bone. As they break off or wear out, new ones grow to replace them.

PECTORAL FINS
These act like wings, lifting the shark's body in the water as it swims.

Tremendous strength and speed, huge gaping jaws, and rows of razor-sharp teeth make the great white shark one of the most feared creatures on Earth. Slamming into attack mode, the great white hits with such speed and force it often thrusts its victim clear out of the water and into the air. The great white swallows small prey whole, but with bigger prey it takes a sample bite, chopping out a great chunk of flesh. If it likes the taste, it soon comes back for more.

Size

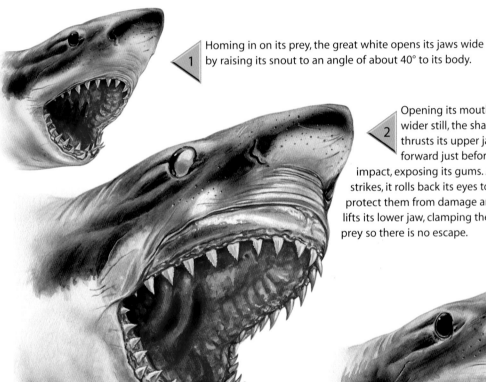

1 Homing in on its prey, the great white opens its jaws wide by raising its snout to an angle of about 40° to its body.

2 Opening its mouth wider still, the shark thrusts its upper jaw forward just before impact, exposing its gums. As it strikes, it rolls back its eyes to protect them from damage and lifts its lower jaw, clamping the prey so there is no escape.

3 The shark then retracts its upper jaw and drops its snout, bringing both sets of teeth together over a huge chunk of flesh. Finally, it shakes its head to shear off the great mouthful, using its bodyweight for extra leverage.

KEY DATA

WEIGHT	Up to 10 tons (3 tonnes)
LENGTH	Up to 23ft (7m)
DIET	Mainly large fish, squid, seals, dolphins, turtles, and seabirds, plus waste from ships and whale carcasses
LIFESPAN	Probably over 30 years

The great white shark lives in all the world's tropical and temperate oceans and seas, including the Mediterranean. It prefers deep coastal waters, where there is plenty of large prey.

Did You Know?

● The great white rarely eats people: it usually takes just one bite and then leaves its victim alone. This may be because people don't have the thick, delicious blubber that covers the bodies of seals and dolphins.

● A hungry great white often raises its head out of the water to scan the surface for signs of prey.

● A great white's first exploratory bite can cut a person in half.

● Neither jaw in the great white's mouth is fixed to its skull. This loose-jaw arrangement means it has a truly awesome biting ability.

WOBBEGONG
Latin name: Family *Orectolobidae*

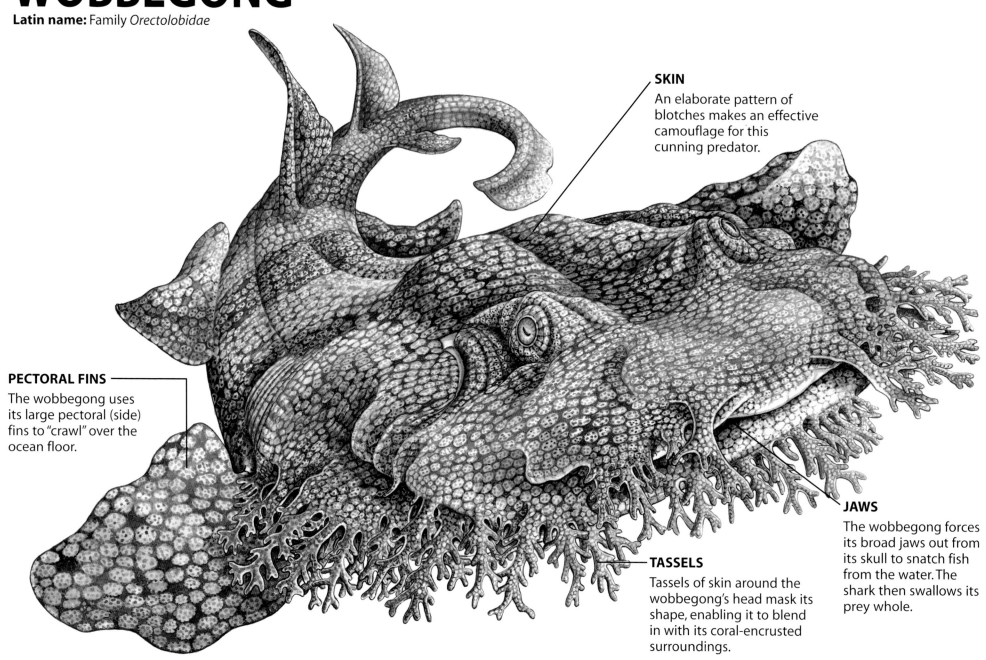

SKIN
An elaborate pattern of blotches makes an effective camouflage for this cunning predator.

PECTORAL FINS
The wobbegong uses its large pectoral (side) fins to "crawl" over the ocean floor.

JAWS
The wobbegong forces its broad jaws out from its skull to snatch fish from the water. The shark then swallows its prey whole.

TASSELS
Tassels of skin around the wobbegong's head mask its shape, enabling it to blend in with its coral-encrusted surroundings.

Cunningly disguised by camouflage that makes it look like a seaweed-encrusted rock, the wobbegong lurks to ambush any tasty prey. The wobbegong is no high-speed hunter, but to its prey it is just as deadly. Its piercing, needle-like teeth are perfectly adapted for stabbing through slippery skin, and once it gets a grip this vicious hunter rarely lets go. The wobbegong's apparent laziness sometimes encourages divers to tease it as if it were harmless. This is a foolish thing to do with any shark that comes armed with razor-sharp, skewer-like teeth.

Size

1 Swimming up to a wobbegong lying innocently on the ocean floor, a mindless diver decides to have a little fun by pulling its tail.

2 In a flash, the shark whips around and grabs the diver by the leg, sinking its teeth into his flesh. The fish clings on tight as the panic-stricken diver flails about, attempting to escape the strong grip of the angry beast.

KEY DATA

LENGTH	Up to 12ft (3.5m)	
LIFESTYLE	Bottom-living ambush predator	
PREY	Fish, squid, mollusks, and crustaceans	The six species of wobbegong live mainly in the warm tropical and subtropical waters of the western Pacific around Australia, New Guinea, Indonesia, China, Japan, and the islands of Polynesia.
TYPICAL ATTACK	Lunging strike from the seabed	
WEAPONS	Sharp teeth	
COMMON HABITATS	Coral reefs, under piers, and on sandy bays	
LIFESPAN	Up to 25 years recorded in captivity	

Did You Know?

● Since wobbegongs sometimes lurk on sandy bottoms in shallow water, bathers occasionally step right into their mouths. No prizes for guessing what happens then!

● Wobbegong is a name given to these sharks by the aboriginal peoples of coastal Australia. The fish is also known as the carpet shark because of its patterned skin.

● Fossil remains (mainly teeth) of sharks almost identical to modern wobbegongs have been found in rocks dating from the early Jurassic period, 190 million years ago.

● The wobbegong is very flexible and could easily bite its own tail.

TIGER SHARK

Latin name: *Galeocerdo cuvier*

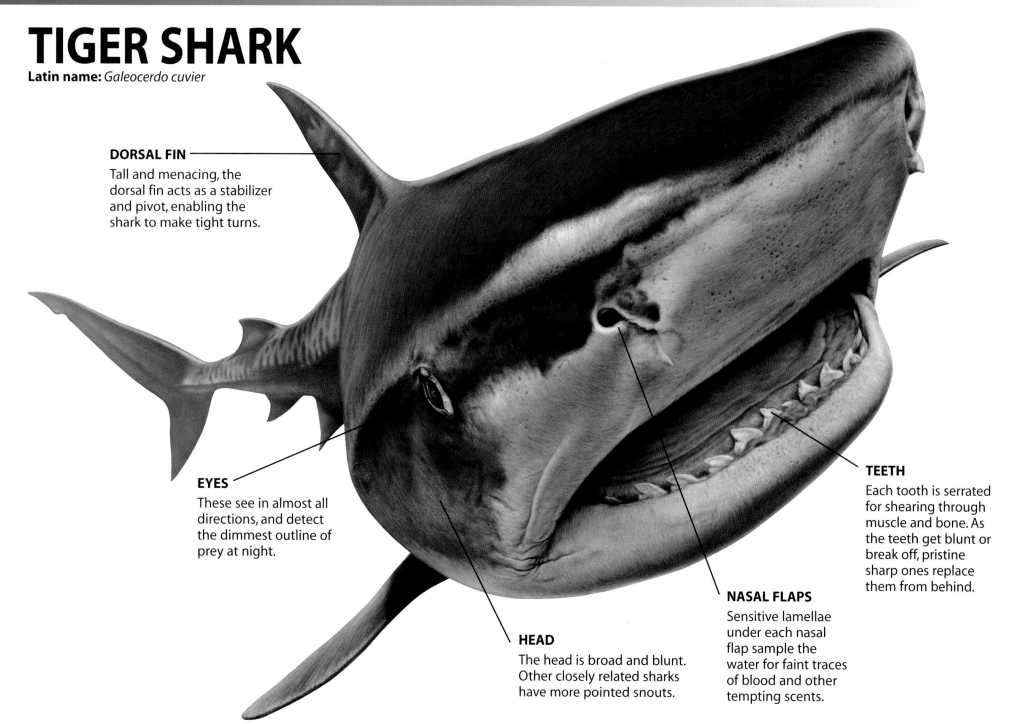

DORSAL FIN

Tall and menacing, the dorsal fin acts as a stabilizer and pivot, enabling the shark to make tight turns.

EYES

These see in almost all directions, and detect the dimmest outline of prey at night.

HEAD

The head is broad and blunt. Other closely related sharks have more pointed snouts.

NASAL FLAPS

Sensitive lamellae under each nasal flap sample the water for faint traces of blood and other tempting scents.

TEETH

Each tooth is serrated for shearing through muscle and bone. As the teeth get blunt or break off, pristine sharp ones replace them from behind.

The tiger shark swims up from the deep ocean to feed in the shallower water of reefs and coasts. As the shark cruises along, scavenging and killing, nothing in its path is safe. The tiger shark circles its prey, waiting and watching from below for the right moment to attack—which it does with sudden and devastating ferocity. The length of two family cars, this massive killer-fish shows no mercy when it spies shipwreck victims in the water—but makes them wait in a state of mind-numbing terror before it finally attacks.

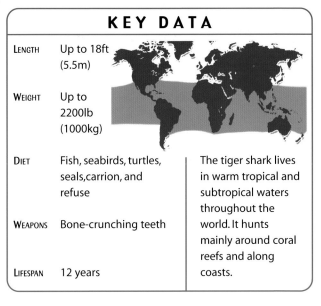

Size

KEY DATA

LENGTH	Up to 18ft (5.5m)	
WEIGHT	Up to 2200lb (1000kg)	
DIET	Fish, seabirds, turtles, seals, carrion, and refuse	The tiger shark lives in warm tropical and subtropical waters throughout the world. It hunts mainly around coral reefs and along coasts.
WEAPONS	Bone-crunching teeth	
LIFESPAN	12 years	

1 Paddling out to catch a wave, a surfer is blissfully unaware that he's in mortal danger, for lurking below is a hungry tiger shark. The shark eyes up the shape of the board and the man's arms and legs, and mistakes them for a turtle.

2 Suddenly the man is hurled into the air as the shark slams into the attack, biting through the board and smashing it into smithereens. Failing to taste fresh turtle blood, the shark swims away. The surfer has had a narrow escape this time.

Did You Know?

● The tiger shark takes its name from the stripes on its back.

● If it finds a young tiger shark, a large adult has no qualms about turning cannibal—so long as it can fit the smaller shark in its mouth!

● Tiger sharks gather off beaches where turtles come ashore to lay eggs. As the turtles drag their heavy, exhausted bodies back into the surf, the sharks pounce, cracking through the thick, hard shells of the reptiles as if they were walnuts.

● Off the shores of Hawaii, tiger sharks ambush young albatrosses making their first flights. The birds alight briefly on the water to rest their weary wings, then vanish in a spray of feathers and blood.

● Some of the more unusual items found inside the stomachs of tiger sharks are tin cans, car seats, tIres and number plates, driftwood, a crocodile's head, and lumps of coal.

HORN SHARK

Latin name: *Heterodontus* species

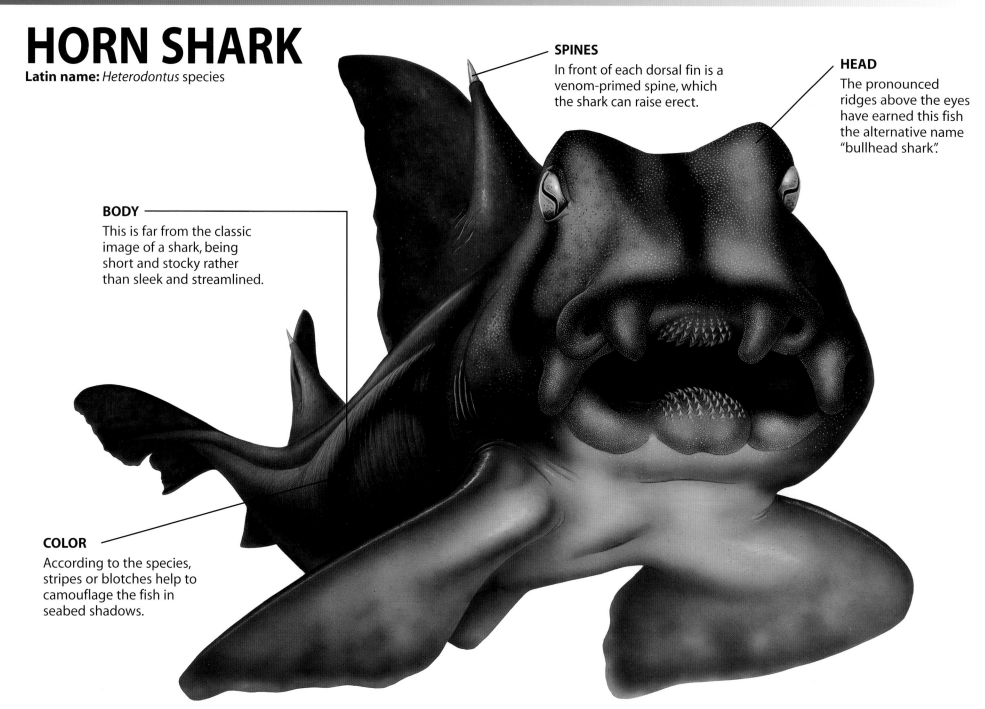

SPINES

In front of each dorsal fin is a venom-primed spine, which the shark can raise erect.

HEAD

The pronounced ridges above the eyes have earned this fish the alternative name "bullhead shark".

BODY

This is far from the classic image of a shark, being short and stocky rather than sleek and streamlined.

COLOR

According to the species, stripes or blotches help to camouflage the fish in seabed shadows.

any sharks are sleek, swift killers bristling with jagged teeth, but

Many sharks are sleek, swift killers bristling with jagged teeth, but certainly not the horn shark. This blunt-headed, thickset beast swims sedately, munches mollusks, and has defense, not attack, as its number one priority. However, no one should be fooled by the horn shark's apparent docility as it goes about its business, for when placed in jeopardy it fights fiercely for its freedom. A slash from one of its spines is enough to leave an agonizing and freely bleeding wound.

Size

KEY DATA

LENGTH	22in–5ft 6in 55cm–1.7m)
PREY	Mainly mollusks; also crabs, urchins, starfish, and other invertebrates, and small fish
DEFENSES	Two short, sharp, venom-primed spines on its back
LIFESPAN	Unknown

At least eight species of horn shark are known to live in the warm coastal waters of the Indian and Pacific oceans, at depths down to about 650ft (200m).

A diver toting a spear-gun closes in on a horn shark and fires his weapon from point-blank range, skewering the fish like a kabob. Blood gushes from the mortally wounded animal.

Did You Know?

● The horn shark can breathe without actually opening its mouth, by pumping water in through the first of its gill slits and out through the four behind. This enables the fish to chomp food without losing any morsels through its gills.

● This shark doesn't often come into conflict with people, but its avid appetite for mollusks makes oyster beds an irresistible target, and its depredations can severely deplete commercial oyster stocks.

● All species of horn shark cope well in captivity, and because they even breed in aquariums they are among the few kinds of sharks that have been closely observed mating. The male clasps one of the female's pectoral fins firmly in his teeth and curves his tail across her back.

● Some horn sharks eat so many purple sea urchins that juices from their crunchy prey stain all their teeth the same dark color.

2 The shark turns and thrashes against the man, slicing a leg with one spine. As he reels in pain, his blood mingles with that of his victim—and may draw killer sharks to the scene…

COOKIE-CUTTER SHARK
Latin name: *Isistius brasiliensis*

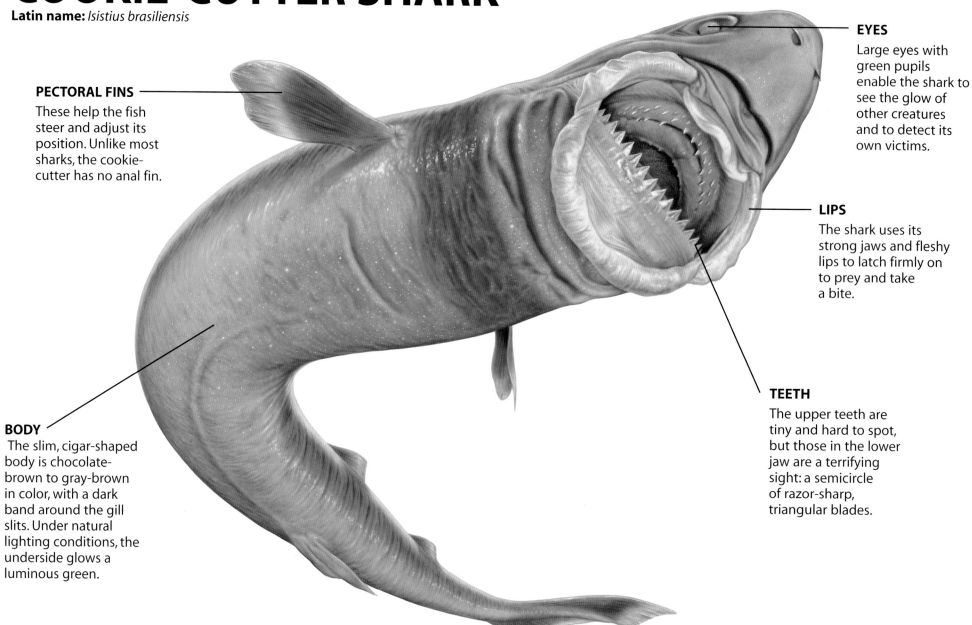

EYES

Large eyes with green pupils enable the shark to see the glow of other creatures and to detect its own victims.

PECTORAL FINS

These help the fish steer and adjust its position. Unlike most sharks, the cookie-cutter has no anal fin.

LIPS

The shark uses its strong jaws and fleshy lips to latch firmly on to prey and take a bite.

BODY

The slim, cigar-shaped body is chocolate-brown to gray-brown in color, with a dark band around the gill slits. Under natural lighting conditions, the underside glows a luminous green.

TEETH

The upper teeth are tiny and hard to spot, but those in the lower jaw are a terrifying sight: a semicircle of razor-sharp, triangular blades.

The cookie-cutter shark is more of a parasite than a true predator. Its larger victims usually escape with their lives—but not before it has left its bloody, disk-shaped signature in their skin. This tiny shark lures much larger animals closer, so that it can bite neat plugs of flesh from them. To a dolphin searching the waters for prey, the cookie-cutter's small, glowing body is irresistibly attractive. But the light show is just a trick to lure the dolphin within range of the shark's savage bite.

Size

KEY DATA

LENGTH	Up to 21in (51cm), but 14–16in (35cm–40cm) usually	
DIET	Flesh of whales, dolphins, porpoises, seals; large fish including marlin, tuna, swordfish, other sharks; also smaller fish and squid	As a deep-water fish, the cookie-cutter shark is seldom fished up, but it has been found in scattered sites throughout the oceans, mainly in the tropics and often near islands.
LIFESPAN	Unknown	

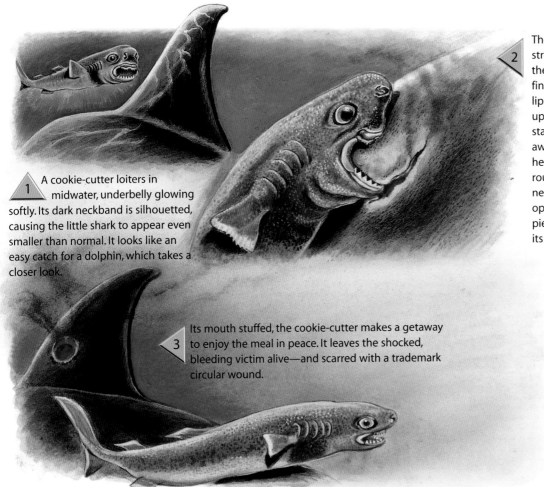

1 A cookie-cutter loiters in midwater, underbelly glowing softly. Its dark neckband is silhouetted, causing the little shark to appear even smaller than normal. It looks like an easy catch for a dolphin, which takes a closer look.

The cookie-cutter strikes, latching on to the dolphin's dorsal fin with its rubbery lips and hooklike upper teeth. The startled dolphin darts away. This movement helps the shark swing round in an arc and, neatly as a can-opener, score out a piece of the fin with its lower teeth. **2**

3 Its mouth stuffed, the cookie-cutter makes a getaway to enjoy the meal in peace. It leaves the shocked, bleeding victim alive—and scarred with a trademark circular wound.

Did You Know?

● The cookie-cutter shark is related to the various species of dogfish. These include many small, harmless coastal creatures, such as those sold in fish restaurants under the name "rock salmon."

● Other names for the cookie-cutter shark are cigar shark and luminous shark.

● Although cookie-cutter sharks cannot kill humans, they bite viciously if caught. But there are not many recorded attacks on swimmers, as they live in deep ocean waters and avoid shallow coasts.

● A second species of cookie-cutter, *Isistius plutodus*, has very similar habits to its close relative. It's often known as the large-tooth cookie-cutter shark—and with good reason. It has the biggest teeth, relative to its overall size, of any shark. For example, its tooth-height to body-length ratio is twice that of the great white shark.

MAKO SHARK

Latin name: *Isurus oxyrinhus & I. paucus*

SNOUT
The mako's pointed snout is peppered with detector cells for locating prey.

TEETH
Rows of long, pointed teeth are ideal for grasping slippery fish and holding them securely as they struggle to get away.

TAIL
Short strokes of the powerful tail propel the shark forward.

PECTORAL FINS
The long pectoral (side) fins keep the mako stable. By manipulating them, the shark steers itself up or down.

The awesome mako shark is one of the deadliest killers in the world. It targets prey with unerring accuracy, strikes with destructive speed—and grips its victims with such tenacity that escape is almost impossible. Notorious for its spine-chilling array of sharp teeth, the mako shark is one of the most lethal predators in the ocean—it even attacks and eats other sharks. Sport fishermen love the mako for the way it fights when hooked, and this feisty shark will fight to the last.

Size

KEY DATA

LENGTH	Up to 12ft 6in (4m)
WEIGHT	Up to 992lb (450kg)
PREY	Fish such as mackerel and tuna, squid, and porpoise
WEAPONS	Long, piercing teeth
LIFESPAN	Unknown

The mako shark swims throughout the world's temperate, subtropical, and tropical seas and oceans. It rarely moves into waters less than about 61°F (16°C).

1 A sport fisherman battles a mako from a boat, trying to control the mighty shark. The fish leaps high into the air in a frantic attempt to free itself from the hook.

2 In desperate fury, the shark throws itself right into the boat—and seizes the fisherman's leg in its unforgiving jaws.

Did You Know?

● Mako sharks and their kin are more intelligent than most fish, as they learn new ways of finding and tackling prey when necessary.

● Big makos attack and kill swordfish, but some swordfish get their revenge. Several dead makos have been found with swordfish bills driven through their bodies.

● The mako shark belongs to the mackerel shark family (*Lamnidae*), which also includes the infamous great white of *Jaws* fame. This huge shark is blamed for more attacks on humans than any other, but most experts agree that tiger and bull sharks are more often the culprits.

● According to data collected by the International Shark Attack File (ISAF), in the seven-year period 1990–1996 there were an average of 50 reliably recorded shark attacks a year on swimmers and divers around the world. On average, these attacks resulted in six deaths each year.

MEGAMOUTH SHARK

Latin name: *Megachasma pelagios*

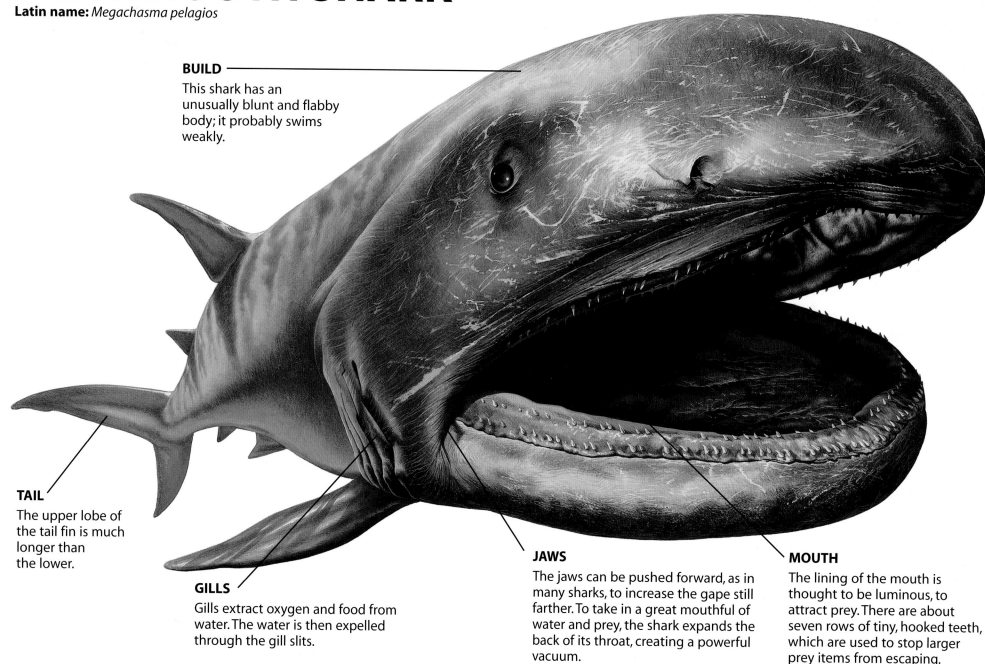

BUILD

This shark has an unusually blunt and flabby body; it probably swims weakly.

TAIL

The upper lobe of the tail fin is much longer than the lower.

GILLS

Gills extract oxygen and food from water. The water is then expelled through the gill slits.

JAWS

The jaws can be pushed forward, as in many sharks, to increase the gape still farther. To take in a great mouthful of water and prey, the shark expands the back of its throat, creating a powerful vacuum.

MOUTH

The lining of the mouth is thought to be luminous, to attract prey. There are about seven rows of tiny, hooked teeth, which are used to stop larger prey items from escaping.

Every so often, the ocean yields a living secret, and the megamouth has certainly been the biggest and oddest find of recent times. It was not until 1976 that the first known megamouth shark was hauled from the ocean depths. This king-size filter-feeder preys mostly on the tiny life-forms that swarm in the deep. Some prey may stray deliberately into its jaws, drawn to the spooky glow created by the luminous lining inside its mouth.

Size

KEY DATA

LENGTH	14ft–17ft (4.3–5.2m)	
WEIGHT	Up to 2200lb (1000kg)	
WIDTH OF MOUTH	31in (80cm)	
DIET	Plankton, jellyfish, squid	As far as we know, the megamouth is scarce but widespread across the warm waters of the world. It has been found in the Pacific, Indian, and Atlantic oceans.
LIFESPAN	Unknown	

1 The megamouth cruises through deep, dimly lit waters, probably following the movements of shoals of prey.

2 The shark spots a shoal of small jellyfish and opens its enormous mouth in readiness. By pushing out its flexible jaws, it makes the fearful cavity loom still larger.

Did You Know?

● The ancient origins of the megamouth are as obscure as its lifestyle. All the fossils we have are remains of similar teeth from 20 million years ago, found in rocks in the western United States, and teeth twice as old, found in England and Argentina.

● The first ever megamouth catch was nearly lost before it could be studied. An attempt to winch the dead beast in by its tail caused the tail to sever and the rest of the shark to plunge back into the water. Luckily, a team of divers retrieved it.

● Earlier in the 20th century, another large, mystery fish was hauled from deep water. The discovery of the coelacanth in 1938 showed that creatures known only from ancient fossils could still be at large somewhere in the oceans.

● The first six megamouth specimens were all male. A female was not found until 1994, when one washed up on a Japanese beach.

3 Lured by the glow of the shark's luminous mouth, the jellyfish head straight for it. The beast closes its jaws on them, along with lots of water. After it expels the water through its gills, the stranded jellyfish are swallowed.

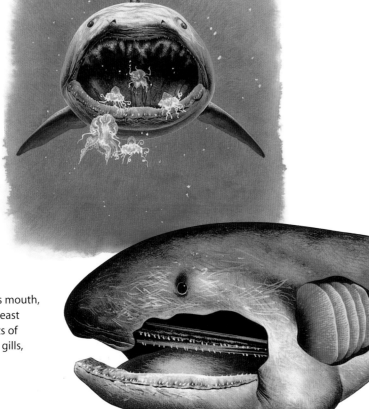

WHALE SHARK

Latin name: *Rhincodon typus*

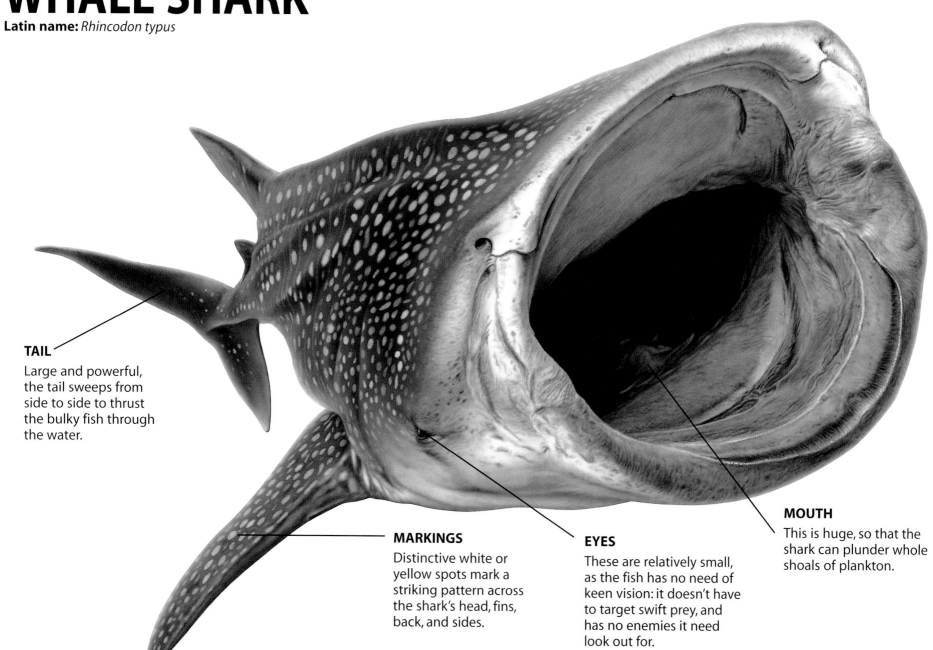

TAIL

Large and powerful, the tail sweeps from side to side to thrust the bulky fish through the water.

MARKINGS

Distinctive white or yellow spots mark a striking pattern across the shark's head, fins, back, and sides.

EYES

These are relatively small, as the fish has no need of keen vision: it doesn't have to target swift prey, and has no enemies it need look out for.

MOUTH

This is huge, so that the shark can plunder whole shoals of plankton.

Despite its formidable size, the whale shark is harmless to anything bigger than a shrimp, and cruises casually past the other creatures sharing its waters—even the occasional inquisitive human diver. The whale shark is the biggest fish in the sea, with a mighty mouth that's cavernous enough to engulf a man—were it not such a gentle giant. Divers can hang on for a ride with the placid whale shark, as it rarely objects. The only dangers are being scraped by the shark's rough skin, being knocked by its huge tail—or forgetting to let go when it dives…

Size

KEY DATA

LENGTH	Up to 46ft (14m)
WEIGHT	Up to 131 tons (40 tonnes)
DIET	Mainly animal plankton, such as krill and the larvae of fish and crabs
LIFESPAN	Unknown, but may be more than 30 years

This gigantic shark is found worldwide in tropical seas on either side of the equator. It is spotted mostly near the Maldives, the Seychelles, and in the Gulf of Mexico.

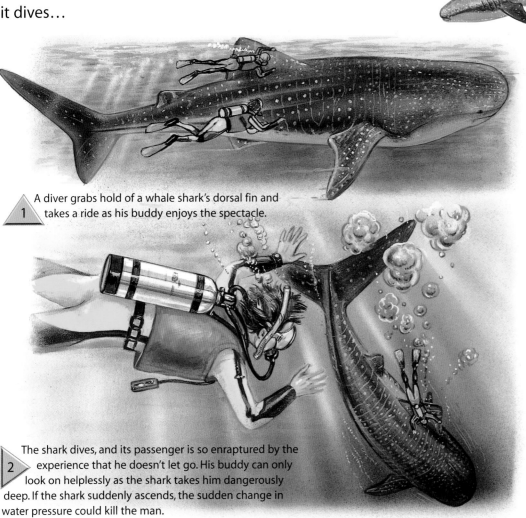

1 A diver grabs hold of a whale shark's dorsal fin and takes a ride as his buddy enjoys the spectacle.

2 The shark dives, and its passenger is so enraptured by the experience that he doesn't let go. His buddy can only look on helplessly as the shark takes him dangerously deep. If the shark suddenly ascends, the sudden change in water pressure could kill the man.

Did You Know?

● At up to 4in (10cm) thick, the skin of the whale shark is thicker and tougher than any other creature's.

● Boats occasionally collide with the broad backs of whale sharks swimming just below the surface. Over 20 such collisions have been recorded worldwide.

● At the other end of the size spectrum to the whale shark is the smallest shark of all, the dwarf shark (*Squaliolus laticaudus*), which grows to a maximum length of 10in (25cm).

● Whale sharks cover enormous distances in their migrations, and in not much more than three years one tagged individual swam an amazing 14,000 miles (22,530km), almost equal to going twice around the world.

● The eggs inside a female whale shark are the world's largest, being an impressive 12in (30cm) or more long.

HAMMERHEAD SHARK
Latin name: *Sphyrna* species

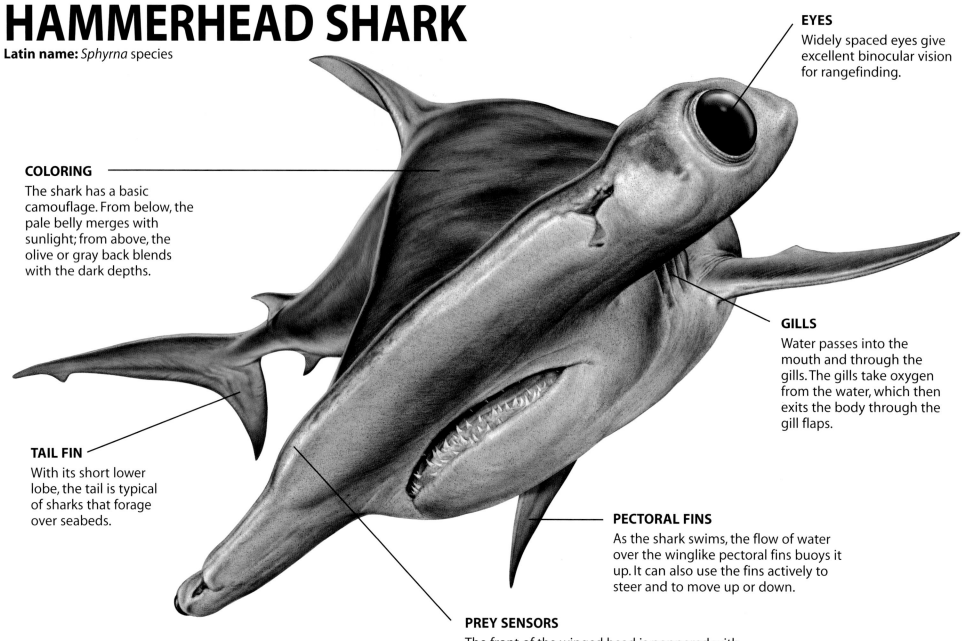

EYES
Widely spaced eyes give excellent binocular vision for rangefinding.

COLORING
The shark has a basic camouflage. From below, the pale belly merges with sunlight; from above, the olive or gray back blends with the dark depths.

GILLS
Water passes into the mouth and through the gills. The gills take oxygen from the water, which then exits the body through the gill flaps.

TAIL FIN
With its short lower lobe, the tail is typical of sharks that forage over seabeds.

PECTORAL FINS
As the shark swims, the flow of water over the winglike pectoral fins buoys it up. It can also use the fins actively to steer and to move up or down.

PREY SENSORS
The front of the winged head is peppered with lots of pressure-sensitive pit organs and electro-receptors for homing in on active prey.

A hammerhead shark may look hideously ugly, but its frightful features have a purpose. The spooky "wings" that form its head are kitted out with sensors so powerful that they make us seem positively primitive. The hammerhead's silhouette is like that of some bizarre undersea alien. For divers, it can be one of the most terrifying sights in the ocean. The great hammerhead eats any fish it can kill, but it especially relishes stingrays. Even buried in sand, rays are easily picked up by the hammerhead's powerful scanners.

Size

KEY DATA

LENGTH	3ft–5ft (1–5m), depending on species	
WEIGHT	Up to 882lb–1014lb (400–460kg) in great hammerhead	Hammerheads may turn up in any of the world's tropical and subtropical seas and oceans. In the northern summer, some individuals range as far north as the Mediterranean.
PREY	Fish, squid, and shellfish	
WEAPONS	Up to 68 saw-edged teeth	
LIFESPAN	20–30 years	

1 As it glides over the seabed, the shark sweeps its broad head from side to side to scan a wide swathe of sandy terrain. It may be too dark to see clearly, but the electro-receptors in the shark's snout have no trouble locating a buried stingray. When it has the ray's precise location, the shark strikes.

Did You Know?

● Although the great hammerhead feeds mainly on rays and small bony fish, it has also been known to attack and eat other sharks.

● The shark's skin is studded with tiny sharp, toothlike spikes called denticles. In the past, people used the skin like sandpaper. The coarse material, known as shagreen, was also wrapped around sword hilts, to give a good grip in the sweat and blood of battle.

● The oil from a hammerhead's liver is rich in Vitamin A. The sharks were once caught in huge numbers to supply the fish-oil industry.

● Hammerhead sharks are hated by sport fishermen for the habit of chasing baits set for fish such as marlin. Once a shark has located a source of food, it's very hard to shake off. Hammerheads also make a nuisance of themselves among reef fishermen, stealing catches as the lines are hauled in.

2 The ray tries to flee, but its enemy is too quick. The shark pins the ray to the sand with one side of its head. Then it twists round until it can bite into a wing. The shark circles the crippled ray, chopping into it, until the victim is all eaten up—even the venomous tail-spine.

ANGEL SHARK

Latin name: *Squatina* species

DENTICLES

Small, toothlike denticles cover the skin. On the back they're spiked, to deter attackers, while on the belly they're scalelike, to prevent chafing on rocks.

PECTORAL FINS

These are greatly extended and account for most of the shark's body. They also account for its name, reminding people of an angel's wings.

Sharks are closely related to skates and rays and, like its flat-bodied cousins, the angel shark is shaped for life on the seabed. Don't be fooled by its name, though; this shark is no angel. A relentless hunter at night, by day it lurks in ambush mode on the seafloor, ever ready to dart up and catch fish swimming by—or attack humans intruding on its patch. It's one thing for an expert wearing special gloves to handle an angel shark, but anyone in ordinary diving gear is advised to steer clear. Some people won't be told, though, and have to learn the hard way…

Size

KEY DATA

LENGTH	Up to 8ft (2.5m)
WEIGHT	Up to 176lb (80kg)
PREY	Fish, lobsters, crabs, squid, and shelled mollusks
WEAPONS	Strong jaws, sharp teeth
LIFESPAN	Unknown

The dozen or so species of angel shark have been recorded in coastal and continental shelf waters in most of the world's seas and oceans, including the Atlantic and Pacific, from 10ft (3m) down to 4265ft (1300m).

1 An angel shark lies buried in the sandy seabed, just its eyes and snout showing. While it scans the water above for potential prey, a diver swims toward its head, curious to get a closer look.

2 The diver reaches out to poke the shark, trying to make it stir and reveal itself fully. But the man gets much more than he bargained for—the angel shark rears up out of the sand and bites the startled diver's hand, sinking its devilishly sharp teeth deep into his flesh before he can react. He'll know better in future…

Did You Know?

● In many parts of the world, people catch and eat angel sharks. The fish rarely take a baited hook, so are usually caught by dragging a net across the ocean floor.

● The rough skin of the shark was once dried and used like sandpaper to polish wood and ivory, while eating dried angel shark meat was said to be a good cure for itching.

● The angel shark is also called the monkfish, because the shape of its head is thought to look like the hood of a monk's cloak. And in some places it is known as the fiddle fish, because when seen from above, the shape of its body resembles a violin.

● The angel shark is secretive and little is known about it. To discover more, scientists once fitted radio transmitters to several angel sharks and tracked them. They found that the sharks are territorial, spending most of their time inside a home range of only 0.5sq mile (1.5 sq km) or so.

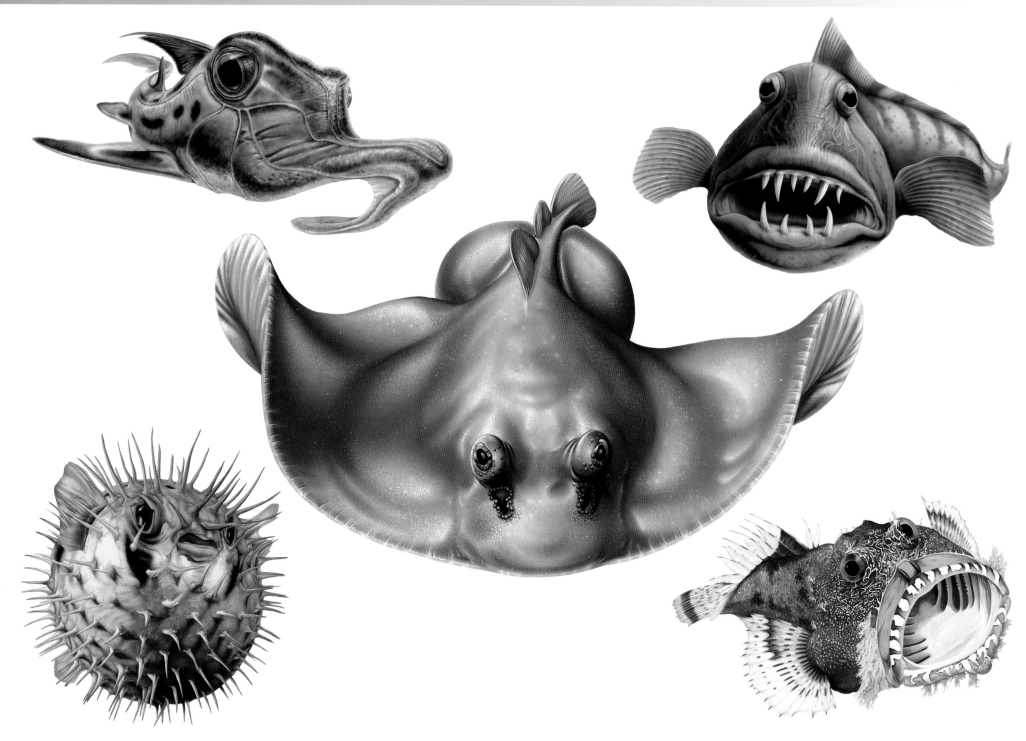

Other Saltwater Fish

*Saltwater fish possess a variety of features to help them
survive in the harsh sea and ocean environment
that they inhabit.*

They are in constant danger of attack by predators so they carry their own defenses, such as the sharp spines of the Porcupine fish or the camouflage that makes the Frogfish look like a plant or coral. On the other hand, saltwater fish also have to eat and they carry weapons to break through the defenses of their prey. For example, the Wolf Fish and the Stingray have no problems with the shells of the crustaceans they consume. They can bite through or crush the hardest shell and feast on the soft flesh inside. The Electric Ray has the best of both worlds: the electrically charged cells on either side of its head can both fight off attack and paralyze prey. Other saltwater fish live in special conditions that require special remedies. The Gulper Eel lives with the pitch-black freezing waters and crushing water pressure found at great depths. To cope with the darkness, it carries its own pulsating light on its tail. Food is hard to find in this unfriendly environment, but the light attracts small fish toward the Eel's mouth, which can open to a vast size so that it has the best chance of catching and eating it.

SPOTTED EAGLE RAY

Latin name: *Aetobatus narinari*

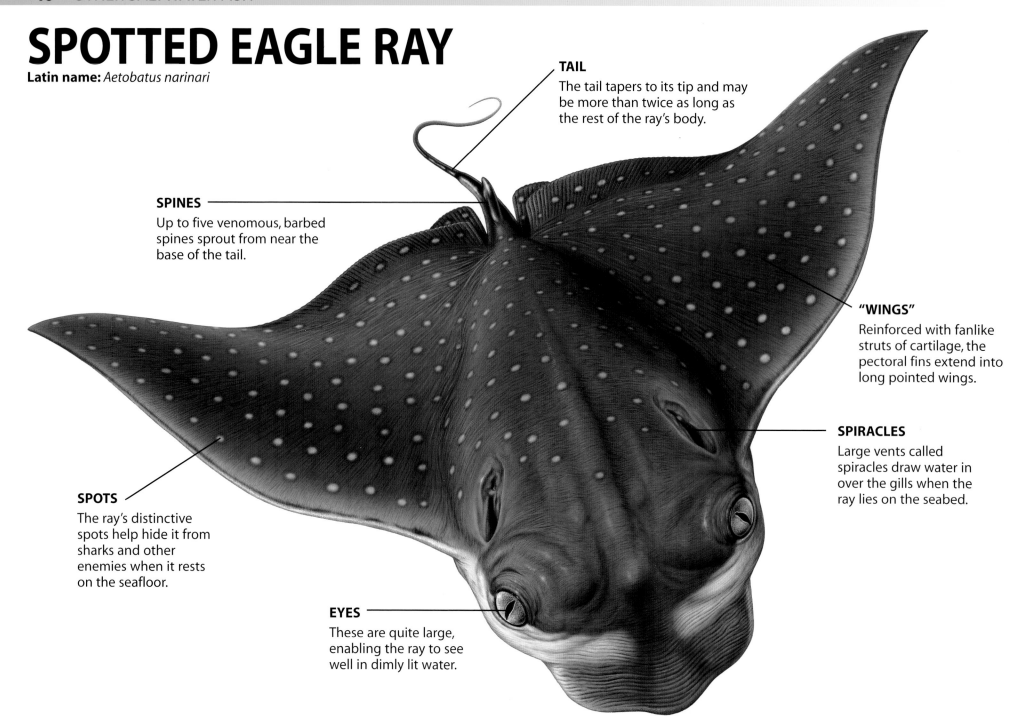

TAIL

The tail tapers to its tip and may be more than twice as long as the rest of the ray's body.

SPINES

Up to five venomous, barbed spines sprout from near the base of the tail.

"WINGS"

Reinforced with fanlike struts of cartilage, the pectoral fins extend into long pointed wings.

SPIRACLES

Large vents called spiracles draw water in over the gills when the ray lies on the seabed.

SPOTS

The ray's distinctive spots help hide it from sharks and other enemies when it rests on the seafloor.

EYES

These are quite large, enabling the ray to see well in dimly lit water.

The spotted eagle ray spends most of its time grubbing about the seabed, searching for shellfish to crush in its millstone teeth. Lying on the seabed, often close to shore, with its broad, speckled body and long, spiny tail half-buried in the muddy sand, it can spring a painful surprise on anyone disturbing it. The venomous spines on the tail of the spotted eagle ray inflict agonizing wounds that often become infected and fester for weeks—as many a trawlerman has discovered to his cost.

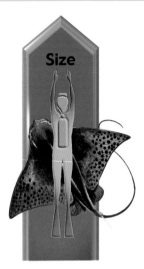
Size

1
A spotted eagle ray is caught in a net with thousands of smaller fish and hauled from the sea. A trawlerman guides the dripping net over the side of the boat.

2
Hard at work, the man doesn't spot the ray's tail flailing through the mesh—until a barbed spine skewers his wrist and breaks off deep in his flesh.

KEY DATA

LENGTH	Body up to 6ft (2m), tail 19ft (6m)
'WINGSPAN'	Usually 6ft (2m), up to 12ft (3.5m)
WEIGHT	Up to 496lb (225kg)
DIET	Mainly mollusks such as clams, plus crabs, shrimp, worms, and small fish
WEAPONS	Up to five barbed tail spines loaded with venom that contains nerve toxins
TYPICAL ATTACK	Single thrashing strike
LIFESPAN	Unknown

One of the most widespread of the eagle rays, the spotted species lives in warm, shallow seas all around the world, straying farther from the tropics in summer.

Did You Know?

● The spotted eagle ray is also sometimes known as the duckbill ray, due to the shape of its snout.

● When courting a mate, the ray sometimes frolics on the surface close to shore. As it does so, its pointed pectoral fins slice through the waves—panicking swimmers into mistaking them for the dorsal fins of cruising sharks.

● The female spotted eagle ray mates with up to four males in the space of one hour. A year later, she bears up to four live "pups"—many of which are instantly snapped up by sharks that have followed her around diligently for several days for precisely this purpose.

WOLF FISH

Latin name: *Anarrhichas lupus*

FINS
Long dorsal and anal fins sweep along the top and bottom to control its movements in confined spaces, such as among rocks, as it seeks its quarry.

TAIL
The tail fin is rather small for such a hefty creature, and too weak to propel the beast at speed, but drives the fish fast enough to catch slow victims.

SKIN
The wolf fish's skin appears naked because it lacks the scales present on most other fish.

TEETH
Conical teeth at the front of the jaws deliver a massive bite. Behind them are rows of thicker teeth for chewing.

The wolf fish spends little time roaming the open sea. It prefers to lurk on the bottom where it can sink its teeth into crunchy prey. Few denizens of the deep look as grotesque as the wolf fish, and its fang-filled face spells death to many sea animals. To a wolf fish, a spider crab's claws, spines, and shell are no deterrent. The predator's deadly dentistry cracks through the prey's shell with ease. The killer then feasts greedily on the flesh inside.

Size

KEY DATA

LENGTH	Up to 4ft 6in (1.3m)
WEIGHT	Up to 551lb (25kg)
WEAPONS	Shell-cracking teeth
PREY	Mollusks, crabs, sea urchins, and other bottom-dwellers
LIFESPAN	Unknown

The wolf fish inhabits cold coastal waters near northern Europe, northeastern North America, and Greenland. It forages on rocky bottoms and muddy or sandy beds at depths of several feet and up to 1650ft (500m) on the fringes of continental shelves.

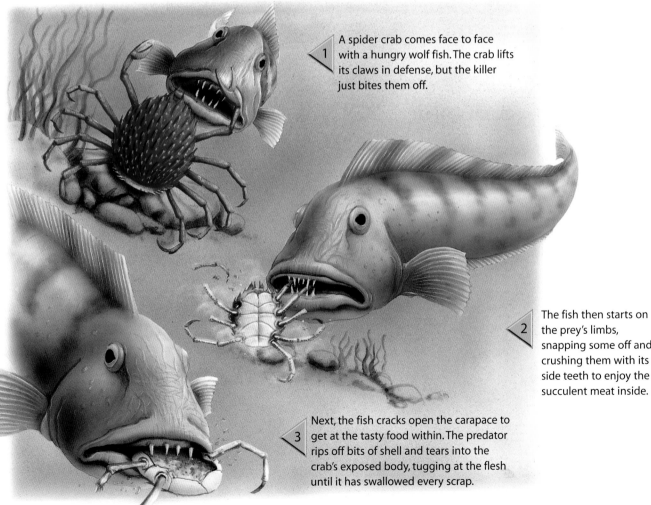

1 A spider crab comes face to face with a hungry wolf fish. The crab lifts its claws in defense, but the killer just bites them off.

2 The fish then starts on the prey's limbs, snapping some off and crushing them with its side teeth to enjoy the succulent meat inside.

3 Next, the fish cracks open the carapace to get at the tasty food within. The predator rips off bits of shell and tears into the crab's exposed body, tugging at the flesh until it has swallowed every scrap.

Did You Know?

● The wolf fish has five close relatives in the genus Anarrhichas, all sharp-toothed fish living in the cold waters of the North Atlantic. The offshore waters of the North Pacific are home to a similar three species in the genus Anarrhichthys, though these have elongated spines with nearly twice as many bones.

● In fish markets, the wolf fish often goes go by the name of "lobo," which is Spanish for wolf. Although it is a tasty food fish with a sweet, firm, flaky flesh like cod, the creature's ugly countenance scares many customers and puts them off buying it. As a result, the wolf fish usually has its head removed before it is displayed for sale. In most fish dealers and supermarkets, wolf fish are now sold mainly as fillets, with the skin removed too.

● Because of its sharp, catlike teeth, the wolf fish is sometimes called the "sea catfish," but it isn't closely related to the true catfish.

FROGFISH

Latin name: *Antennarius* species

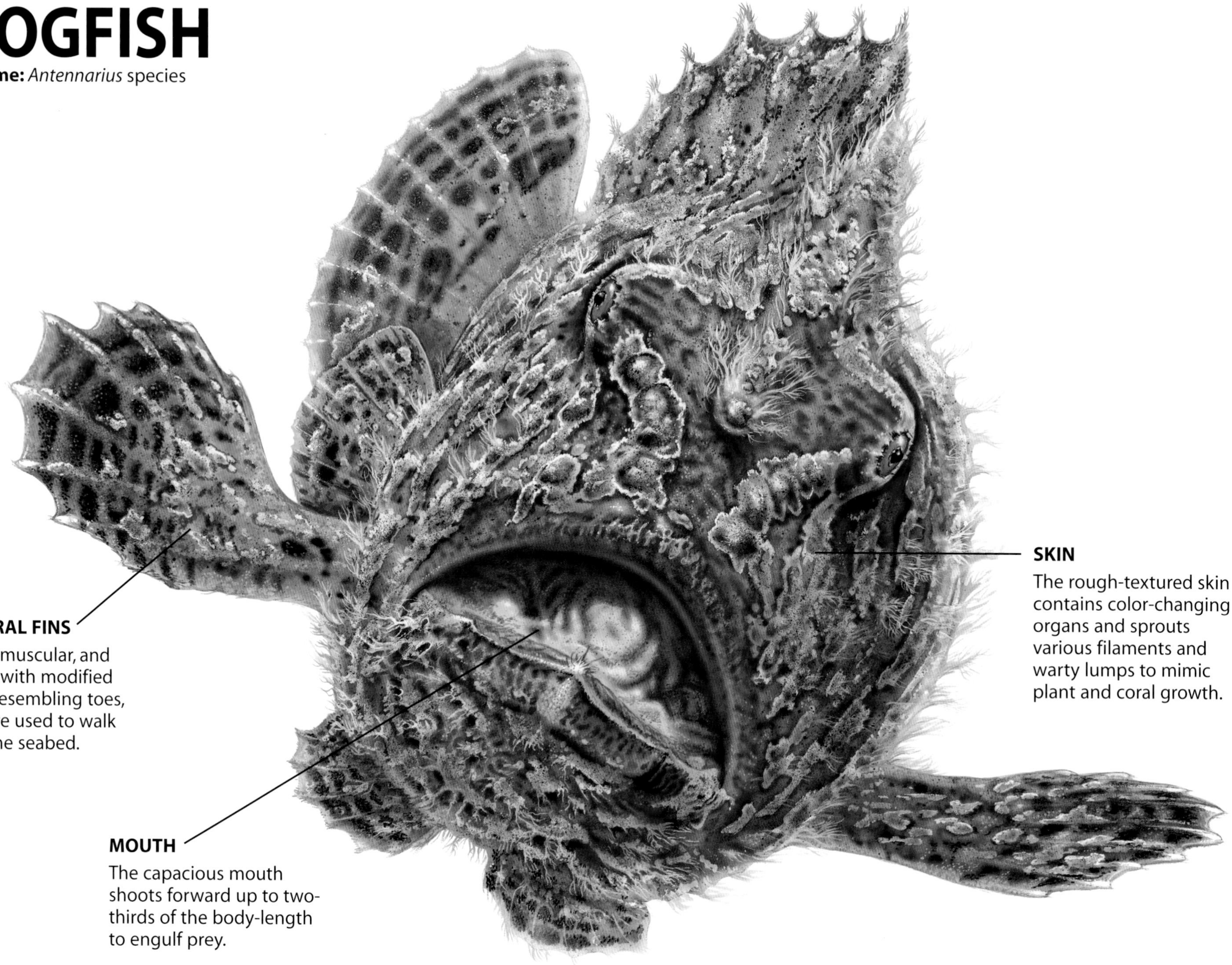

PECTORAL FINS

Stubby, muscular, and jointed, with modified spines resembling toes, these are used to walk along the seabed.

MOUTH

The capacious mouth shoots forward up to two-thirds of the body-length to engulf prey.

SKIN

The rough-textured skin contains color-changing organs and sprouts various filaments and warty lumps to mimic plant and coral growth.

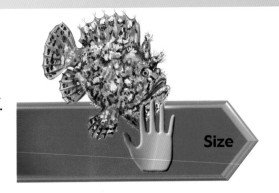

O ne of the ocean's great gluttons, a frogfish is all stretchy stomach and mobile mouth. This underwater eating-machine waits in ambush on the seabed, and easily swallows victims bigger than itself. Heavily disguised, the frogfish fishes with a rod and lure and can engulf its victims in six milliseconds, plucking a fish from a school without the others noticing.

Size

KEY DATA

LENGTH	1.25–16in (3.5–40cm), depending on species	
BAIT	Modified dorsal spine tipped with fleshy lure	
PREY	Fish (including other frogfish) and crustaceans	Frogfish are widely distributed through tropical and subtropical waters around the world, although most prefer temperatures of about 68°F (20°C).
HABITAT	Mainly sandy or rocky sea floors and coral reefs	
DEPTH	Usually 96ft–327ft (30–100m), with a 984 ft (300m) maximum	
YOUNG	Female lays thousands of eggs in rafts at the surface; eggs sink as they hatch	

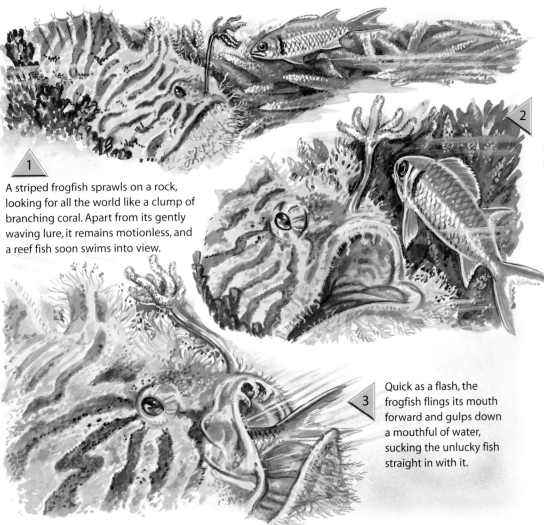

1

A striped frogfish sprawls on a rock, looking for all the world like a clump of branching coral. Apart from its gently waving lure, it remains motionless, and a reef fish soon swims into view.

2

Attracted by the branching lure, the little fish noses closer, entering the danger zone. The frogfish watches with beady eyes and readies for the strike.

3

Quick as a flash, the frogfish flings its mouth forward and gulps down a mouthful of water, sucking the unlucky fish straight in with it.

Did You Know?

● Frogfish are so greedy, they often try to swallow impossibly awkward prey—such as spiny butterfly fish—and have to cough them out again.

● Before they realized that frogfish could change color at will, scientists thought there were far more species.

● When hunting is good, a frogfish will often stay in the same position on the seabed for weeks at a time.

● If a frogfish loses its rod and lure to over-enthusiastic prey, they will totally regenerate within six months—but it may go hungry in the interim.

● When a female frogfish is full of eggs, she floats upward—tail-first.

HATCHETFISH

Latin name: *Argyropelecus* species

SPINE

A prominent, double-pointed spine projects in front of the pelvic fin.

TAIL

Like many deep-sea fish, the hatchetfish has a short, slender tail, reducing the bodyweight so it needs less food.

EYES

The tubular eyes have a spherical lens and point upward, enabling the fish to spot prey against the dim glow from above.

BODY

The body is deep and flattened, with a sharp-edged belly. The overall shape is like the blade of a hatchet—hence the name.

SKIN

The skin on the flanks has a shiny, mirror-like finish that reflects light.

MOUTH

Like its eyes, the hatchetfish's capacious mouth points upward, so the fish can scoop up unsuspecting prey from below.

PHOTOPHORES

These organs on the belly produce a gentle light that disguises the fish's silhouette. They work in much the same way as the light-producing organs of a firefly.

It's a cruel world of eat or be eaten in the deep ocean, so while the hatchetfish spends its time in pursuit of microscopic prey, it relies on lurid lights to protect itself from larger predators. Glowing with eerie blue light in the dim waters of the deep, it looks like a tiny invader from another planet. In the barren wastes of the deep ocean waters, food is scarce, so the hatchetfish must gorge itself whenever it gets the chance.

Size

KEY DATA

LENGTH	Up to 4in (10cm)
DIET	Animal plankton, including tiny crustaceans and fish
HABITS	Migrates toward surface at night, sinks back at dawn
DEFENSES	Luminous organs that disguise silhouette

Hatchetfish live in all the oceans of the world beyond the edges of the continental shelves, in the mid-waters of the deep sea. They are most common in the cooler, food-rich waters of the north and south, away from the tropics.

1 As the hatchetfish swims slowly through the dim water, a surge of nervous energy makes its luminescent organs glow with light.

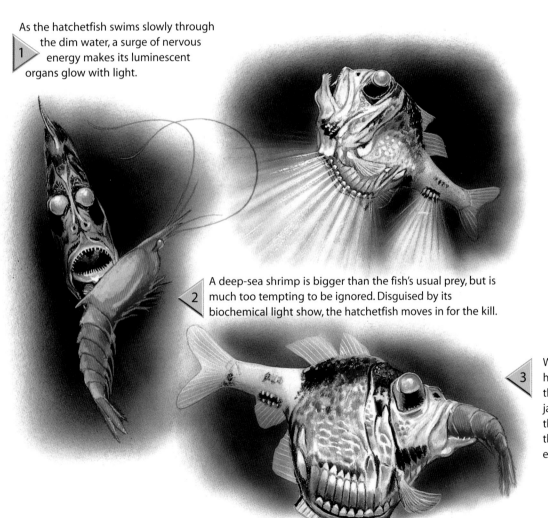

2 A deep-sea shrimp is bigger than the fish's usual prey, but is much too tempting to be ignored. Disguised by its biochemical light show, the hatchetfish moves in for the kill.

3 With a swift snap, the hatchetfish catches the shrimp in its wide jaws, and starts forcing the body down its throat and into its expandable stomach.

Did You Know?

● A hatchetfish's photophores (light organs) convert more than 98 percent of the energy they use into light. Just 3 percent of the electrical energy used by a domestic light bulb is turned into light.

● During its quest for food, the hatchetfish migrates considerable distances every morning and evening, traveling up to 1310ft (400m) up and down through the water as it follows its plankton prey.

● Nerve signals control the light produced by the photophores, and the hatchetfish continually adjusts the level so that it matches the light from the surrounding water.

● Hatchetfish may be seldom seen, but they're a vital part of the ocean food chain. First they eat tiny organisms such as the drifting plankton; then they digest the food and convert it into fish flesh; finally they fall prey to bigger fish, passing on the nutrients.

VIPERFISH
Latin name: *Chauliodus* species

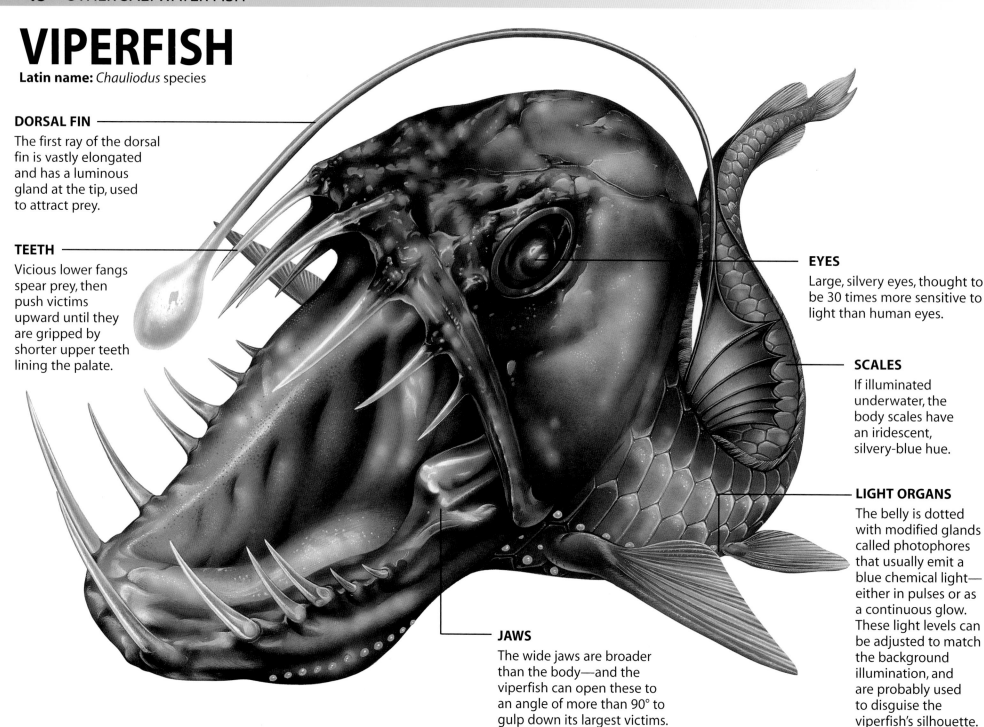

DORSAL FIN

The first ray of the dorsal fin is vastly elongated and has a luminous gland at the tip, used to attract prey.

TEETH

Vicious lower fangs spear prey, then push victims upward until they are gripped by shorter upper teeth lining the palate.

EYES

Large, silvery eyes, thought to be 30 times more sensitive to light than human eyes.

SCALES

If illuminated underwater, the body scales have an iridescent, silvery-blue hue.

LIGHT ORGANS

The belly is dotted with modified glands called photophores that usually emit a blue chemical light—either in pulses or as a continuous glow. These light levels can be adjusted to match the background illumination, and are probably used to disguise the viperfish's silhouette.

JAWS

The wide jaws are broader than the body—and the viperfish can open these to an angle of more than 90° to gulp down its largest victims.

A viperfish may not be the largest predator, but stalking through the glimmering deep or hanging in the darkness with its treacherous lure aglow, this voracious killer is the scourge of many mid-water creatures. A slimy, eel-like fish with a great, gaping mouth bristling with wicked fangs, the viperfish tempts scarce prey near with a devious trick. Resting almost motionless, it extends a built-in fishing line and dangles a glowing bait in front of its jaws.

Size

KEY DATA

LENGTH	10–14in (25–35cm)	
PREY	Fish and crustaceans	
WEAPONS	Fearsome fangs	
HABITAT	Mid-waters of the deep sea, down to more than 3280ft (1000m)	The six known species of viperfish live in the mid-waters of tropical and temperate oceans throughout the world, between 60° North and 40° South.
LIFESPAN	Unknown	

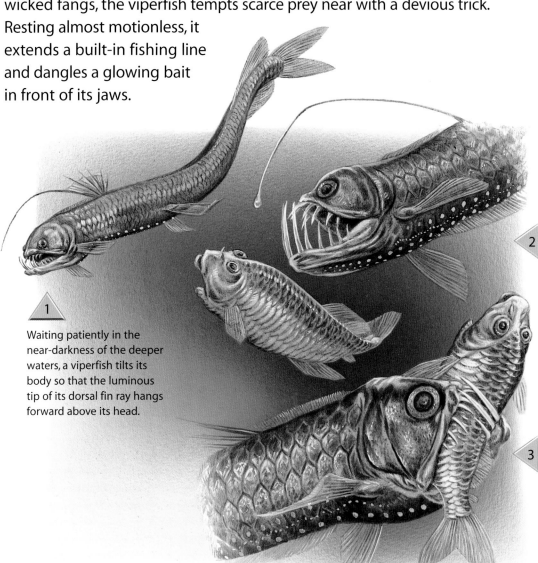

1

Waiting patiently in the near-darkness of the deeper waters, a viperfish tilts its body so that the luminous tip of its dorsal fin ray hangs forward above its head.

2

Light organs dotting its belly emit a faint glow, disguising any slight shadow the viperfish casts below and making it almost invisible. All an approaching tube-eyed fish sees is the enticing blob of light from the dangling lure.

3

Drawn like a moth to a flame, the tube-eyed fish swims closer. In a flash, the viperfish throws back its head and spears its prey with one swift stab of its stiletto teeth, clamping it fast between the gruesome spikes.

Did You Know?

● One remarkable feature of this odd fish is the size of the first bone in its spine, which is several times larger than the adjacent vertebrae. When the viperfish is eating, this enlarged bone takes the strain as it throws its upper jaw backward. It also provides muscle attachments that enable it to dislocate sections of its head and gills to swallow.

● The viperfish has many strange illuminations, but the most curious of all are light organs that actually shine into its eyes. Some scientists suggest that the dim glow from these organs ensures the eyes are prepared to cope with flashing signals from other fish, preventing the viperfish from being dazzled by any sudden bursts of light in the darkness.

● Fish such as the viperfish often eat prey with light-producing organs, so their stomachs are lined with a special black membrane that stops any light from shining through their stretchy skin after a meal.

CONGER EEL

Latin name: *Conger conger*

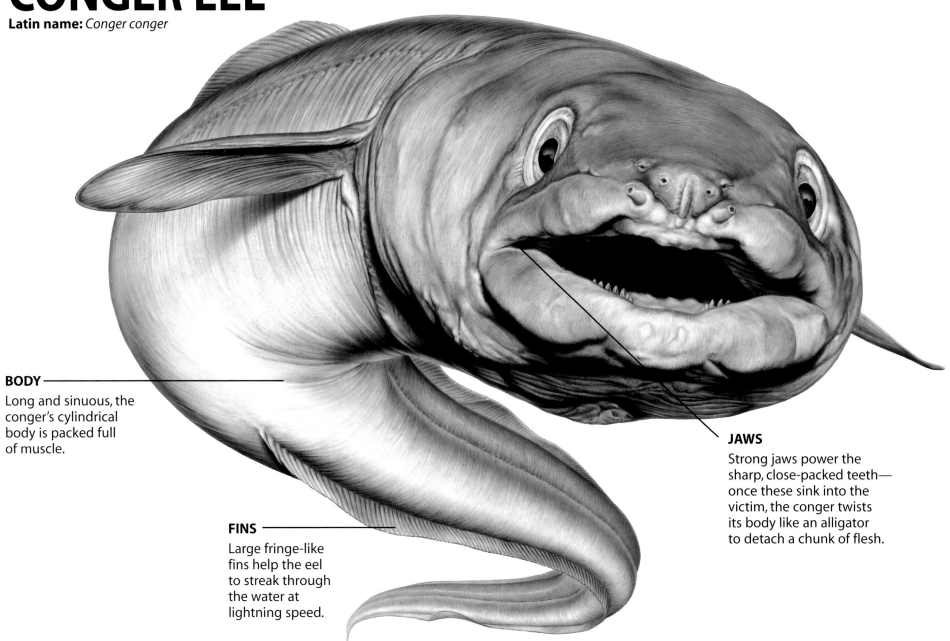

BODY

Long and sinuous, the conger's cylindrical body is packed full of muscle.

FINS

Large fringe-like fins help the eel to streak through the water at lightning speed.

JAWS

Strong jaws power the sharp, close-packed teeth— once these sink into the victim, the conger twists its body like an alligator to detach a chunk of flesh.

For centuries, fisherfolk have told stories of the flesh-shearing teeth and powerhouse strength of the mighty conger. Even armed divers today are wary of this legendary creature. Lithe and muscular, the serpent-like conger eel slips through inshore caves and threads in and out of sunken shipwrecks, hunting prey at night. A conger eel is known to attack the closest target when caught. And the danger isn't over once the eel is "dead." A fisherman not in the know may learn this the hard way…

Size

KEY DATA

LENGTH	3ft–10ft (1–3m) (females usually twice as long as males)
WEIGHT	Up to 242lb (110kg)
HABITAT	Rocky inshore seabeds up to 1638ft (500m) deep, including reefs, caverns, and submerged wrecks
DIET	Fish (including smaller congers), large crabs, lobsters, squid, octopus, and some carrion
LIFESPAN	Up to 15 years, maybe more

The conger eel is found in the eastern Atlantic Ocean, from Iceland toward the north to as far south as Senegal in western Africa. It also resides in the North, Baltic, Mediterranean, Adriatic, Aegean, and Black seas.

1

A fisherman anticipates a tasty meal as he cuts off the head of his enormous catch in his bathtub.

2

Once the eel is decapitated, the man reaches down to pick up the severed head—unaware that the conger's reflexes are still active. The head bites his wrist viciously, and as he screams in agony the body continues to writhe in the bathtub.

Did You Know?

● Conger eels and their larvae are so dissimilar that, until the late 19th century, scientists believed they were entirely separate species.

● Large hard-shelled crustaceans ,such as crabs and lobsters, pose no problem for a hungry conger eel. It seizes its prey and smashes the shell open against rocks before gulping down the contents.

● The Channel Islands once had a large conger fishing and exporting industry that was recorded in the famous Domesday Book of 1086.

● The conger eel has perhaps the easiest Latin name of all creatures, simply being called *Conger conger*.

PORCUPINE FISH

Latin name: *Diodon* species

FINS

The fins are too small for fast swimming, but the fish can make delicate maneuvers in narrow crevices.

SPINES

Each bony spine is formed by a modified scale and can grow up to 2in (5cm) long.

A porcupine fish may happily munch its way through all kinds of heavily armored prey, but it makes sure it seldom suffers the same fate. Its defense lies in an inflatable coat of sharp spines and organs packed with toxins. The porcupine fish presents a prickly problem to any marine predator rash enough to try to eat it. In "relaxed" pose, the porcupine fish looks like any other tasty ocean titbit. A dolphin using its echolocation detects a salmon-sized "blip" in the waters and homes in for the kill, but it's in for a nasty surprise…

SIZE

KEY DATA

LENGTH	Up to 3ft (90cm); typically 1ft (30cm)
LIFESTYLE	Solitary, night-active
PREY	Coral polyps, shellfish, and marine worms
DEFENSES	Spines, swelling, toxins
TOXICITY	Toxin can kill humans

Porcupine fish are found in warm seas throughout the world, particularly among coral reefs and seagrass beds. They are sometimes carried into cooler waters by ocean currents.

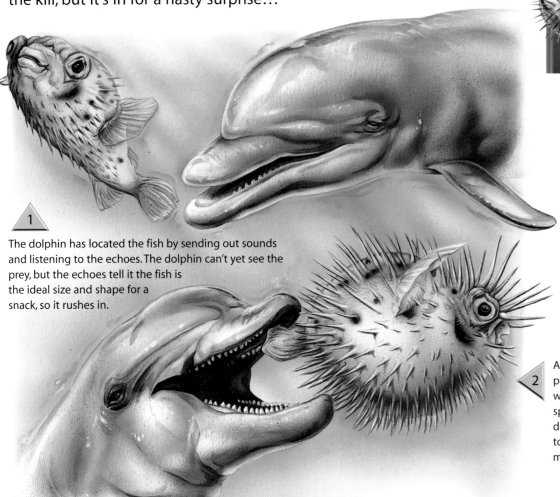

1

The dolphin has located the fish by sending out sounds and listening to the echoes. The dolphin can't yet see the prey, but the echoes tell it the fish is the ideal size and shape for a snack, so it rushes in.

2 At the last moment, the porcupine fish gulps in water and swells like a spiny football. The dolphin is smart enough to see it's made a huge mistake, and backs off.

Did You Know?

● An inflated porcupine fish is an impossible mouthful, and most predators won't even attempt to eat it. But a few have tried, and have been found dead, with their spiny prey wedged firmly in their throat.

● When a porcupine fish browses on coral, the crushed remains often stay in its system for some time. One fish was found with 18oz (500g) of powdered coral rock in its gut, the equivalent of swimming around with a bag of sand in your stomach.

● Although adult porcupine fish have few enemies, youngsters are far more vulnerable. In some areas they gather in vast shoals containing thousands of fish, which form an important food source for predators such as dolphins, tunas, and marlins.

● The death puffer (*Canthigaster solandri*), a toxic relative of the porcupine fish, is a great delicacy in Japan. But unless it is expertly prepared, a grisly death can follow.

DEEP-SEAGULPER EEL

Latin name: *Eurypharynx & Saccopharynx* species

TAIL ORGAN
The organ on the end of the eel's whip tail pulsates and glows spookily.

BODY
The muscles and many organs are greatly reduced in size so the eel needs little food to sustain them.

EYES
A pair of tiny eyes is adequate for detecting the glow from luminous neighbors in the dark.

MOUTH
The vast funnel mouth is lined with small, sharp teeth, probably for gripping any small fish the eel is lucky enough to come across.

GUT
The eel's stomach can expand to hold a large meal—if it finds one.

All mouth and stomach, the deep-sea gulper eel is equipped with massive jaws and a bucket-like gut for feeding in the dark depths of the ocean. As it cruises along, it gobbles shrimp and other small animals. The gulper eel is adapted to survive in perhaps the most inhospitable conditions on Earth: pitch-dark, freezing cold, and crushing pressure. In the dark ocean depths, light is irresistible. The deep-sea gulper eel may use the luminous organ on its tail to entrance prey. By waving the lure, it could grab inquisitive fish that come to investigate.

Size

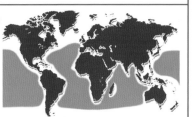

KEY DATA

LENGTH	Up to 2ft (60cm)
PREY	Animal plankton, small crustaceans, and small fish
WEAPONS	Large mouth, luminous lure
DEPTH	3280–9840 ft (1000–3000m)
LIFESPAN	Unknown

Gulper eels have been dredged up by fishing trawlers in oceans all over the warmer parts of the world.

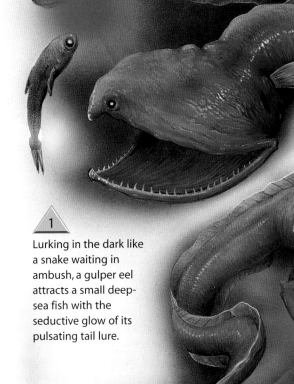

△1
Lurking in the dark like a snake waiting in ambush, a gulper eel attracts a small deep-sea fish with the seductive glow of its pulsating tail lure.

Slowly and tantalizingly, the eel moves the lure in front of its mouth. Unaware of the danger, the fish hovers just inside the cavernous space between the eel's gaping jaws. The predator closes its mouth in a single lethal movement, gulping down the helpless prey. ◁2

Did You Know?

● The leaf-shaped young of the gulper eel live nearer to the ocean surface than their parents. They change into their adult shape when they are just under 1.5in (4cm) long, and already have huge mouths.

● The gulper eel lives too deep in the ocean to be studied in its natural environment. Scientists have to deduce its behavior mainly from a study of badly damaged specimens hauled up in deep-sea trawl nets.

● As much of the gulper eel's life story is unknown, scientists can only speculate on the function of the luminous organ on its tail. The idea that it is a lure is only one theory. The eel might also use it to confuse predators, or to attract a mate.

● Unlike in most other fish, the gulper eel's lateral line organ, which detects vibrations, stands out from the surface of its skin. This may make the organ more sensitive to the movements of approaching prey.

CHIMAERA

Latin name: Families *Chimaeridae, Rhinochimaeridae & Callorhynchidae*

SPINE
Some chimaeras have a venomous spine in their dorsal fin.

TAIL
The plow-nosed chimaera has a tail like a shark's. Other chimaeras have a long, narrow tail.

EYES
These are largest in the blunt-nosed chimaera.

GILL COVERS
The chimaera's delicate gills are protected by covers, like the gills of bony fish.

TEETH
The teeth are fused into beaklike plates, giving the fish a powerful bite for crushing the thick shells of its prey.

SNOUT
The snout of the plow-nosed chimaera is ideally shaped for probing sand and mud for buried prey.

A chimaera may be slow and ungainly, but it is superbly adapted for finding mollusks and other prey on the seabed—and some species have a painful surprise in store for any shark or other predator that attacks. The bizarre-looking chimaera is one of the funniest-looking fish in the sea—but the venomous dorsal-fin spine of some species of this strange creature is no joke! Nosing its way over the seabed, the chimaera has special adaptations for finding tasty titbits hiding in the mud, weed, and murk. Some families of the fish live and hunt in shallow seas; others lurk in the gloom deeper down.

Size

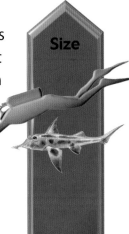

KEY DATA

LENGTH	Up to 4.5ft (1.5m), depending on species	
DIET	Mollusks, crustaceans, small fish, and starfish	
WEAPONS	Some species have a venomous dorsal spine	All the known species of chimaera live close to the seabed. They are found all around the world, in the colder seas and oceans of both the Northern and Southern Hemispheres.
LIFESPAN	Unknown	

1

The plow-nosed chimaera (family Callorhynchidae) lives in shallow coastal water, where it uses its plough-shaped and sensitive snout to find mollusks buried in the seabed.

2

The blunt-nosed chimaera (family Chimaeridae) lives in the murky twilight of deeper water, some 984–1638ft (300–500m) down. Its very sensitive eyes enable it to spot starfish and other prey on the surface of the seabed.

3

The long-nosed chimaera (family Rhinochimaeridae) lives even deeper down. It has a long, sensitive snout for locating mollusks in the permanently dark water.

Did You Know?

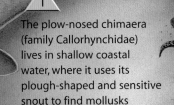

● Around the world, the chimaera has many other names that reflect its peculiar appearance, including ratfish, ghost shark, rabbit fish, leopard fish, and elephant fish.

● To compensate for wear and tear, the sharp, beaklike plates in the chimaera's mouth grow continuously throughout its life.

● The fire-breathing chimaera of Ancient Greek mythology was part lion, part goat, and part dragon. Today, the word "chimaera" has come to mean any extraordinary looking creature, real or imagined.

● Chimaeras are often caught in nets but in Europe are usually considered inedible and discarded. In China and South Africa, however, they are regarded as a delicacy and cooked in a variety of ways. In New Zealand, they are known as "silver trumpet" and are fried and served with fries, and in Australia they are eaten as "white fillet."

HAGFISH

Latin name: Family *Mixinidae*

SKIN

The soft, scaleless skin is white to pale brown.

BODY

Rows of pores along each flank contain glands that exude vast quantities of glutinous slime.

TENTACLES

These are sensitive both to touch and chemical traces in the water.

MOUTH

Although it has no jaws, the mouth conceals a rasping tongue equipped with comb-shaped teeth.

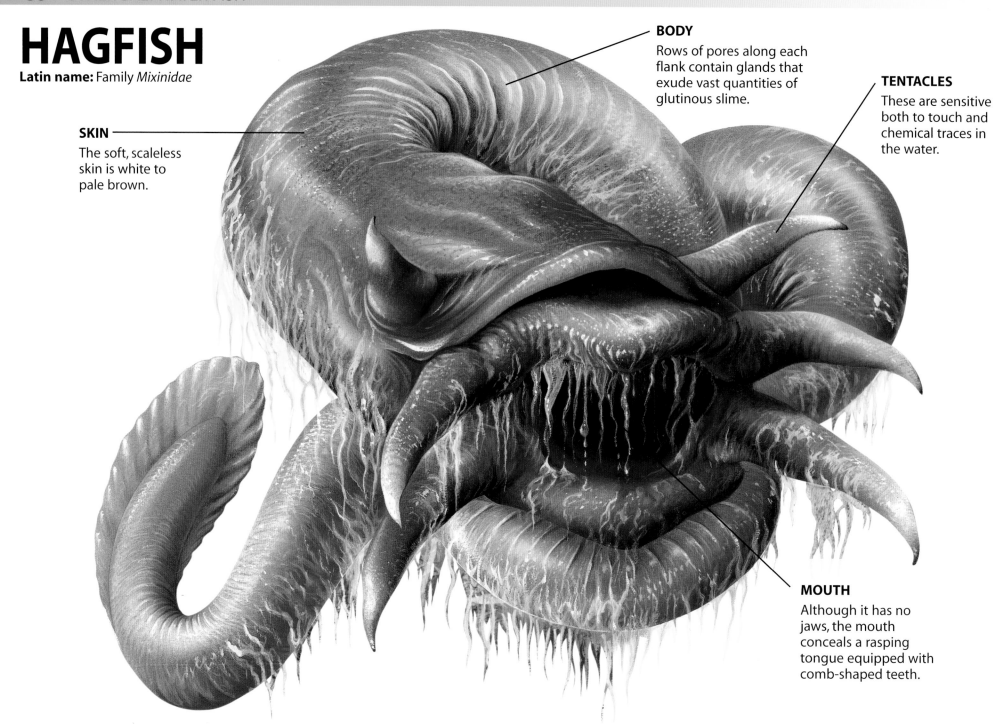

A hagfish is known as the slime-hag because it uses gobs of it to clog the gills of other fish to smother them. It also sneaks into fishing nets to gorge on the helpless occupants. This wormlike creature is a fish: a scavenger that attacks living victims and eats them from the inside out. If a bigger fish attacks, the hagfish makes slime with long filaments to form a sticky mesh to entangle and smother the unfortunate predator.

Size

KEY DATA

SPECIES	More than 40	
LENGTH	Up to 28in (70cm)	
PREY	Mollusks, worms, and dead and dying fish	Hagfish prefer water temperatures of 55°F (13°C) or under, and live in cooler areas of the Atlantic, Pacific, and Indian oceans. They are most commonly found over the continental shelves, to depths of 1968ft (600m).
WEAPONS	Rasping jaws and slime	
LIFESPAN	Unknown	

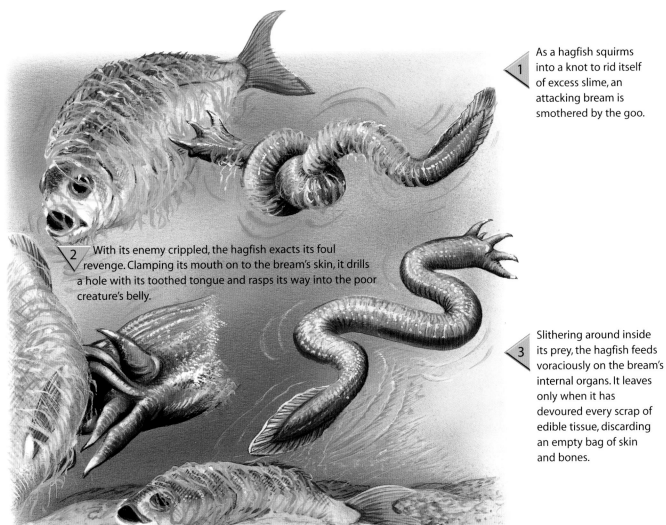

1 As a hagfish squirms into a knot to rid itself of excess slime, an attacking bream is smothered by the goo.

2 With its enemy crippled, the hagfish exacts its foul revenge. Clamping its mouth on to the bream's skin, it drills a hole with its toothed tongue and rasps its way into the poor creature's belly.

3 Slithering around inside its prey, the hagfish feeds voraciously on the bream's internal organs. It leaves only when it has devoured every scrap of edible tissue, discarding an empty bag of skin and bones.

Did You Know?

● The hagfish keeps its single nostril clear of clogging mucus by blowing it out with a slimy sneeze.

● Trawlers sometimes bring up fish that have been entirely eaten out by hagfish—cutting them open to find the slimy killers still coiled up inside.

● As the hagfish punches into a victim's body, it often coils itself into a knot to obtain more leverage.

● A hagfish can create five gallons of slime in just a few seconds—and a single specimen placed in a large bucket of seawater can rapidly turn the entire contents into gooey gloop.

● The hagfish has such a slow metabolism that it can survive for up to seven months without eating.

● Hagfish are a popular dish in Asia—especially Korea. But in North America people generally hunt them for their tough, leathery skin, which is used to make purses and belts.

GROUPER

Latin name: Family *Serranidae*

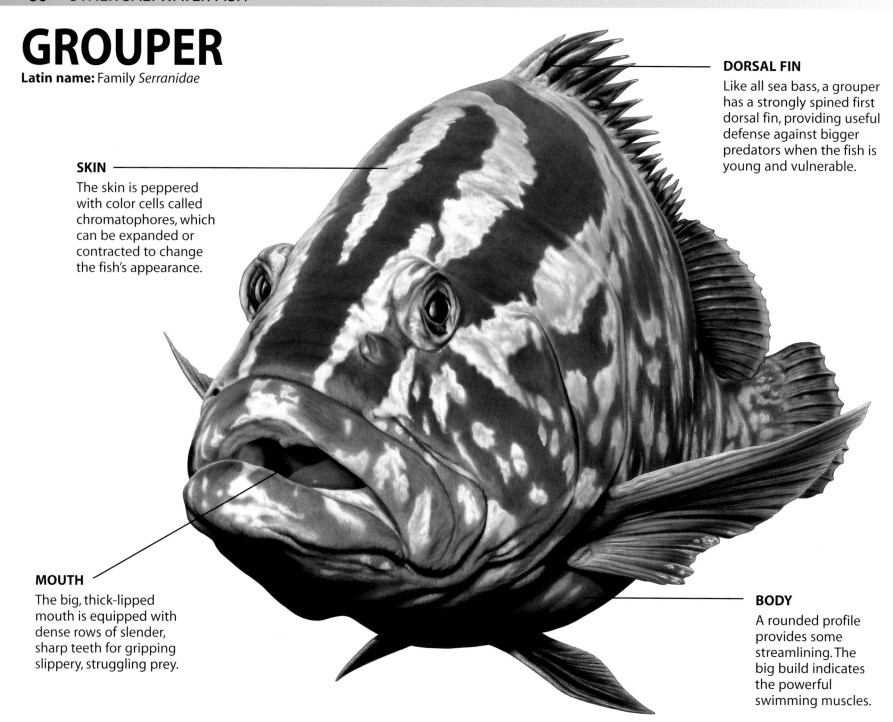

DORSAL FIN

Like all sea bass, a grouper has a strongly spined first dorsal fin, providing useful defense against bigger predators when the fish is young and vulnerable.

SKIN

The skin is peppered with color cells called chromatophores, which can be expanded or contracted to change the fish's appearance.

MOUTH

The big, thick-lipped mouth is equipped with dense rows of slender, sharp teeth for gripping slippery, struggling prey.

BODY

A rounded profile provides some streamlining. The big build indicates the powerful swimming muscles.

Groupers are counted as kings of the coral reef: ruthlessly efficient killers whose success can be measured by their often enormous sizes. Thickset and slow, a grouper may look like a chubby vegetarian, but it is a murderous meat-eater, with a talent for super-fast surprise attacks.

Size

KEY DATA

LENGTH	Up to 9ft (2.7m) depending on species
WEIGHT	Up to 1102lb (500kg)
LIFESTYLE	Ambush predator
PREY	Fish, shellfish, octopus, squid
LIFESPAN	70 years or more

Groupers live in warm shallow seas all around the world, but they are most numerous in coral reefs—where the teeming shoals of small fish provide them with plenty of prey.

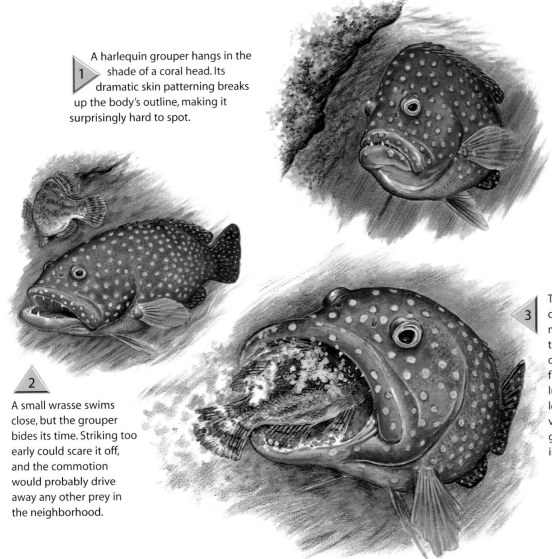

1 A harlequin grouper hangs in the shade of a coral head. Its dramatic skin patterning breaks up the body's outline, making it surprisingly hard to spot.

2 A small wrasse swims close, but the grouper bides its time. Striking too early could scare it off, and the commotion would probably drive away any other prey in the neighborhood.

3 The little wrasse comes closer still. Judging its moment to perfection, the grouper suddenly opens its mouth. Water floods in, carrying the luckless wrasse with it. In less than a second it has vanished, and the grouper slips back into hiding.

Did You Know?

● In the *Sydney Morning Herald* of November 30, 1943, a report told of massive groupers making repeated attacks on salvage divers. One fish clamped its jaws around a diver's helmet and carried him off.

● Spotted groupers are sometimes found with the blackened remains of sharp-tailed eels lodged in odd parts of their bodies. Swallowed alive, these wriggling, knife-edged fish slice though the grouper's gut and become trapped in its body cavity—and as they cannot be digested here, they gradually become mummified.

● The biggest of all groupers is probably the Queensland grouper, found off the northeast coast of Australia. A full-grown specimen can tip the scales at half a tonne!

● Cousins of the groupers include the soapfish. These fish are able to ooze a coat of slime containing grammistin, a foul-tasting poison that puts off would-be predators.

ELECTRIC RAY

Latin name: Family *Torpedinidae*

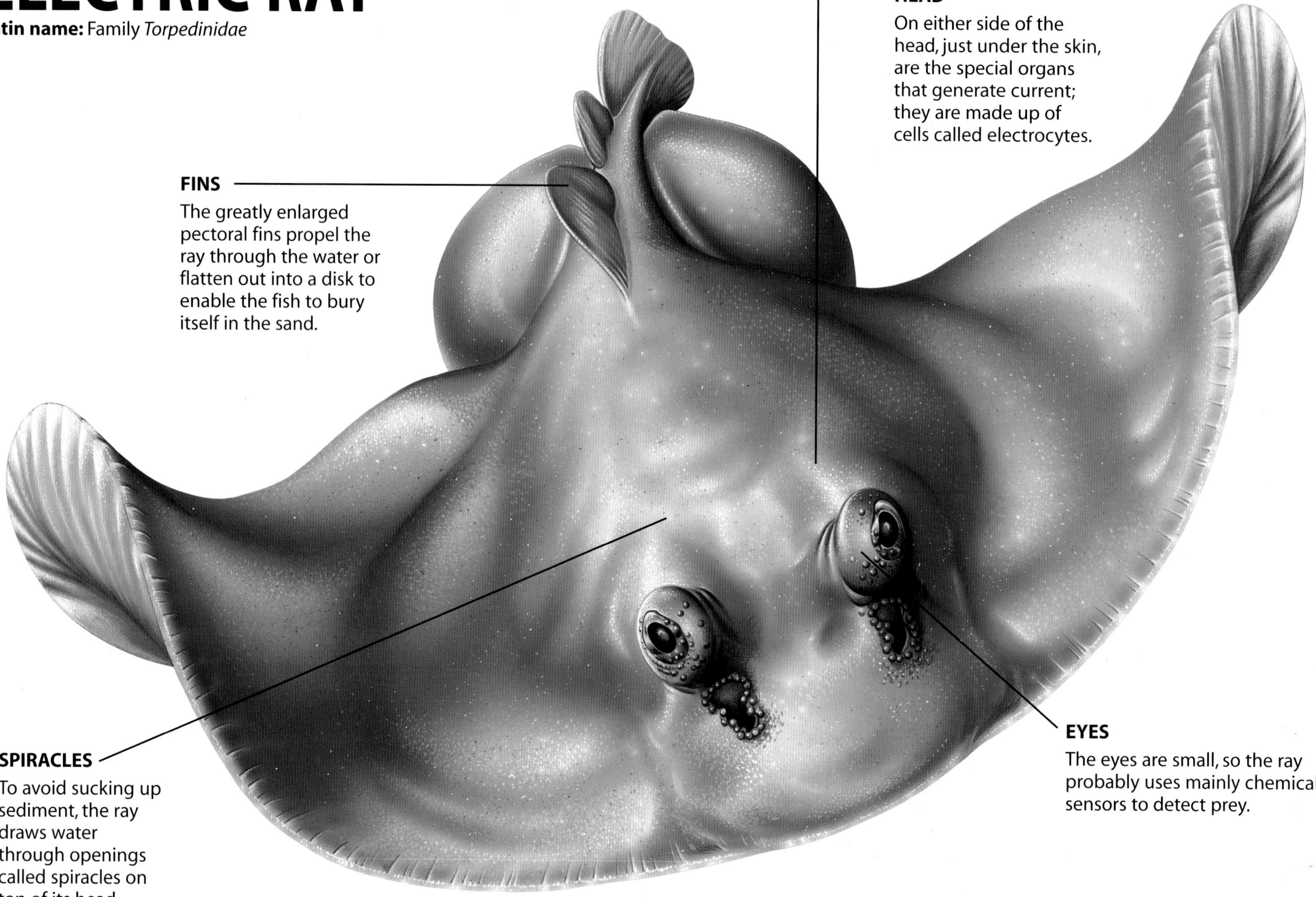

HEAD

On either side of the head, just under the skin, are the special organs that generate current; they are made up of cells called electrocytes.

FINS

The greatly enlarged pectoral fins propel the ray through the water or flatten out into a disk to enable the fish to bury itself in the sand.

SPIRACLES

To avoid sucking up sediment, the ray draws water through openings called spiracles on top of its head.

EYES

The eyes are small, so the ray probably uses mainly chemical sensors to detect prey.

The secret of the electric ray's deadly power lies in the banks of current-generating cells either side of its head. Discharging in unison, the cells emit electric pulses that are strong enough to deter enemies and immobilize prey. When this ugly fish heads for coastal waters in search of victims, all other sea animals should keep away. The electric ray's favorite ploy is to drift into the shallows, flatten itself on the seabed, and wait for prey.

Size

KEY DATA

LENGTH	Up to 6ft (1.8m)	
WEIGHT	Up to 198lb (90kg)	
PREY	Small fish and marine invertebrates, including snails, worms, and small crustaceans such as crabs	The electric ray inhabits all the tropical, subtropical, and temperate seas and oceans. Most species are found in shallow coastal zones, but some live on the seabed in deep water.
LIFESPAN	Unknown	

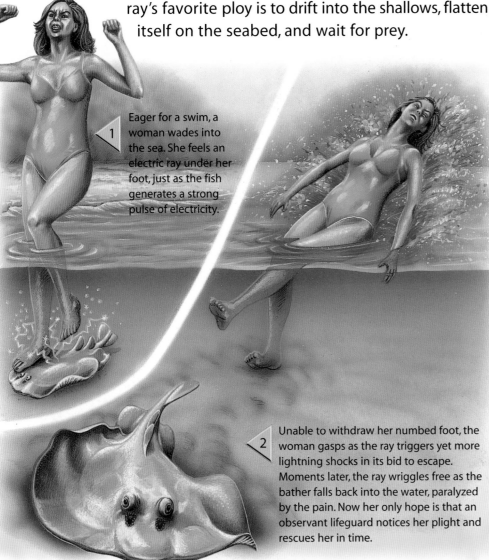

1 Eager for a swim, a woman wades into the sea. She feels an electric ray under her foot, just as the fish generates a strong pulse of electricity.

2 Unable to withdraw her numbed foot, the woman gasps as the ray triggers yet more lightning shocks in its bid to escape. Moments later, the ray wriggles free as the bather falls back into the water, paralyzed by the pain. Now her only hope is that an observant lifeguard notices her plight and rescues her in time.

Did You Know?

● The electric ray may not be entirely immune to its own shocks. Close observation shows that each discharge triggers a contraction of the muscles in the fish's body.

● The electric ray is relatively harmless on dry land. However, if someone pours water onto a living fish the current can travel up the stream and give the pourer a shock.

● The ray's greedy appetite for stunned fish can be its undoing. Dead specimens of the short-tail electric ray (*Hypnos monopterygium*) have been found with large fish wedged in their throats. It seems the rays died trying to engulf prey that were just too big to swallow.

● The electric ray was well known to the ancient Greeks, and it appears in pottery and writing dating back over 2000 years. During ancient Roman times, doctors even administered shocks from electric rays to treat chronic foot ailments such as gout.

WEEVER FISH

Latin name: Family *Trachinidae*

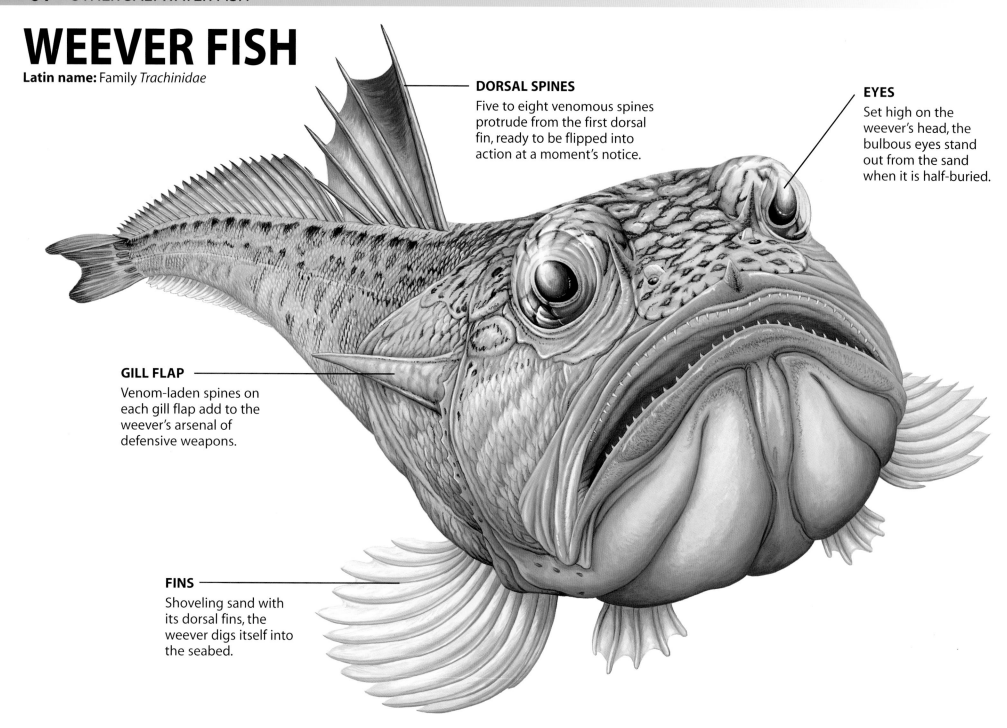

DORSAL SPINES
Five to eight venomous spines protrude from the first dorsal fin, ready to be flipped into action at a moment's notice.

EYES
Set high on the weever's head, the bulbous eyes stand out from the sand when it is half-buried.

GILL FLAP
Venom-laden spines on each gill flap add to the weever's arsenal of defensive weapons.

FINS
Shoveling sand with its dorsal fins, the weever digs itself into the seabed.

Bristling with venomous spines to protect it from enemies, the weever fish has a nasty reputation. It stabs bathers who stumble on its sandy hideaway and fishermen who snare it in their nets. Hidden in the sand with just its venom-loaded spines showing, the weever fish springs a shocking surprise on anyone paddling barefoot. Weever fish like to hunt at night, but by day, they'll happily snap up passing fish and shrimp.

Size

KEY DATA

LENGTH	Up to 6ft (45cm) (greater weever)	
PREY	Shrimp, crabs, and small fish	
INJURY	Usually a pierced foot	
VENOM	Injected by spines on fins and gill covers	
VIRULENCE	Painful but not lethal	

The four species of weever fish are found in the mild waters of the northeastern Atlantic Ocean and the Mediterranean Sea, in coastal waters up to depths of about 328ft (100m). There are also unconfirmed reports of weever fish living in Pacific waters around China and Chile.

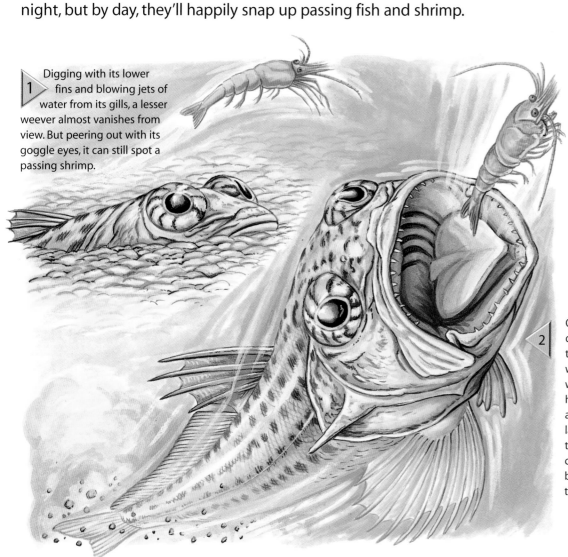

1 ▷ Digging with its lower fins and blowing jets of water from its gills, a lesser weever almost vanishes from view. But peering out with its goggle eyes, it can still spot a passing shrimp.

2 ▷ Oblivious to the hidden danger lurking below, the shrimp paddles within range. The weever bursts from its hiding place, mouth agape. A split second later, the weever sucks the shrimp into its cavernous throat and burrows back into the sand.

Did You Know?

● Weever fish are often caught in the trawl nets used by shrimp boats, and removing them from the mass of shrimp is difficult, dangerous work.

● The lesser weever has stronger venom than the greater weever, and is also more dangerous because it moves closer to shore in summer—just when the beaches are packed with holidaymakers.

● Despite their dangerous venom, greater weevers have tasty flesh and are often caught for food in Europe. As a precautionary measure, their heads and fin spines are normally removed as soon as they are caught.

● Many fish have an air-filled swim bladder to keep them afloat, but as the weever spends most of its time on the seabed, it doesn't need one.

ANGLERFISH

Latin name: *Lophius* species

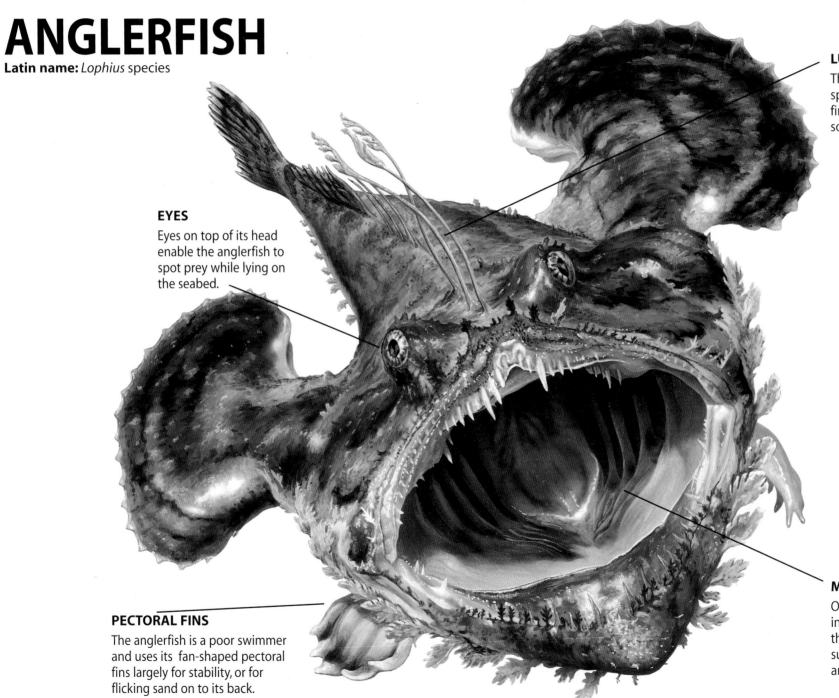

LURE
The anglerfish has several spines along its back, the first one topped by a fleshy, sometimes wormlike, lure.

EYES
Eyes on top of its head enable the anglerfish to spot prey while lying on the seabed.

MOUTH
Opening and closing in the blink of an eye, the cavernous mouth sucks in small fish in an instant.

PECTORAL FINS
The anglerfish is a poor swimmer and uses its fan-shaped pectoral fins largely for stability, or for flicking sand on to its back.

The popular idea of a marine predator is a muscular shark slipping through water after fast prey. The ugly anglerfish does things differently, but it's as mean and lethal as they come. Flopped on the seabed and looking like a clod of mud, this big, flabby fish reacts explosively to grab any prey that wanders near. The anglerfish uses a slender spine between its eyes to fish for prey. It wiggles the fleshy lure at the tip to attract the attention of potential prey or waves it gently to imitate the ripples of a swimming fish.

Size

KEY DATA

LENGTH	Up to 6ft (1.8m); teeth 1in (2.5cm)
WIDTH	3ft (90cm)
WEIGHT	Up to 991lb (45kg)
DEPTH	1968ft (600m); 6560ft (2000m) if breeding
PREY	Fish, crustaceans, squid, seabirds, and even turtles

The common anglerfish, *Lophius piscatorius*, lives around European coasts from Norway to the Mediterranean. The American species *Lophius americanus* occurs along the Atlantic coast from Nova Scotia to Brazil.

1 After flicking sand and pieces of shell on to its back, the anglerfish settles on the seabed, where it is camouflaged by its mottled skin. A silvery-gray bass soon swims into view, and the anglerfish begins to twitch its lure enticingly, gradually tempting the smaller fish toward its mouth.

2 As the little bass swims closer, the anglerfish waits for the perfect moment. Seconds later, it whisks the lure out of the way and opens its enormous mouth, gulping in a huge quantity of water and sucking the bass in with it. The unfortunate creature passes easily over the predator's spiked teeth as it shoots inside, because they bend down out of the way on fibrous hinges. But immediately afterward, they flip back up again to form an impenetrable wall of inward-curving barbs—and the bass has had its chips.

Did You Know?

● An anglerfish was once found floating on the surface with a seagull stuck in its mouth, after choking to death on its over-large meal.

● Sometimes, other fish damage or even amputate the anglerfish's lure by biting at the tempting morsel. Fortunately for the anglerfish, it soon grows back, ready to be used again.

● Despite its distinctly grotesque appearance, the anglerfish has delicately flavored flesh. Its tail is said to taste like crayfish, and some unscrupulous fishermen have even been known to substitute scoops of anglerfish flesh for scampi.

● The anglerfish was known as the fishing frog for many centuries, and is also called the goosefish. Its flesh is sold as monkfish in Britain.

● Scientists have identified anglerfish fossils that date back to the latter part of the Eocene period, more than 38 million years ago.

MANTA RAY

Latin name: *Manta birostris & M. hamiltoni*

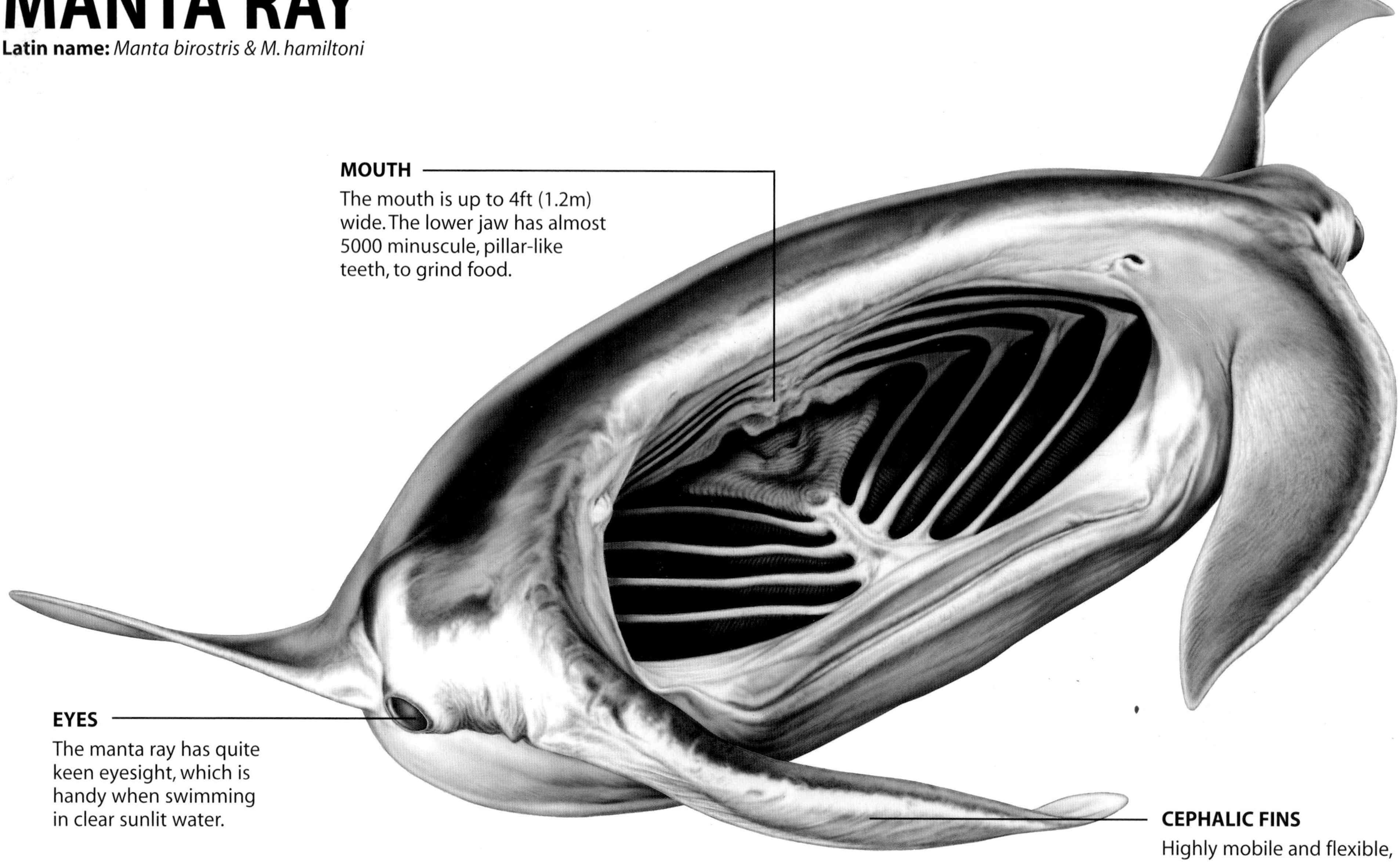

MOUTH

The mouth is up to 4ft (1.2m) wide. The lower jaw has almost 5000 minuscule, pillar-like teeth, to grind food.

EYES

The manta ray has quite keen eyesight, which is handy when swimming in clear sunlit water.

CEPHALIC FINS

Highly mobile and flexible, these funnel water and food into the manta ray's open mouth.

A gentle giant, the graceful manta ray cruises the surface waters of the warm oceans, sunning its back and filling its belly with fresh seafood. For a diver, swimming with this marine marvel is the experience of a lifetime. Ghosting through the sea like an alien spacecraft, the monstrous but harmless manta ray is one of the wonders of the natural world. The manta's great wings can launch the fish high above the waves, to bellyflop or flip over and land full on its back. The aim may be to dislodge lice, but it can spell disaster for a small boat.

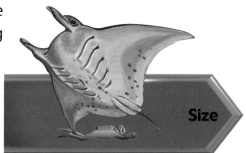

Size

KEY DATA

LENGTH	Up to 16ft (5m), half body, half tail	
WINGSPAN	Up to 23ft (7m), possibly more	
WEIGHT	Up to 5 tons (1.6 tonnes)	Manta rays live in all the warm seas and oceans of the world. Although they are not common, they are widespread, wandering over a vast area: mainly far offshore but occasionally along coasts.
DIET	Mainly shrimp and plankton	
LIFESPAN	Unknown	

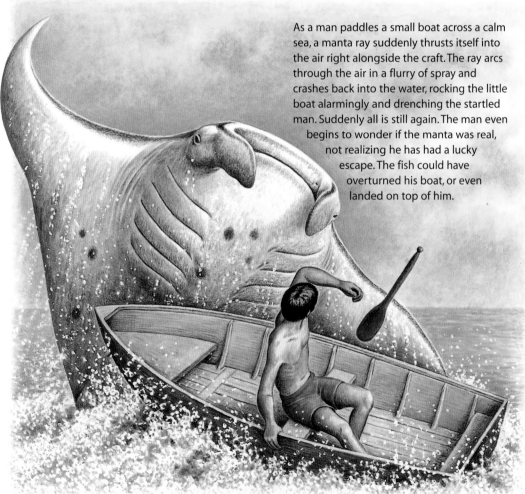

As a man paddles a small boat across a calm sea, a manta ray suddenly thrusts itself into the air right alongside the craft. The ray arcs through the air in a flurry of spray and crashes back into the water, rocking the little boat alarmingly and drenching the startled man. Suddenly all is still again. The man even begins to wonder if the manta was real, not realizing he has had a lucky escape. The fish could have overturned his boat, or even landed on top of him.

Did You Know?

● "Manta" derives from a Spanish word meaning cloak or blanket.

● The manta ray was once widely called the giant devil ray because of its diabolical-looking "horns." People thought that it could envelop them in its wings and devour them alive.

● The female manta ray gives birth to a single, fully formed baby with a 3ft 3in (1m) wingspan. The young ray can fend for itself straight away.

● Everywhere the manta goes, the remora fish goes too, clinging to the underside of the ray's body with the powerful sucker on top of its head. Now and then, it darts forward to steal some of the manta's food, before returning to its station and continuing to hitch a free ride.

● People once hunted the manta for its meat and rich liver oil and for shark bait. Reportedly, a harpooned manta could tow a small boat for hours at high speed before it tired.

MORAY EEL

Latin name: *Muraenidae* family

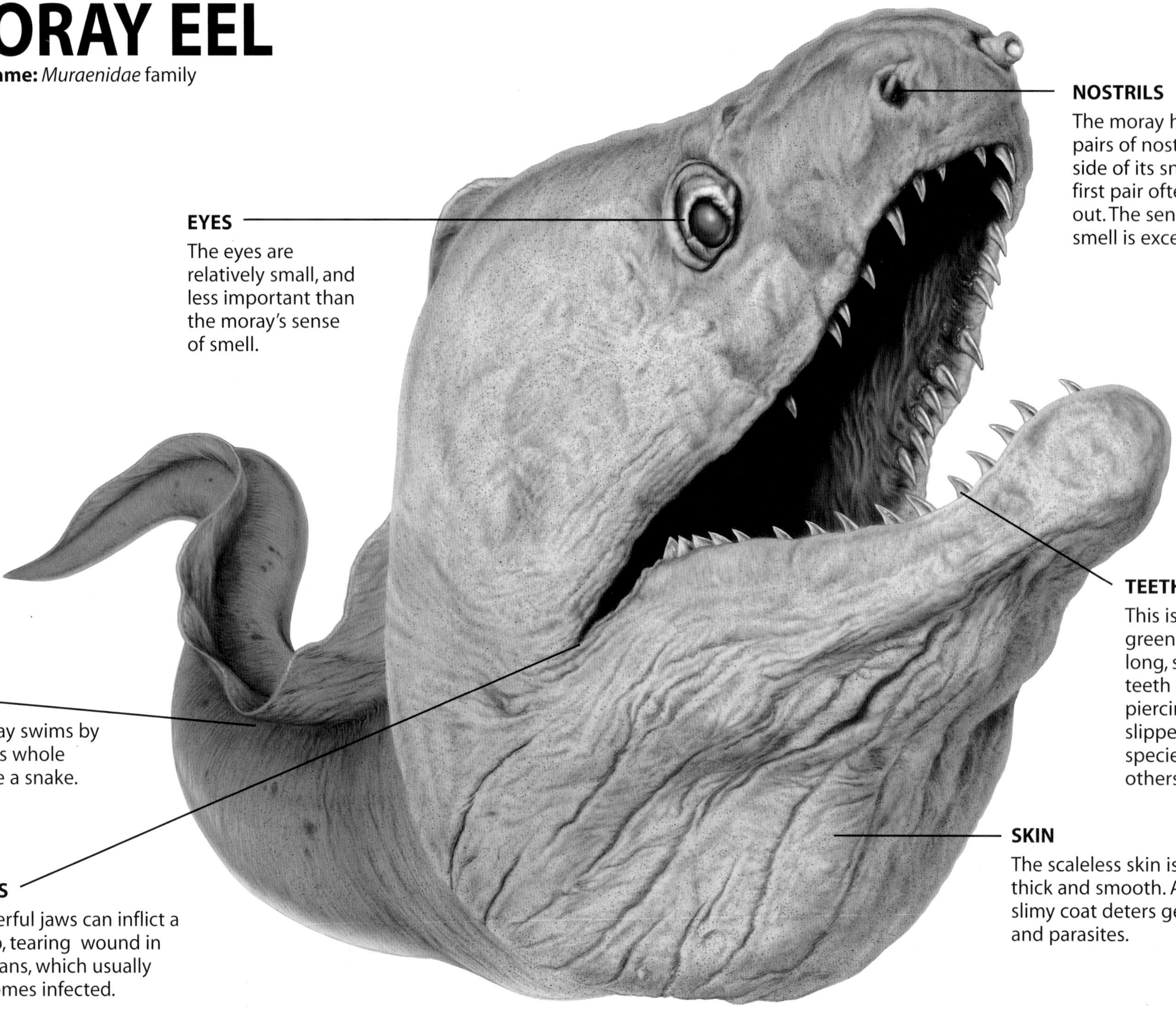

NOSTRILS

The moray has two pairs of nostrils either side of its snout. The first pair often stick out. The sense of smell is excellent.

EYES

The eyes are relatively small, and less important than the moray's sense of smell.

TEETH

This is the Atlantic green moray, whose long, slender, pointed teeth are ideal for piercing and holding slippery fish. Some species have longer teeth; others have short pegs.

BODY

The moray swims by flexing its whole body, like a snake.

SKIN

The scaleless skin is thick and smooth. A slimy coat deters germs and parasites.

JAWS

Powerful jaws can inflict a deep, tearing wound in humans, which usually becomes infected.

Lurking in its lair, with bloodhound nostrils sampling every trace of a likely meal, the moray eel is always ready to snatch passing prey in its vicelike jaws. A moray eel is ready to attack any animal that comes its way, but its favorite prey is a juicy octopus. Scenting a victim, the moray launches a ferocious attack. It coils its slippery body into a knot to enable it to shrug off the fiercely clinging tentacles.

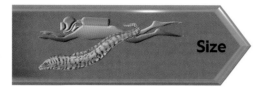

Size

KEY DATA

LENGTH	Usually 5ft (1.5m) or so; the Pacific species *Thyrsoidea macrurus* reaches 11.5ft (3.5m)	
WEIGHT	Up to 77lb (35kg)	Moray eels are found worldwide in warm, shallow seas, and are particularly numerous on tropical coral reefs. Occasionally morays stray into the cooler waters of the North Atlantic or North Pacific in summer.
PREY	Fish, octopus, shrimp, and crabs	
LIFESPAN	Up to 25 years	

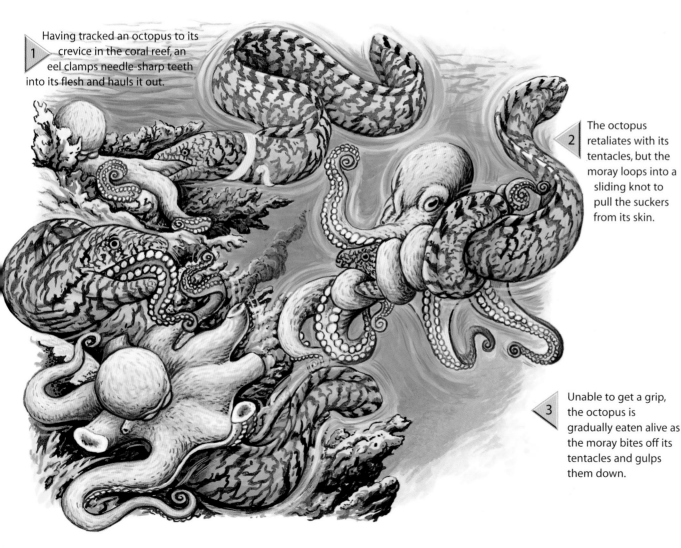

1 Having tracked an octopus to its crevice in the coral reef, an eel clamps needle-sharp teeth into its flesh and hauls it out.

2 The octopus retaliates with its tentacles, but the moray loops into a sliding knot to pull the suckers from its skin.

3 Unable to get a grip, the octopus is gradually eaten alive as the moray bites off its tentacles and gulps them down.

Did You Know?

● Moray eels may bite savagely if disturbed. The bite is often laced with bacteria, and a few divers have died from infected moray bites.

● There are about 80 species of moray. Some are drab, like the dark brown Californian moray. Others have vivid patterns and glowing colors, like the white-striped zebra moray and the dragon moray, both found on Indo-Pacific coral reefs.

● Some moray eels have strange horns and leaflike extensions to their nostrils, which may help them "sniff out" their prey.

● The parrotfish (*Pseudoscarus* species) goes to sleep each night on the coral reef in a "cocoon" of its own mucus. This prevents even the keen-nosed moray from tracking it down.

● The moray often has its mouth open to breathe, so to complete its camouflage the inside of the mouth is the same color as the outside.

SEA LAMPREY

Latin name: *Petromyzon marinus*

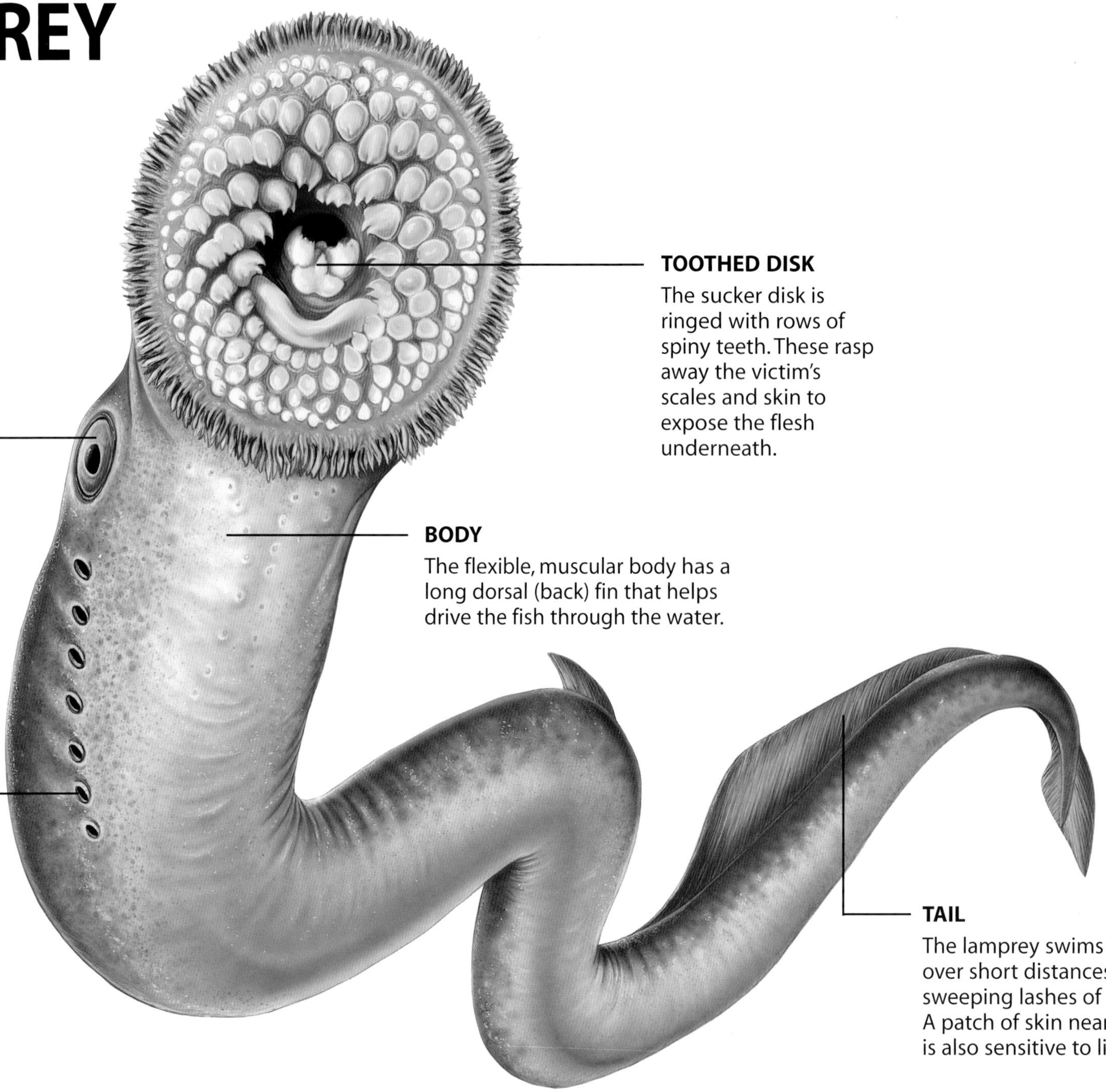

TOOTHED DISK

The sucker disk is ringed with rows of spiny teeth. These rasp away the victim's scales and skin to expose the flesh underneath.

EYES

The lamprey's eyes develop only when the fish finally turns into an adult. For the first seven years of its life, the larval lamprey is almost blind, detecting only light and dark.

BODY

The flexible, muscular body has a long dorsal (back) fin that helps drive the fish through the water.

GILLS

The gills take oxygen from water drawn into openings behind the mouth, so the fish can breathe while it feeds. The water then exits through seven gill holes on each side of its body.

TAIL

The lamprey swims rapidly over short distances with sweeping lashes of its tail. A patch of skin near the tip is also sensitive to light.

Clinging to its host like a giant leech, the sea lamprey gnaws at living flesh with boneless, toothy jaws. Young lamprey eat small organisms, but the adult lamprey is an avid bloodsucker. A vampire of the sea, this primitive creature latches on to other fish with its sucker mouth, then rasps holes in their flanks and drinks their blood. Hunting its victims by sight and smell, the lamprey targets the juiciest fish. As it closes in, the bloodsucking predator opens its mouth to use rows of vicious teeth to bore through skin and flesh.

Size

KEY DATA

LENGTH	Up to 36in (90cm)	
WEIGHT	Up to 5lb (2.5kg)	
BREEDING	Spawns in fresh water, after upriver migration	
DIET	Adult sucks the blood of living fish; larva filters tiny organisms from water	Adult sea lampreys live in the coastal waters of the European and American North Atlantic. They are also found in the North Sea, the Baltic, and the western Mediterranean.
HOST	Cod, trout, and salmon	
DEFENSE	Toxic mucus secreted by glands in the skin	
LIFESPAN	7 years as larval fish, 2 years as adult	

1 Wiggling rapidly toward a large sea trout, the lamprey bares its teeth, ready to latch on to the victim's scaly skin.

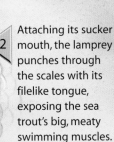

2 Attaching its sucker mouth, the lamprey punches through the scales with its filelike tongue, exposing the sea trout's big, meaty swimming muscles.

3 The lamprey sucks out blood and tissue fragments from the raw wound, and releases the victim only when its stomach is full. As it drops away, the wounded fish sinks bleeding through the water.

Did You Know?

 ● A sea lamprey drinks about 3lb (1.4kg) of blood during its adult life. A vampire bat drinks ten times as much.

● Sea lampreys have been found attached to sharks, but as they cannot penetrate the close-set denticles (sharp scales) covering the skin, they were probably just hitch-hiking.

● Lampreys were once known as "nine-eyes," because of the row of seven round gill openings behind each eye and the single round nostril between them.

● When some lampreys become adults, they don't feed, but lay their eggs and die soon afterward.

SCORPIONFISH

Latin name: *Scorpaena* group

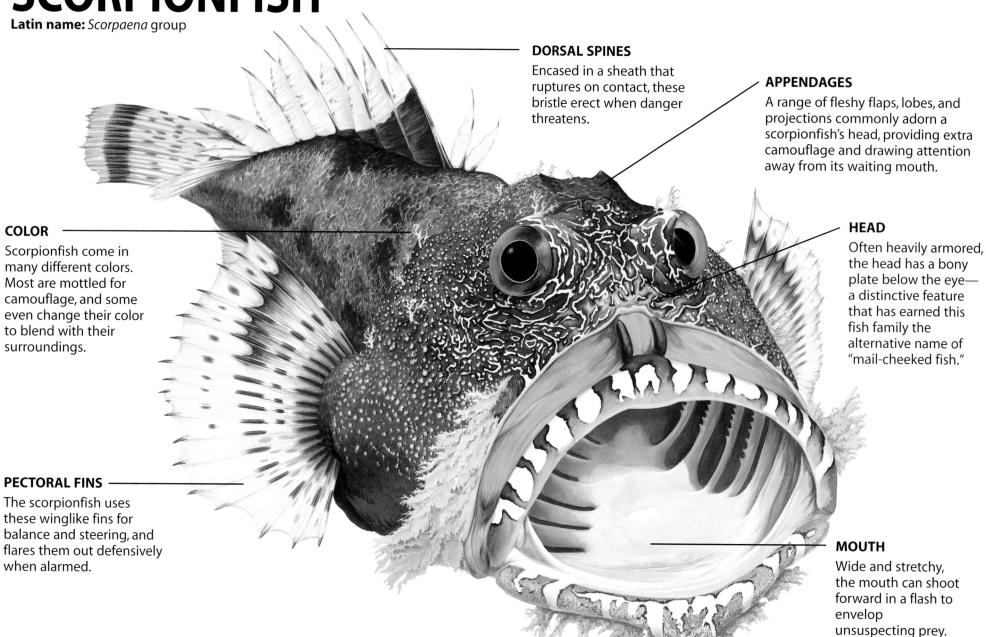

DORSAL SPINES

Encased in a sheath that ruptures on contact, these bristle erect when danger threatens.

APPENDAGES

A range of fleshy flaps, lobes, and projections commonly adorn a scorpionfish's head, providing extra camouflage and drawing attention away from its waiting mouth.

COLOR

Scorpionfish come in many different colors. Most are mottled for camouflage, and some even change their color to blend with their surroundings.

HEAD

Often heavily armored, the head has a bony plate below the eye—a distinctive feature that has earned this fish family the alternative name of "mail-cheeked fish."

PECTORAL FINS

The scorpionfish uses these winglike fins for balance and steering, and flares them out defensively when alarmed.

MOUTH

Wide and stretchy, the mouth can shoot forward in a flash to envelop unsuspecting prey.

Lurking in a crevice or masquerading as an algae-coated rock, the scorpionfish has deadly powers of disguise, but its spines are for protection only. Scorpionfish are caught commercially for their tasty flesh, but they must be handled with care, for like their landliving namesakes they can deliver an excruciating sting. Even the most experienced fisherman can fall foul of their bristling spines.

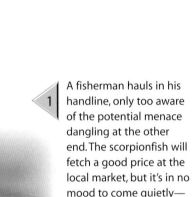

Size

KEY DATA

LENGTH	4–14in (10–35cm)
WEIGHT	Up to 3.5lb (1.5kg)
PREY	Small fish and crustaceans
WEAPONS	Venomous spines
HABITAT	Intertidal zone to depths of 295ft (90m)

Scorpionfish are found in temperate, subtropical, and tropical seas, with most species in the Indian and Pacific oceans. They usually live in shallow bays, along the coast or on coral reefs.

1 A fisherman hauls in his handline, only too aware of the potential menace dangling at the other end. The scorpionfish will fetch a good price at the local market, but it's in no mood to come quietly—spreading its fins and erecting its spines as it prepares for a violent encounter.

2 As he tries to remove his hook, the fish's desperate struggles force one of its venomous spines right into his hand—causing excruciating pain.

Did You Know?

● After a scorpionfish has been caught and killed, its spines remain dangerous for several days, even when it is kept in cold storage.

● After discharging its contents, the venom gland of a scorpionfish can regenerate and be ready for action again within six days.

● The red scorpionfish of the northwestern Atlantic regularly sheds its skin like a snake. The faster it feeds and grows, the more often it loses the upper layer, sometimes replacing it twice every month.

● Scorpionfish are also known as bullrouts, sulkies, waspfish, and kroki.

● Scorpionfish usually have longer spines than stonefish, with ductless venom glands located near the tips.

● Some species of scorpionfish expel tens of thousands of fertilized eggs inside a jello-like balloon that may reach up to 8in (20cm) in diameter.

BARRACUDA

Latin name: *Sphyraena* species

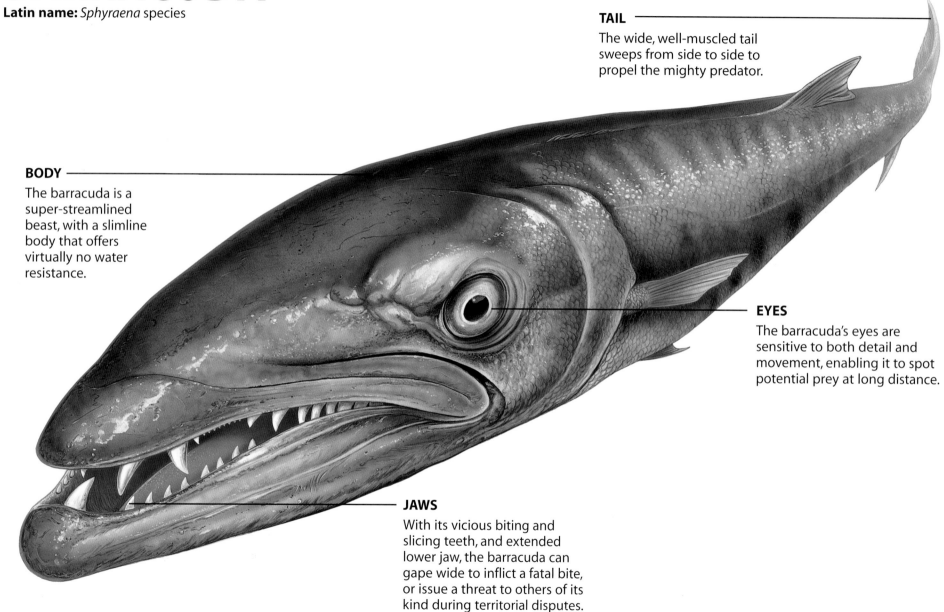

TAIL
The wide, well-muscled tail sweeps from side to side to propel the mighty predator.

BODY
The barracuda is a super-streamlined beast, with a slimline body that offers virtually no water resistance.

EYES
The barracuda's eyes are sensitive to both detail and movement, enabling it to spot potential prey at long distance.

JAWS
With its vicious biting and slicing teeth, and extended lower jaw, the barracuda can gape wide to inflict a fatal bite, or issue a threat to others of its kind during territorial disputes.

Hunting in groups or on its own, the voracious barracuda is a lurking menace in the warm coastal waters of the world. Once this sleek killer spots a potential victim, it locks on to its target and blasts through the sea like a missile. The barracuda's flesh-ripping jaws, keen vision, and lightning speed make it one of the most formidable hunters around tropical coasts. The barracuda has large eyes and hunts by sight. As it cruises its hunting area, it watches for signs of weakened prey, such as the erratic movements of an injured fish.

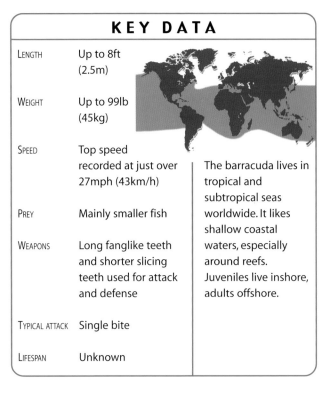

Size

KEY DATA

LENGTH	Up to 8ft (2.5m)
WEIGHT	Up to 99lb (45kg)
SPEED	Top speed recorded at just over 27mph (43km/h)
PREY	Mainly smaller fish
WEAPONS	Long fanglike teeth and shorter slicing teeth used for attack and defense
TYPICAL ATTACK	Single bite
LIFESPAN	Unknown

The barracuda lives in tropical and subtropical seas worldwide. It likes shallow coastal waters, especially around reefs. Juveniles live inshore, adults offshore.

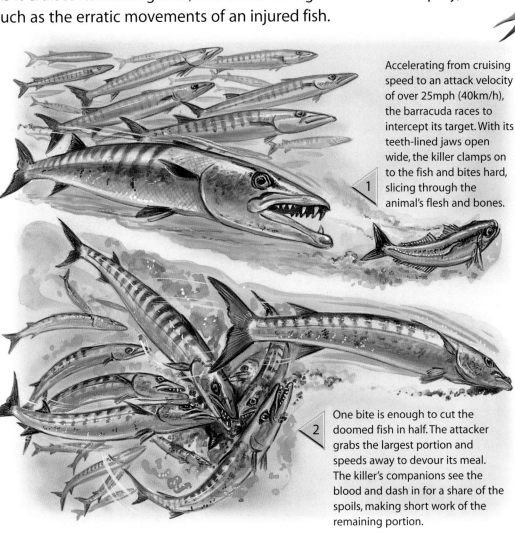

Accelerating from cruising speed to an attack velocity of over 25mph (40km/h), the barracuda races to intercept its target. With its teeth-lined jaws open wide, the killer clamps on to the fish and bites hard, slicing through the animal's flesh and bones.

1

2

One bite is enough to cut the doomed fish in half. The attacker grabs the largest portion and speeds away to devour its meal. The killer's companions see the blood and dash in for a share of the spoils, making short work of the remaining portion.

Did You Know?

● In some parts of the world, it is unsafe for humans to eat an adult barracuda, as it can result in the deadly *ciguatara* disease. This is caused by a build-up of toxins from fish that the barracuda has eaten.

● Barracudas that have eaten their fill of a shoal of small fish have been seen to herd the remainder into shallow water and guard their prey until they feel hungry again.

● Barracuda attacks on humans mostly occur in murky water, and may be due to mistaken identity. More often, an inquisitive barracuda will follow a diver around, watching intently and making the diver nervous, but without attacking.

TOADFISH

Latin name: Subfamily *Thalassophryninae*

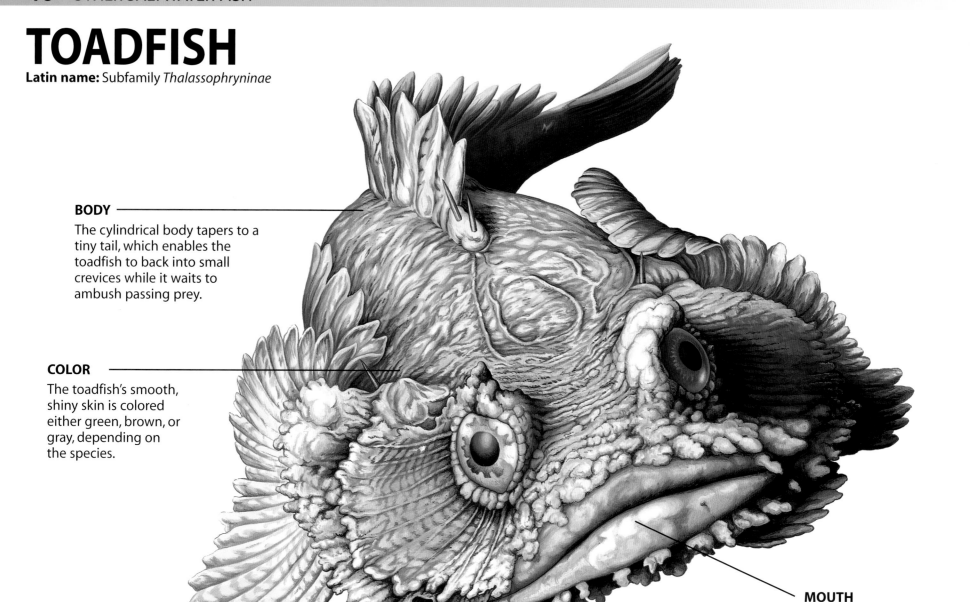

BODY

The cylindrical body tapers to a tiny tail, which enables the toadfish to back into small crevices while it waits to ambush passing prey.

COLOR

The toadfish's smooth, shiny skin is colored either green, brown, or gray, depending on the species.

MOUTH

The "turned down" mouth has large fleshy barbels that help the fish detect its food.

With a face that only a mother could love, and a taste for ambushing prey and gobbling it whole, a toadfish seems to lack redeeming features. Yet the male shows such dedication as a parent that he puts many animals to shame. This ugly denizen of coastal waters likes to find a cosy niche where it can hunt and breed and raise its young—and it sports nasty spines to ensure it's left alone. The shy toadfish is always looking for secret places to hide. Unfortunately, its choice of hidey-hole often brings it into contact with humans.

Size

1 As the sun rises over the warm Caribbean sea, a fisherman looks in his lobster pot, checking the previous night's catch. Unknown to him, an opportunistic toadfish has chosen his pot as a cozy hiding place and is lurking inside. The fisherman reaches in to pluck out a lobster.

2 The man has been attacked by lobsters many times and knows how to handle them—but he fails to spot the toadfish. Suddenly, he lets out a shriek and recoils in pain. As he pulls his hand from the pot, he finds the toadfish is still attached, its agonizing spines penetrating deep into his palm.

KEY DATA

SIZE	Length 3–9in (7.5–22cm), depending on species; weight up to 3lb (1.5kg)
PREY	Crabs, shrimp, octopus, fish, and shelled mollusks
DEFENSES	Venom-primed spines
LIFESPAN	About 3 years

Venomous toadfishes, members of the subfamily *Thalassophryninae*, are found off Central and South America. They dwell in crevices under rocks and in reefs, and even occupy discarded items such as jars. Other, non-venomous, toadfish live around the Americas, Africa, Australia, and southern Asia.

Did You Know?

● Some members of the toadfish subfamily *Porichthyinae* have small light-emitting organs along the sides of their head and body. These fish have been nicknamed "midshipmen" because the lights look like the shiny buttons on a naval officer's uniform.

● In captivity, toadfish have been able to survive out of water for over 24 hours. In the wild, they have been observed using their ventral fins as proto-legs to drag themselves over mudflats to get from pool to pool.

● People who live near a toadfish neighborhood dread the creature's mating season. The croaking noise the males make during courtship is so loud that it often keeps people living near the sea awake at night.

● The toadfish creates its unique call using an adapted air sac, called a swimbladder. This internal organ is found in nearly all fish and helps them to stay buoyant in the water.

STONEFISH

Latin name: *Synanceia horrida, S. verrucosa*

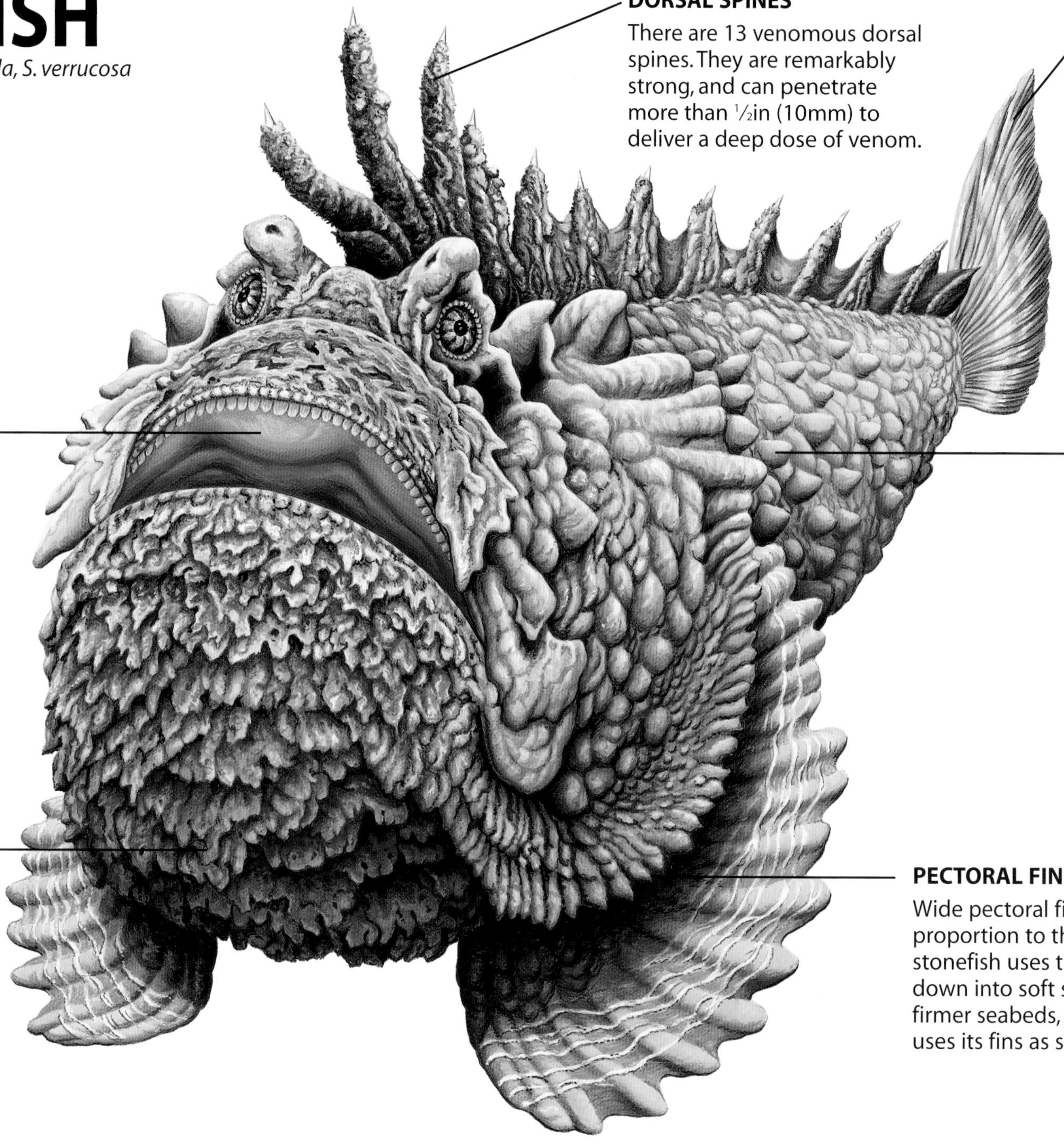

DORSAL SPINES

There are 13 venomous dorsal spines. They are remarkably strong, and can penetrate more than ½in (10mm) to deliver a deep dose of venom.

TAIL

The tail is small and unstreamlined, and can't propel the heavy, unwieldy body at any great speed.

MOUTH

The huge mouth bears a permanent scowl because the corners are downturned for efficient feeding. When the fish gulps down a meal, it opens its mouth and sucks in its prey at enormous speed. The process takes only 0.015 seconds.

TUBERCLES

Wartlike tubercles not only help to break up the fish's outline, but also secrete a toxic fluid that is a second line of defense against predators.

SKIN

The slimy, scaleless skin soon collects a camouflaging crust of seabed scraps and weed.

PECTORAL FINS

Wide pectoral fins are large in proportion to the body, and the stonefish uses them to dig its way down into soft sand and mud. Over firmer seabeds, a stonefish simply uses its fins as stabilizers.

Every year, holidaymakers enjoying a Pacific Ocean beach may be just a footstep away from a painful death. Nestling in the seabed of the warm shallows is a true nightmare of the marine world: the stonefish. Lying still in the shallows, the stonefish looks like a piece of muddy rubble. But one sting from its spines can bring hours of unbearable agony— sometimes death. The deadly spines are designed to keep a stonefish safe from predators, but they can stab deeply into the flesh of a human hand or foot, forcing the contents of the venom glands directly into the wounds.

Size

1 ▷ Lurking motionless in the shallows, a stonefish senses movement close by: a holidaymaker is reaching out for a pretty shell. The fish stealthily erects the spines of its dorsal fin. The three largest spines at the front are held almost vertical; the rear ten are angled backward.

Each spine is encased within a warty sheath. Near its base are two bulbous venom sacs, with narrow ducts that run up grooves on each spine, reaching almost to the tip. Fibrous tissue seals the top of each duct like a bottle stopper: this retains the venom under pressure.

2 ▷ A finger is impaled on the spines. As it presses down, the human tissue strips back the spine-sheaths and rips away the tip seals. It also crushes the venom glands. The venom (shown here in blue) explodes along the ducts and into the finger to inflict agonizing pain—or worse. The spines themselves are recharged after a few weeks.

KEY DATA

LENGTH	8–15in (20–38cm)
HABITAT	Tidal shallows to depths of 131ft (40m), including sandy seabeds, rocky reefs, and coral
DIET	Small fishes, crustaceans
VENOM DELIVERY	13 dorsal fin spines

Stonefish live in coastal waters in the Indo-Pacific region, in the Red Sea, along the east coast of Africa, across the Indian Ocean to the north of Australia, and around the French Polynesian reefs of the South Pacific.

Did You Know?

● The Australian Aborigines enact a traditional stonefish dance. Carrying clay fish with 13 wooden spines, the dancers wade about in the shallows and mime stepping on stonefish and dying in agony.

● A stonefish can remain alive for up to ten hours out of water. And the spines can still inject a lethal dose of venom for several days after a fish has died.

● It is possible—though extremely unwise—to pick up a live stonefish without injury, by gently slipping a hand into the sand beneath the fish and slowly raising it.

STINGRAY

Latin name: *Urolophidae & Dasyatidae* families

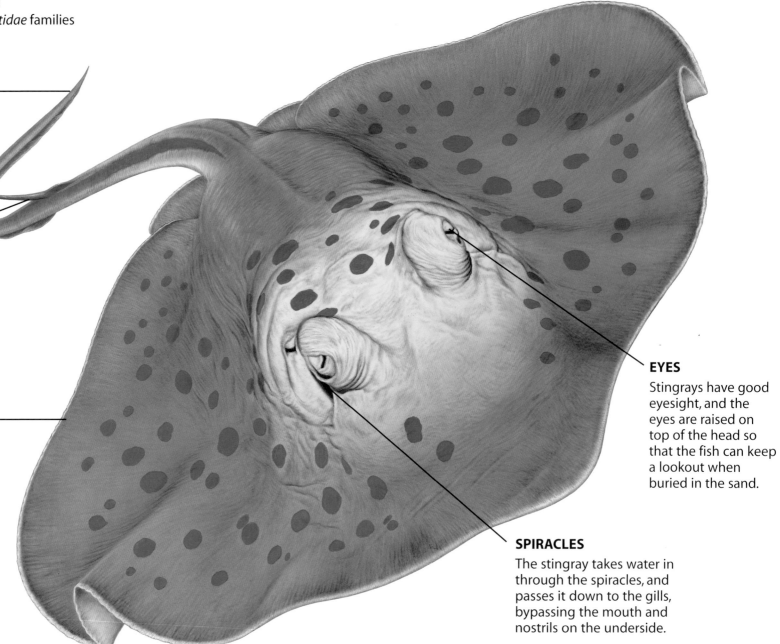

TAIL

Although capable of powerful strikes, the muscular tail is normally used for steering. Some species have a fringelike fin at the end.

SPINE

Hooked barbs cover the sharp spine, which is primed with venom from glands at the base. Some species of stingray have two spines.

PECTORAL FINS

Millions of years ago, the pectoral fins evolved into a continuous mantle around the flattened body.

EYES

Stingrays have good eyesight, and the eyes are raised on top of the head so that the fish can keep a lookout when buried in the sand.

SPIRACLES

The stingray takes water in through the spiracles, and passes it down to the gills, bypassing the mouth and nostrils on the underside.

A stingray spends much of its time foraging for food, skimming across the sea floor with an elegant flight-like motion. Favorite meals are mollusks and crustaceans, crunched between hard jaw plates. Often the wily ray uncovers its prey by wafting away the sand with its fins, or by squirting a jet of water from its mouth. When not on the move, the ray buries itself in the sand for a spot of rest and relaxation. Normally the ray relies on camouflage for protection, but if humans blunder too close, it strikes with a lightning flick of its venomous whiplike tail.

Size

KEY DATA

LENGTH	Largest species up to 15ft (4.5m) including tail	
WINGSPAN	Largest species up to 7ft (2m)	
SPINE	Largest species up to 14in (37cm)	Stingrays inhabit shallow waters in tropical, subtropical, and warm temperate seas around the world. Although stingrays are most common on the continental shelf, they are sometimes found in deeper waters.
WEIGHT	Largest up to 771lb (350kg)	
DEPTH OF HABITAT	656ft (200m), but usually less than 229ft (70m)	
PREY	Crabs, snails, shrimp, clams, and other shellfish, worms; occasionally small fish	
LIFESPAN	Unknown	

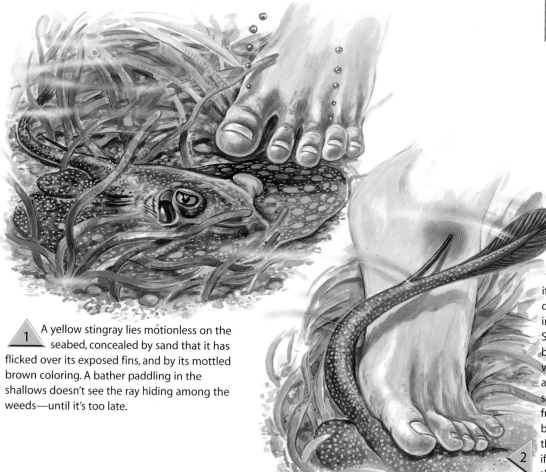

△1 A yellow stingray lies motionless on the seabed, concealed by sand that it has flicked over its exposed fins, and by its mottled brown coloring. A bather paddling in the shallows doesn't see the ray hiding among the weeds—until it's too late.

2 As the bather steps on the ray's flattened fin, it attacks in a flash. Striking over its back with an upward lash of its muscular tail, the ray drives the barbed spine into the intruder's foot. Severed blood vessels bleed copiously, and venom from the glands and sheath causes severe pain. Barbs and fragments of spine become embedded in the deep wound, which if left untreated, will rot the victim's flesh.

Did You Know?

● Scientists once uncovered a complete stingray fossil known as *Xiphotrygon* ("sword-tailed") in Wyoming, USA, in deposits dating back about 58 million years.

● When stingrays damage their spines, they grow new spines to replace the broken ones. Sometimes they have up to four spines on the tail at various stages of growth.

● Baby stingrays are born with their spines sheathed, to stop them damaging their mother during birth.

● Stingrays are intelligent fish and become very tame in aquariums, gently accepting food from the hands of their keepers.

SWORDFISH
Latin name: *Xiphias gladius*

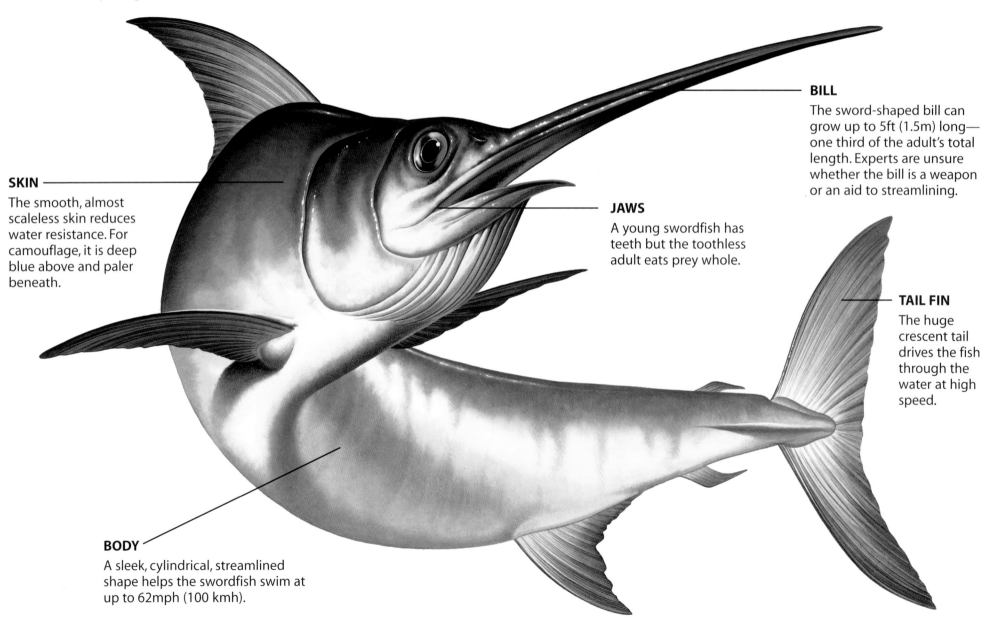

BILL

The sword-shaped bill can grow up to 5ft (1.5m) long—one third of the adult's total length. Experts are unsure whether the bill is a weapon or an aid to streamlining.

SKIN

The smooth, almost scaleless skin reduces water resistance. For camouflage, it is deep blue above and paler beneath.

JAWS

A young swordfish has teeth but the toothless adult eats prey whole.

TAIL FIN

The huge crescent tail drives the fish through the water at high speed.

BODY

A sleek, cylindrical, streamlined shape helps the swordfish swim at up to 62mph (100 kmh).

A swordfish is a solitary hunter that patrols large areas of sea in search of prey. Armed and deadly, this streamlined assassin blasts through the ocean as it seeks out more victims to savage with its lethal lance. Biologists still debate the exact purpose of the swordfish's immensely long bill. One theory is that it uses its "sword" as a slashing weapon to maim shoaling fish so that the killer can gobble up a greater number of prey.

Size

KEY DATA

LENGTH	7–16.5ft (2–5m)	
WEIGHT	Up to 1433lb (650kg)	
PREY	Fish and squid	The swordfish has one of the largest ranges of any species of fish. It is found throughout the tropical, subtropical, and temperate oceans of the world at depths down to 1968ft (600m).
WEAPONS	Long, swordlike bill; teeth in young swordfish	
LIFESPAN	25 years	

1 While hunting for prey, an alert swordfish discovers a shoal of fish. Before its prey can scatter, the predator rushes headlong into their midst, thrashing its bill about as it plunges through the heart of the group.

2 As the killer swivels round, most of the shoal flee the scene, leaving several wounded companions writhing in their wake. The predator now has an easy task to swim around gobbling up each injured fish in turn.

Did You Know?

● A very young swordfish has jaws of equal length, and it is only as it becomes a juvenile that the upper jaw outgrows the lower. As the fish continues to mature, the difference in the length of the two jaws grows ever more pronounced.

● Swordfish "attacks" on ships are legendary. A 19th-century British warship, *HMS Dreadnought*, once sprung a leak after a swordfish holed its wooden hull. The British Museum of Natural History has a piece of a ship's wooden hull on display showing a hole 22in (56cm) deep made by a swordfish. These were probably not deliberate attacks, however. It is more likely that the swordfish were simply traveling too fast to avoid ramming the ships.

● Small fish called remoras, which have strange sucker-like dorsal fins, sometimes attach themselves to the swordfish and hitch a ride as the giants power through the ocean.

Freshwater Fish

*Saltwater fish do not have a monopoly on bloodthirsty
behavior. Freshwater fish living in rivers, lakes, and
other inland waters can be just as savage.*

Take pikes, for example. They have wickedly spiked teeth for grasping their prey and a large mouth that can swallow it whole. Pikes specialize in surprise raids and can seize a victim without warning, and so fast that it has no chance of escape. Another freshwater fish, the Stargazer, has a different method, but is no less deadly. The Stargazer lies quietly on a river or lake bed under a camouflage of mud and sand, and can lure its prey by sticking a red filament out of its mouth. The prey mistakes this for a red worm and approaches, and before it knows what is happening, the Stargazer has gobbled it up. Some freshwater fish are equipped with curious features to help them find their food. The Elephant Fish, for example, has a long trunk with sensors, the Wels Catfish carries its sensors in thick "whiskers" called barbels, the Sawfish's head has a sawlike projection, and the Electric Eel is equipped with high voltage power cells sited along its tail. Whatever their equipment, freshwater fish are proof of Nature in all her ingenious variety.

ALLIGATOR GAR

Latin name: *Atractosteus spatula*

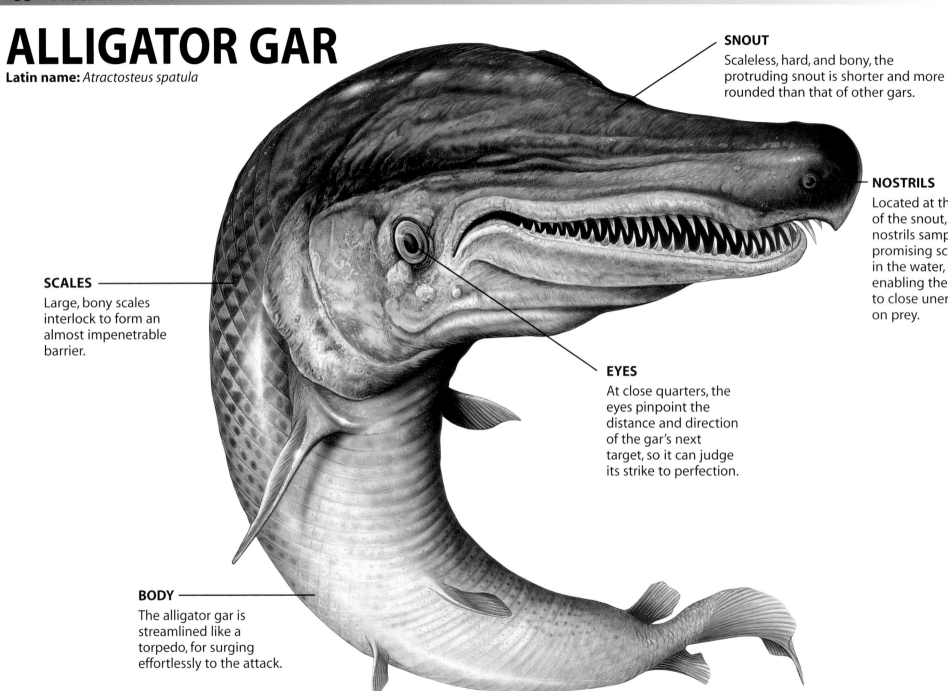

SNOUT
Scaleless, hard, and bony, the protruding snout is shorter and more rounded than that of other gars.

NOSTRILS
Located at the tip of the snout, the nostrils sample promising scents in the water, enabling the gar to close unerringly on prey.

SCALES
Large, bony scales interlock to form an almost impenetrable barrier.

EYES
At close quarters, the eyes pinpoint the distance and direction of the gar's next target, so it can judge its strike to perfection.

BODY
The alligator gar is streamlined like a torpedo, for surging effortlessly to the attack.

Protected by enameled scales, the alligator gar spends most of its life doing what it has done since the day of the dinosaurs— drifting lazily in silty river waters in search of food. One of the largest freshwater fish in the world, the snapping, slashing jaws of an adult alligator gar make short work of smaller prey such as fish and waterbirds. Even larger animals, such as young alligators, are no match for its needle teeth.

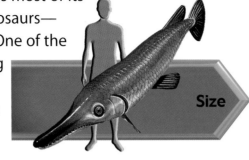

Size

KEY DATA

LENGTH	Up to 10ft (3m)
WEIGHT	Up to 298lb (135kg)
PREY	Fish, crabs, waterbirds, turtles, and small alligators
WEAPONS	Numerous pointed teeth
LIFESPAN	Probably 50 years or more

The alligator gar is found in lakes, swamps, backwaters, and bayous (creeks) of large rivers on the Gulf-Coast plain of Mexico and the USA. It is found mainly in the lower Mississippi basin, but also lives as far south as Veracruz and as far east as western Florida. It is scarce throughout its range.

1 Cruising through the sluggish backwaters of the Mississippi River like a patrolling submarine, a huge alligator gar intercepts a young alligator sunning itself at the surface. With a burst of speed, the fish surges to the attack.

2 As the gar rushes in with mouth wide open, the sleepy reptile is caught completely off-guard and has no time to escape or fight back. In an instant, the mighty fish clamps its powerful jaws around its victim, biting the alligator almost clean in half. Within seconds, it's all over, and the gar starts tearing at the 'gator's bloody guts as they spill into the water.

Did You Know?

● The flesh of the alligator gar is highly prized by some people, who usually bake the fish whole as its bony scales make it difficult to skin.

● A young alligator gar has a dark band running down each side of its body and a white stripe along its back, but loses these as it matures. As an adult, it is simply a dull green or brown—ideal for stalking prey unseen in murky waters.

● The alligator gar is frequently found in the brackish waters of river estuaries, and on rare occasions it even ventures out to sea.

● Some Native American tribes traditionally hunted the alligator gar with bows and arrows as it basked on the surface—frequently using its tough, diamond-shaped scales as arrowheads. Today, craftspeople more commonly use the gar's scales to make brooches and other items of novelty jewelry, while its skin is made into luxury leather goods.

ELECTRIC EEL

Latin name: *Electrophorus electricus*

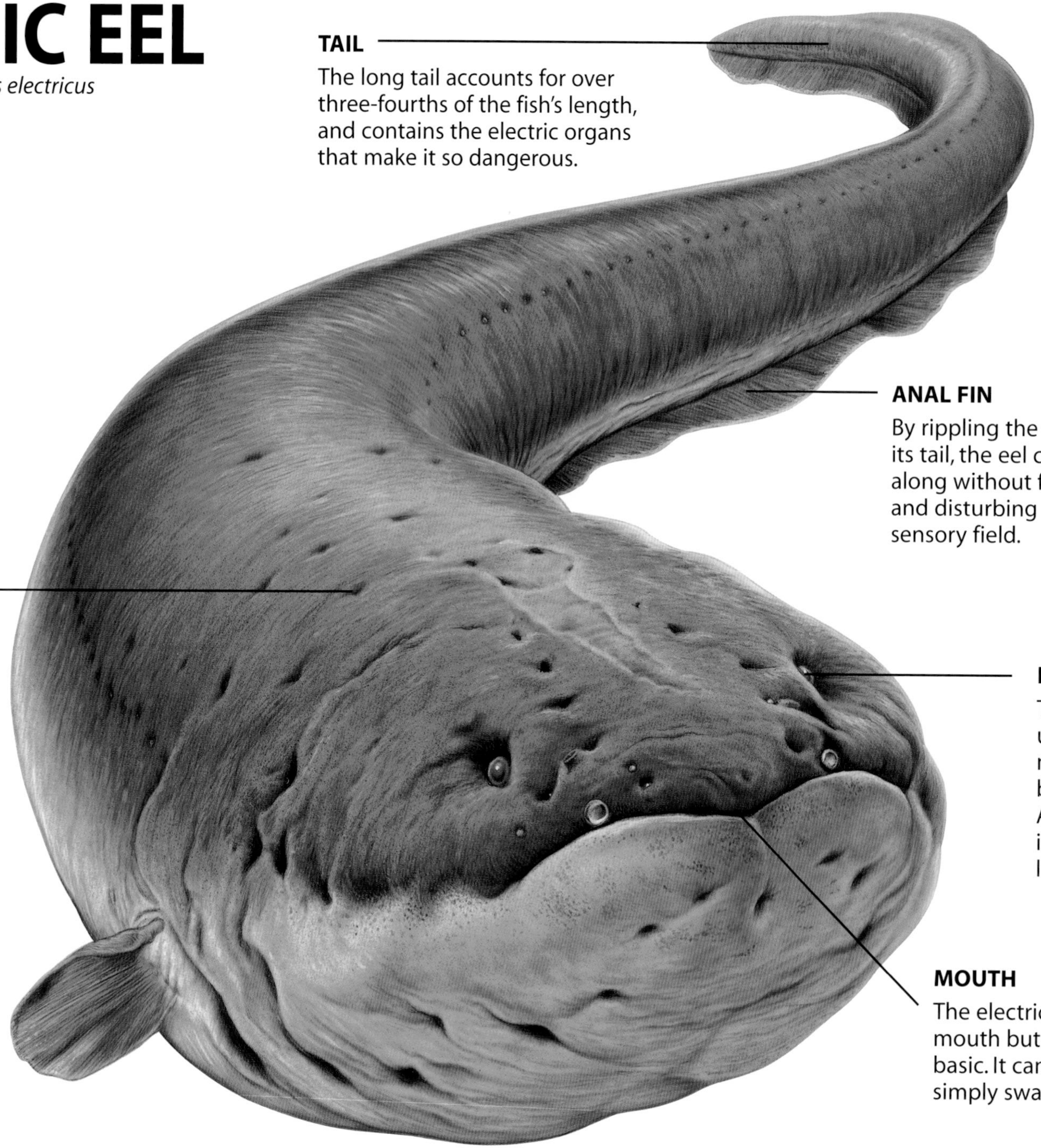

TAIL

The long tail accounts for over three-fourths of the fish's length, and contains the electric organs that make it so dangerous.

ANAL FIN

By rippling the long fin beneath its tail, the eel can drive itself along without flexing its body and disturbing its electric sensory field.

SENSORY PITS

Pits lined with sensor cells detect tiny electrical field distortions caused by other animals and by obstacles.

EYES

The small blue eyes face upward, and do little more than distinguish between light and dark. As the eel gets older, its eyes become even less important.

MOUTH

The electric eel has a huge mouth but its teeth are very basic. It cannot chew and simply swallows its prey whole.

A harmless-looking electric eel is, in fact, a high-voltage killer. The electric eel has banks of power cells along its tail, which serve two quite different functions: they help it navigate through the murky waters of its native swamps, and they produce a shock wave that can stun or even kill its prey. It has a battery of cells that generate a shock powerful enough to poleaxe anyone who unwittingly steps on it. An invisible menace, the electric eel lives in waterholes favored by land creatures such as the tapir. When this gentle mammal visits the water to drink, it risks stepping on an eel by accident; this may be the last move it makes.

Size

1 Disguised by their drab color, three electric eels glide through the overgrown, muddy waters of a shallow stream toward a tapir wading in the water. The tapir then blunders into the eels and they retaliate with a massive triple dose of electricity.

2 The shock stuns the tapir's nervous system, dropping it in its tracks and causing convulsions. These movements provoke more shocks which stop its heart beating.

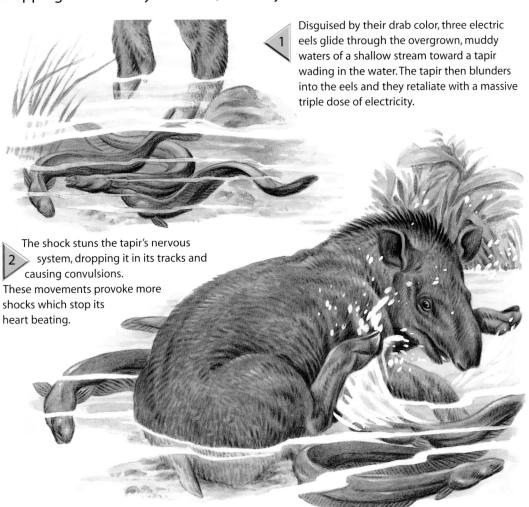

KEY DATA

LENGTH	Up to 10ft (3m)		
WEIGHT	Up to 88lb (40kg)		
PREY	Fish, frogs, and other small aquatic animals		
WEAPON	Electric pulses of up to 650 volts each		The electric eel lives in the muddy backwaters of the Amazon and Orinoco river systems, in the rainforests of tropical South America. The main concentrations are in Venezuela and Brazil. Its preferred habitats are marshland areas, shallow pools, and the stagnant arms of river tributaries.
POWER	Can kill a man or even a horse		
PARENTING	Gives birth to live young cared for by both parents		
LIFESPAN	Not known		

Did You Know?

● The devastating shock of the electric eel is actually a series of short pulses, each lasting less than 1/500th of a second but enough to power a color television.

● The eel's electricity-generating organs account for about half the entire weight of its body.

● Because of the way its electric cells are arranged, the electric eel is positive at its head and negative at its tail—like an animated battery.

● The long, rippling anal fin beneath the eel's tail can push it in any direction—forward, back, up, or down—so it can maneuver in the tightest corners.

PIKE

Latin name: *Esox lucius*

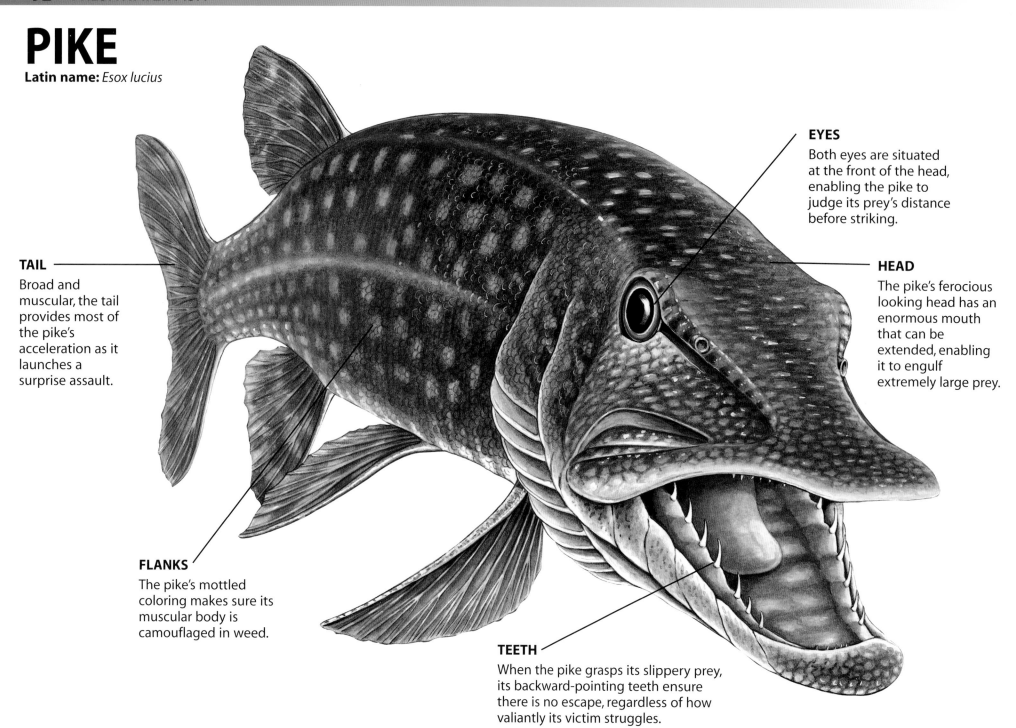

EYES
Both eyes are situated at the front of the head, enabling the pike to judge its prey's distance before striking.

HEAD
The pike's ferocious looking head has an enormous mouth that can be extended, enabling it to engulf extremely large prey.

TAIL
Broad and muscular, the tail provides most of the pike's acceleration as it launches a surprise assault.

FLANKS
The pike's mottled coloring makes sure its muscular body is camouflaged in weed.

TEETH
When the pike grasps its slippery prey, its backward-pointing teeth ensure there is no escape, regardless of how valiantly its victim struggles.

When anglers gather after a day's fishing, tales of large pike become common—with the fish growing larger the later it gets. However, not all these stories are fanciful… A lily-fringed lake on a summer's day is an idyllic scene, but when a huge pike is stalking its prey, nothing in or around the water is safe. A large pike can swallow prey up to half its own weight. The victims are usually fish, but the pike is an opportunist and may attack any animal that enters its watery abode.

Size

1 A woman is exercising her beloved dog, throwing a stick into a lake for it to fetch. Suddenly the woman notices a dark shape approaching her pet…

2 The dog's enthusiastic paddling attracts the attention of the lake's largest resident, a hungry old pike. Before the dog knows what has hit it, the huge fish grabs the unfortunate animal in its mighty jaws.

3 The dog's owner gets a glimpse of the pike rolling at the surface, then her poor dog vanishes—if the pike doesn't let go quickly, her pet may well drown.

KEY DATA

LENGTH	Female up to 4.5ft (1.5m); male much smaller
WEIGHT	Female up to 77lb (35kg); male much smaller, up to 13lb (6kg)
DIET	Live fish (including other pike), amphibians, small mammals and waterbirds, and some carrion
WEAPONS	Razor-sharp, backward-facing teeth
HUNTING METHOD	Ambush and chase
LIFESPAN	Up to 30 years

The pike is found throughout northern Europe and Asia as far north as the Bering Sea. In North America, the pike lives north of a line from Pennsylvania in the east to Nebraska in the west, as well as throughout Canada and Alaska.

Did You Know?

● Pike sometimes choke to death when they ambitiously try to swallow fish (including other pike, see picture left) that are too big for their mouths.

● In the northern Baltic Sea, the pike has adapted to live in brackish water. Some experts think large pike may have evolved to live in the sea.

● In North America, the pike is known as the northern pike, to distinguish it from its close relative, the ferocious hunter called the muskellunge.

STURGEON

Latin name: Family *Acipenseridae*

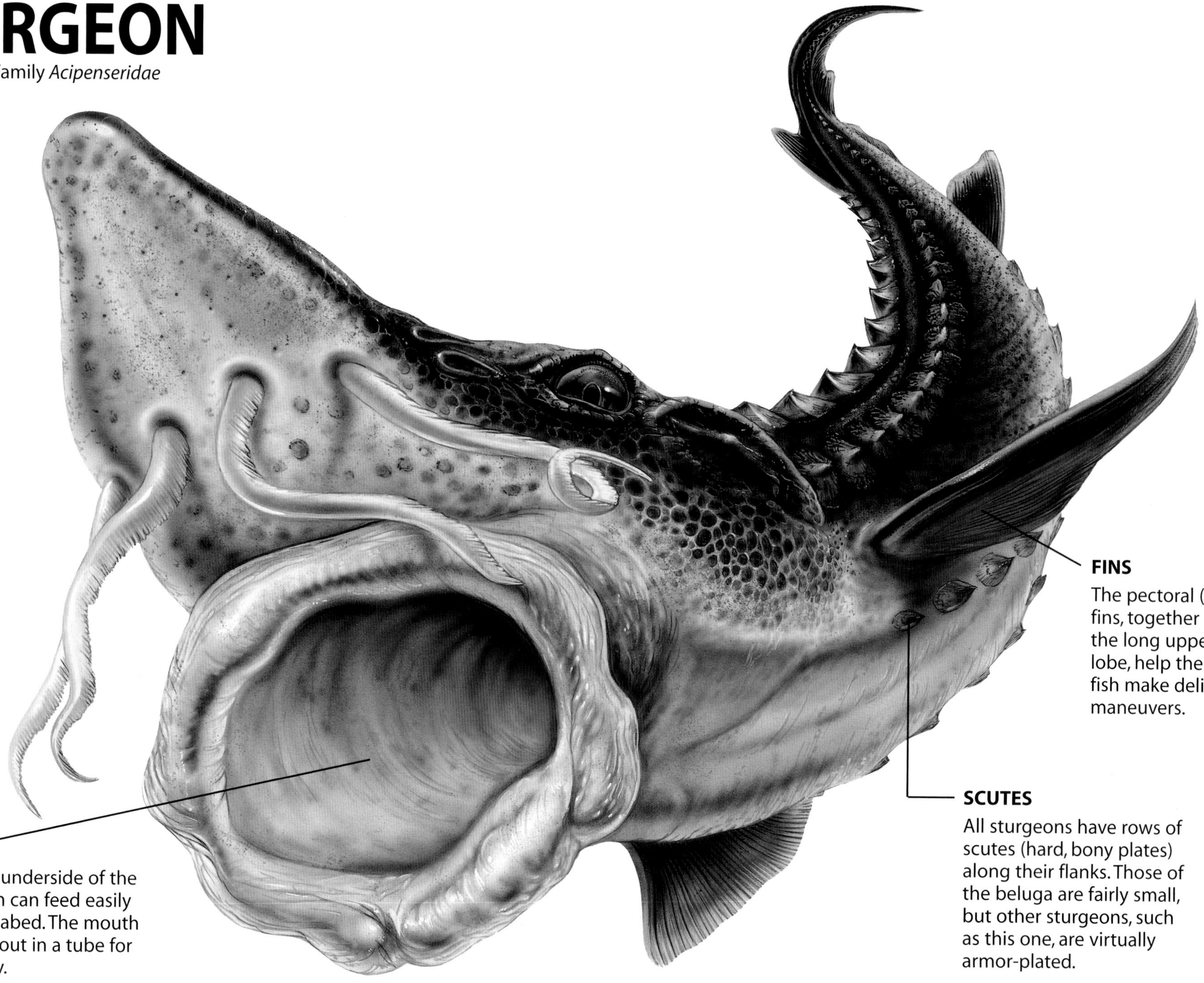

FINS

The pectoral (side) fins, together with the long upper tail lobe, help the big fish make delicate maneuvers.

SCUTES

All sturgeons have rows of scutes (hard, bony plates) along their flanks. Those of the beluga are fairly small, but other sturgeons, such as this one, are virtually armor-plated.

MOUTH

This lies on the underside of the head, so the fish can feed easily on a river- or seabed. The mouth can be pushed out in a tube for sucking up prey.

From the slender, delicate sterlet to the mighty beluga, the sturgeons that breed each year in the big, icy lakes and rivers of the north are among the world's most extraordinary freshwater fish. Sturgeons are armor-plated survivors from the age of the dinosaurs. Some grow to a ripe old age and reach a tremendous size as they skulk in deep, dark waters in search of prey. Sturgeons are equipped for sucking small animals out of the bottom mud, but the giant beluga is just as likely to cruise through the water taking in small shoaling fish. Its feeding method is devastatingly simple—and effective.

Size

1 A small fish swims after its own prey in mid-water. Preoccupied with catching its meal, it seems unaware of the vast shadowy form looming up behind it—a beluga, or giant sturgeon, is on the prowl. Beating its tail slowly but powerfully, the beluga slips effortlessly after its intended victim, its streamlined snout reducing drag.

2 As the beluga comes within range, it extends its lips to form a fleshy, flexible tube. With a gulp, it sucks the fish into oblivion.

KEY DATA

LENGTH	Up to 16ft (5m) or more (beluga)	
WEIGHT	Up to 5 tons (1.5 tonnes) (beluga)	
DIET	Worms, shellfish, shrimp, and small fish	
LIFESPAN	150 years, but few reach this age nowadays, due to poisoning or overfishing	

The 25 species of sturgeon live in cool northern seas, rivers, and lakes, from the coasts of Europe and Scandinavia, through Russia and Siberia to coastal and inland North America.

Did You Know?

 ● A small freshwater sturgeon, the sterlet, is kept by aquarists and bred in captivity. It is a proper sturgeon in everything but size, growing to a maximum length of 4ft (1.2m).

● A female sturgeon may lay as many as a million eggs during her spring spawning.

● Most of the sturgeon's skeleton is made of rubbery cartilage, just like that of a shark, instead of bone.

● An American lake sturgeon caught in 1953 was estimated at 154 years old. Today a sturgeon would be lucky to survive half as long.

● Sturgeons yield a substance called isinglass, which is used to remove the cloudiness from wines.

● As a result of overfishing and pollution, the population of adult sturgeons in the Caspian Sea fell from 142 million in 1978 to 43.5 million in 1994.

STARGAZER

Latin name: Family *Uranoscopidae*

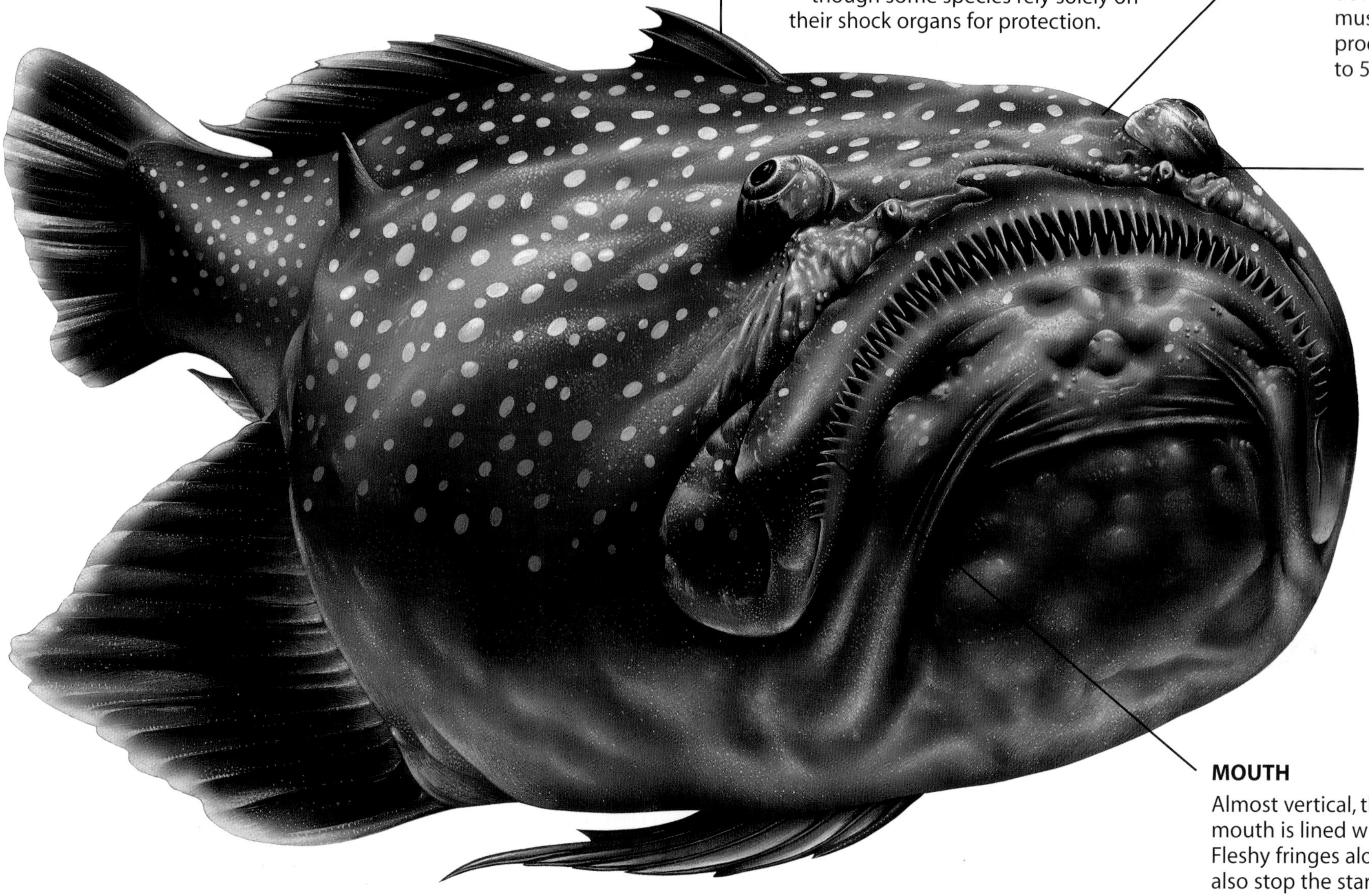

SPINES

Grooved spines above each pectoral fin connect to venom glands at the base, providing a potent defense mechanism —though some species rely solely on their shock organs for protection.

ELECTRICAL ORGANS

Located in a special pouch behind the eyes, the electrical organs develop from eye-muscle tissue and can produce a charge of up to 50 volts.

NOSTRILS

Most fish "breathe" by drawing water in through their mouth, but the stargazer has two nostrils on top of its head. These enable it to "breathe" while almost totally buried, and fleshy, comblike fringes protect these vital waterways from grains of sand.

MOUTH

Almost vertical, the enormous mouth is lined with tiny teeth. Fleshy fringes along the lips also stop the stargazer from swallowing sand as it lies buried on the seabed with its mouth agape.

The stargazer lies silent, still, and covered in sand and mud, its speckled markings providing perfect camouflage. It waits until a likely meal passes by, then darts out from its hiding place to swallow its victim whole. Some have a reddish, wormlike filament in the floor of their mouth to wiggle enticingly to lure prey. When passing fish mistake this for a tasty worm and approach, they are rapidly gobbled up. Although many stargazers rely on their venomous spines for protection, some use another trick. If big fish or crustaceans come too close, they send the intruders packing with a painful bolt from their electrical organs.

Size

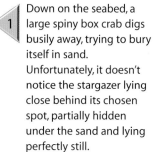

KEY DATA

LENGTH	Up to 28in (70cm)
WEIGHT	Up to 20lb (9kg)
PREY	Crustaceans and fish
WEAPONS	Venom-primed spines and electrical organs
LIFESPAN	Unknown

There are about 50 species of stargazer around the world, living in the tropical and temperate waters of the Atlantic, Indian, and Pacific Oceans, and in the Mediterranean sea.

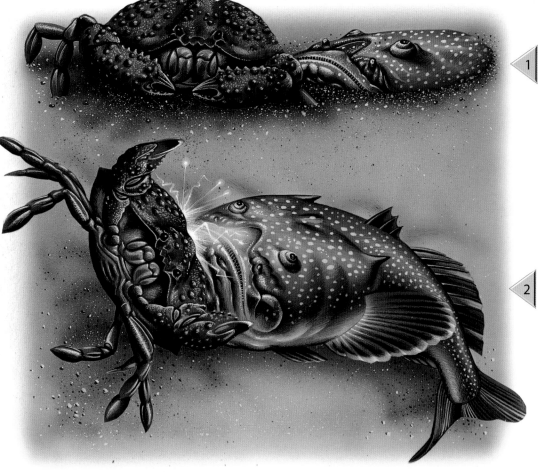

1 Down on the seabed, a large spiny box crab digs busily away, trying to bury itself in sand. Unfortunately, it doesn't notice the stargazer lying close behind its chosen spot, partially hidden under the sand and lying perfectly still.

2 Annoyed by the intrusion, the stargazer explodes from its hiding place and attacks. Its spines cannot penetrate the crab's hard shell, but a surge of electricity from its electrical organs soon has the crustacean scurrying away.

Did You Know?

● Instead of flat gill-flaps like many fish, the stargazer has narrow gills that extend backward to form baggy tubes. These enable it to expel waste water without disturbing the sand and revealing its presence.

● If disturbed by night divers, stargazers bite aggressively.

● Some species of stargazer have been known to eat up to 48 times their own bodyweight every year.

● All animal muscles produce tiny charges of electricity, but only a few creatures have developed the ability to concentrate and use this energy.

● Sharks have an "extra" sense that enables them to detect the tiny currents produced by fish muscles, helping them track down their prey.

● While the stargazer stares at the sky, the lookdown fish gazes down its long nose with downcast eyes as it swims in shallow coastal waters.

ELEPHANT FISH

Latin name: *Gnathonemus petersii*

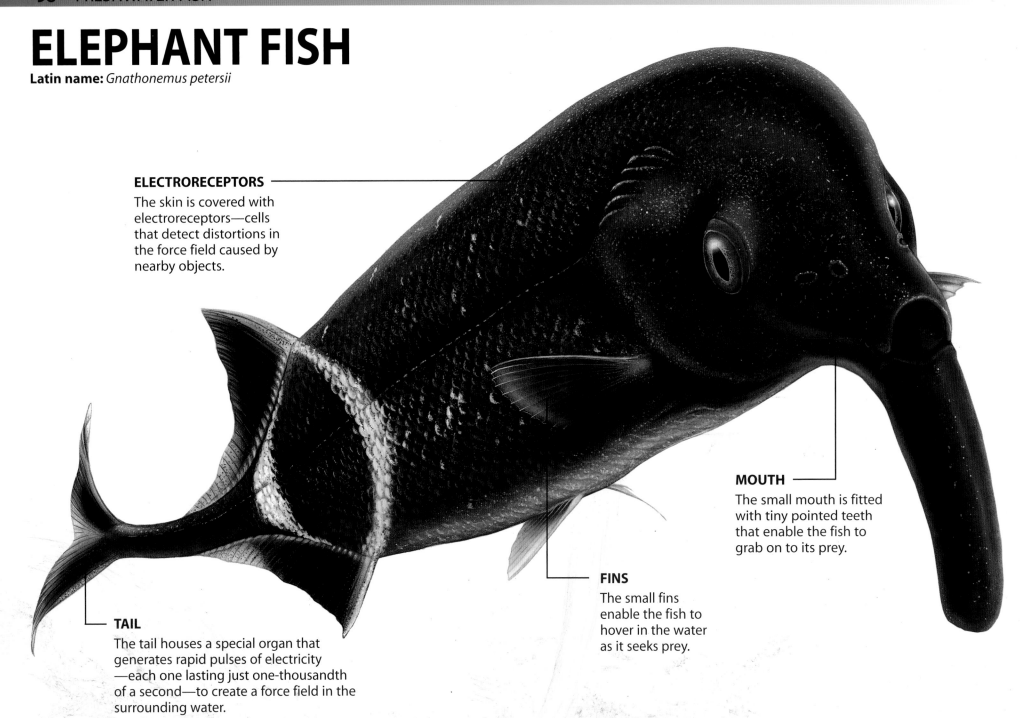

ELECTRORECEPTORS
The skin is covered with electroreceptors—cells that detect distortions in the force field caused by nearby objects.

MOUTH
The small mouth is fitted with tiny pointed teeth that enable the fish to grab on to its prey.

FINS
The small fins enable the fish to hover in the water as it seeks prey.

TAIL
The tail houses a special organ that generates rapid pulses of electricity —each one lasting just one-thousandth of a second—to create a force field in the surrounding water.

The elephant fish has good sight, but as it lives in murky rivers and swamps in Africa and feeds mainly at night, it can't rely on vision to find food to eat. The long "nose" is a jaw that curves down from its tiny mouth. The jaw has chemical and touch sensors to locate prey by taste and by delving for them in mud and weeds. The elephant fish also has a system of hollow tubes connecting bony plates in the skull to the inner ear so the predator can detect sound vibrations from insects in the water. In murky water or at night, the elephant fish's myriad other senses come into play.

Size

As the fish's sharp eyes scan the riverbed for prey, its other senses join in the quest. The lateral line (a) reacts to movement. Electroreceptors in the skin (b) detect changes in the electrical field caused by nearby objects. Chemical sensors (c) pick up waterborne tastes. The hearing organs (d) are sensitive to sound waves.

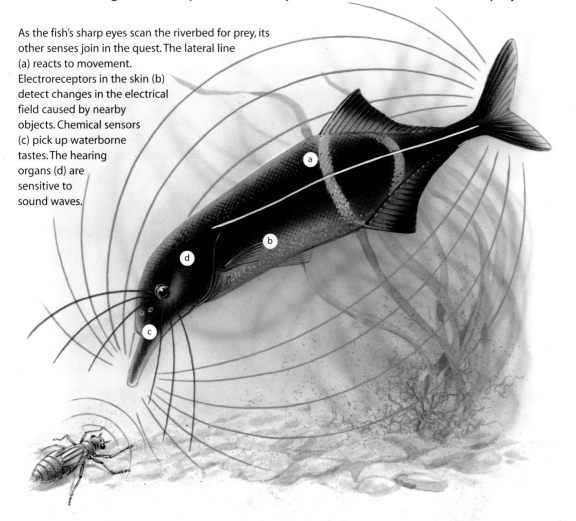

KEY DATA

LENGTH	Up to 10in (25cm)
DIET	Mainly invertebrates such as worms, and insects and their larvae, but occasionally some vegetation
LIFESTYLE	Hunter-tracker
LIFESPAN	Unknown

The long-nosed elephant fish lives in the warm tropical waterways of western and central Africa, from Mali across to Nigeria, Cameroon, and Chad, and southward as far as Zambia. The fish spends most of its time among mud, stones, and weeds on the beds of freshwater rivers, streams, and swamps.

Did You Know?

● The long-nosed elephant fish uses its electrical detection system to recognize other members of its species. It can even tell female and male fish apart, since the different sexes produce their own signals.

● The electrical field the fish generates also acts as a boundary marker. Scientists have found that elephant fish living in neighboring territories generate electrical fields of slightly differing frequencies, so there's no confusion over which territory belongs to which fish.

● The generating organ in the tail produces only a few micro-volts of electricity. This is not enough to shock and stun prey in the way that electric rays and eels hunt for food.

● The long-nosed elephant fish can detect sound vibrations in the water in the range 100–2500Hz. This is good for a fish, but is a long way short of the average human hearing range of 20–20,000Hz.

TIGER FISH
Latin name: *Hydrocynus* species

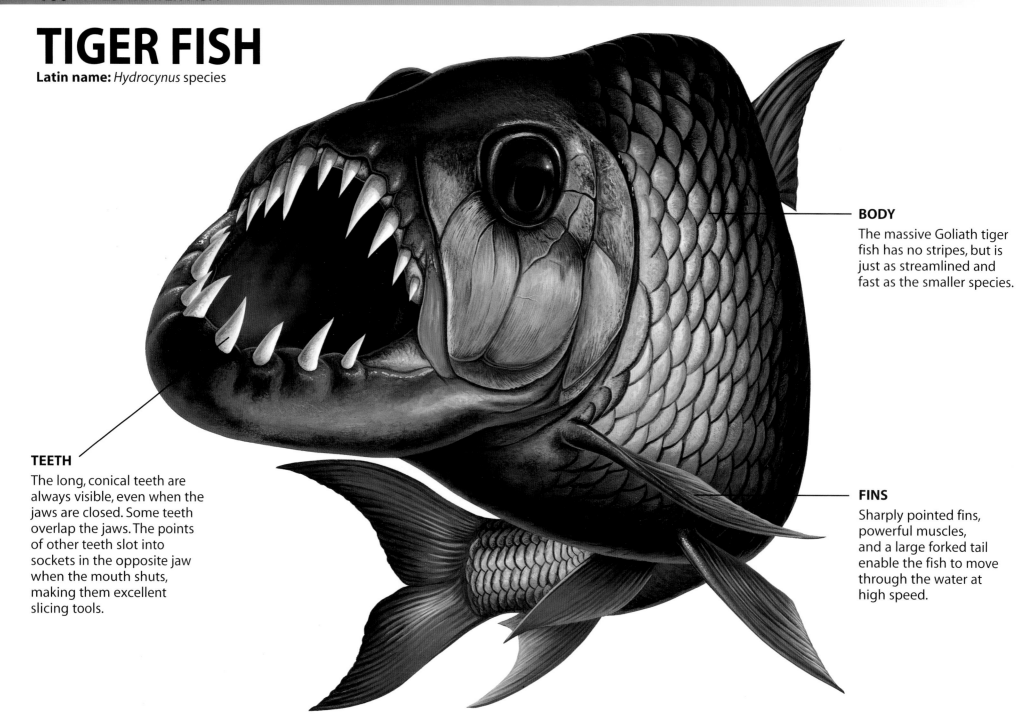

BODY

The massive Goliath tiger fish has no stripes, but is just as streamlined and fast as the smaller species.

TEETH

The long, conical teeth are always visible, even when the jaws are closed. Some teeth overlap the jaws. The points of other teeth slot into sockets in the opposite jaw when the mouth shuts, making them excellent slicing tools.

FINS

Sharply pointed fins, powerful muscles, and a large forked tail enable the fish to move through the water at high speed.

A relative of the deadly South American piranha, the African tiger fish gets its name from the stripes on the body of most species. Its Latin name, *Hydrocynus*, means "water dog," because it prowls in groups like packs of hunting dogs. By hunting in a shoal, the fearsome tiger fish can tackle prey much larger than itself. A disturbance in the water acts like a dinner gong and attracts a prowling shoal of hungry hunters to the scene, all eager to devour fresh meat.

Size

1 ▷ Seeking new food sources, a troop of vervet monkeys begins a perilous journey across a river. At first, the monkeys hop between stones, but as the gap widens they start to swim.

KEY DATA

LENGTH	Up to 7ft (2m) (Goliath)	
WEIGHT	Up to 112lb (50kg) (Goliath)	The tiger fish is found in many of the rivers and lakes in western, central, and southern Africa, and northward along the River Nile. It is rarely found in water that is more than 1968ft (600m) above sea level. The largest of the five species known, the Goliath tiger fish (*Hydrocynus goliath*), lives mainly in Lake Tanganyika and the Congo Basin.
PREY	Fish and many land animals that enter the water	
WEAPONS	Sharp, interlocking teeth	
LIFESPAN	Up to 8 years	

2 ◁ An older monkey is slow climbing out of the water and a tiger fish bites into its leg. The monkey thrashes out in pain, drawing the rest of the shoal. The blood in the water drives the ravenous fish into a feeding frenzy, eagerly slicing strips of flesh from the struggling victim. Other monkeys can only stare as their companion disappears from sight under the ferocious onslaught.

Did You Know?

● There are stories of tiger fish attacking humans, but this has not been proven. It is more likely that attacks occur when anglers attempt to land the fish they have caught.

● Tiger fish sometimes stoop to cannibalism, preying on younger members of the species when there is little else to satisfy their hunger.

● Humans are having a serious impact on tiger fish numbers, as the dams and other irrigation projects built in the upper reaches of many African rivers cause the loss of much of the aquatic vegetation that the fish needs to spawn.

● The tiger fish has an air-filled bag in its body, which is adapted to receive sounds transmitted by movable bones and ligaments near its head. This "hearing-aid" enables the tiger fish to detect the sounds made by animals falling into the water so that the predator can rush over to investigate.

STRIPED CATFISH

Latin name: *Plotosus lineatus*

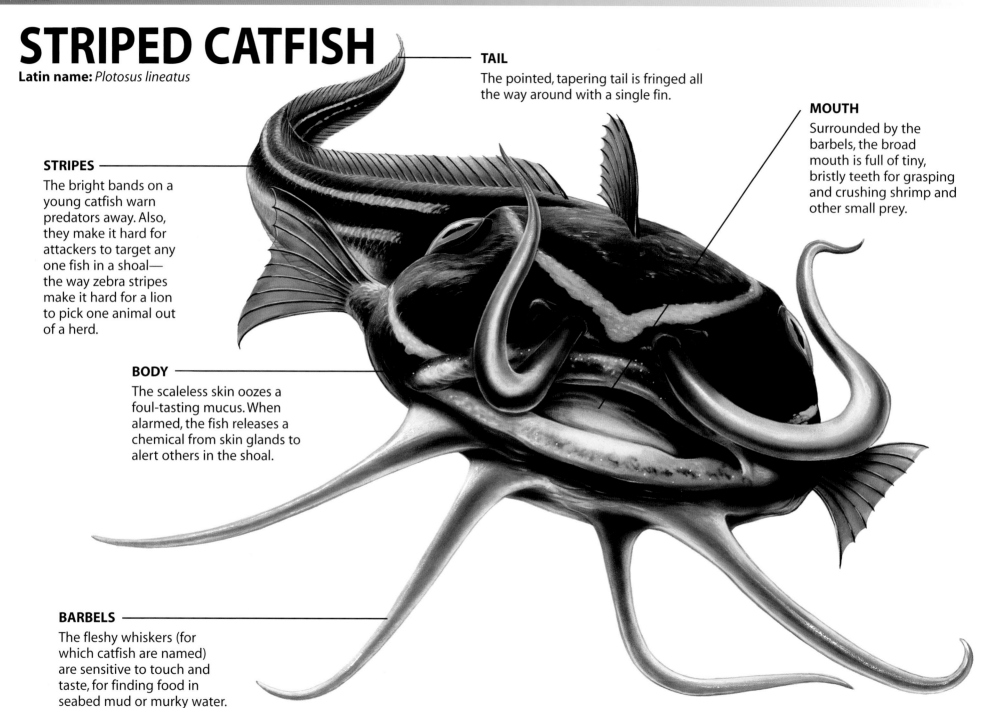

TAIL

The pointed, tapering tail is fringed all the way around with a single fin.

MOUTH

Surrounded by the barbels, the broad mouth is full of tiny, bristly teeth for grasping and crushing shrimp and other small prey.

STRIPES

The bright bands on a young catfish warn predators away. Also, they make it hard for attackers to target any one fish in a shoal—the way zebra stripes make it hard for a lion to pick one animal out of a herd.

BODY

The scaleless skin oozes a foul-tasting mucus. When alarmed, the fish releases a chemical from skin glands to alert others in the shoal.

BARBELS

The fleshy whiskers (for which catfish are named) are sensitive to touch and taste, for finding food in seabed mud or murky water.

Size

Young striped catfish travel in style, bowling through the ocean in dense, ball-shaped schools, looking like an underwater kaleidoscope. The yellow bars on a young catfish warn enemies that this harmless-looking creature carries vicious venomous spines. Their older relatives live a much less exciting life—but their defenses are just as deadly. For the striped catfish, survival isn't just a matter of self-preservation: ensuring the safe arrival of the next generation is as important as saving its own skin. So the father devotes himself to guarding the defenseless offspring.

KEY DATA

LENGTH	Up to 1ft (30cm)		
WEIGHT	Up to 2lb (1kg)		
DIET	Small fish, shrimp, and worms		
WEAPONS	Venomous spines		The striped catfish is found in river estuaries and warm coastal waters and around coral reefs throughout the Indo-Pacific region, from eastern Africa and the Red Sea east across to Samoa, and from Japan south to northern Australia.
LIFESPAN	Up to 6 years		

1 Fresh fish eggs are a favorite snack of many marine predators and scavengers. To keep his own future family off the menu, the male striped catfish never lets them out of his sight. When courting a female, he scours out a pit in the seabed with vigorous wriggles, then invites her to shed her eggs in it. After fertilizing them, he keeps constant watch until they hatch. All the while he flares his fins, with their venomous spines, at any creature that approaches.

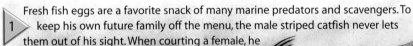

2 Like many fish, newly hatched striped catfish swim in shoals for protection. Young striped catfish take shoaling to the extreme, swimming so close together that to a predator they might look like a single large animal—one too big to attack. If danger does threaten, each catfish twists and turns this way and that, making it hard for an enemy to pick out an individual target.

Did You Know?

● This fish is also known as the coral catfish, oriental catfish, striped-eel catfish, eel-tail catfish, catfish eel, and barber eel. This last name suggests that its stripes look like the traditional spiral signs outside barbers' shops.

● Worldwide there are more than 2,000 species of catfish.

● Male catfish of the oceanic Ariidae family are even better fathers than male striped catfish. After a female ariid catfish lays her eggs, the male scoops them up in his mouth, where they stay safe until they hatch after about two months. Then, the young fish shelter in his mouth for another two weeks.

● Like many eels, the striped catfish can survive in freshwater as well as saltwater, and sometimes swims up rivers. It has even been seen in Lake Nyasa in eastern Africa —having swum nearly 620 miles (1000km) up rivers from the Indian Ocean.

SAWFISH

Latin name: *Pristis* species

SAW BLADE
The long flat blade is made of cartilage and extends over 3ft 3in (1m) in front of the mouth.

SHAPE
The sawfish has a slender, sharklike tail and rear body, but its foreparts show the flattened shape and greatly expanded pectoral fins of its close relatives—the rays.

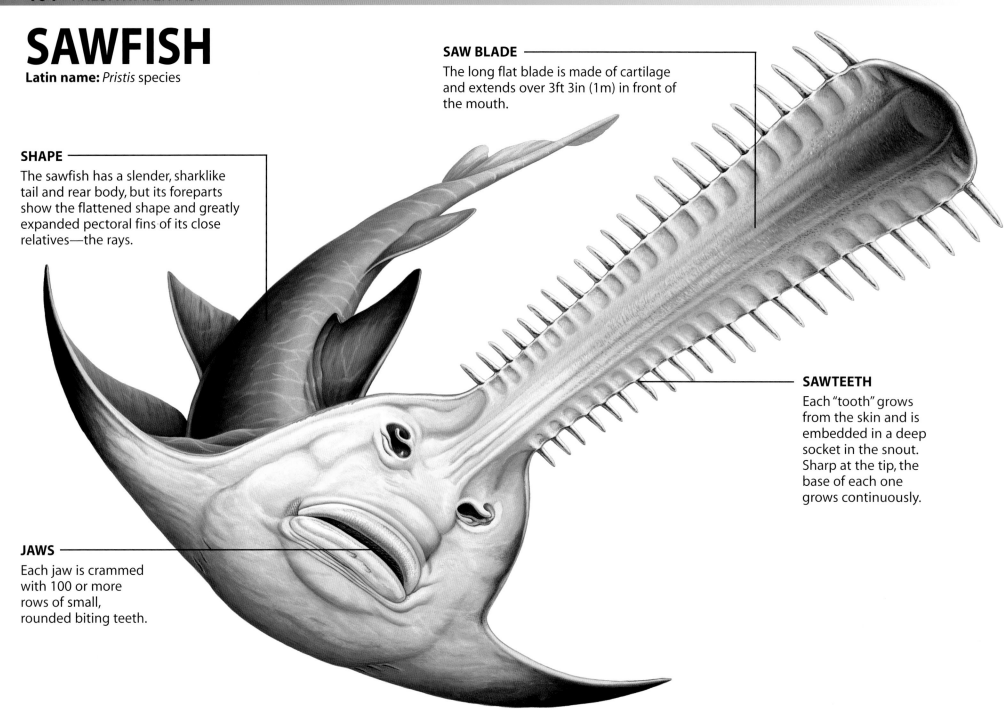

SAWTEETH
Each "tooth" grows from the skin and is embedded in a deep socket in the snout. Sharp at the tip, the base of each one grows continuously.

JAWS
Each jaw is crammed with 100 or more rows of small, rounded biting teeth.

A sawfish's mighty weapon is a versatile tool. By slashing its huge snout from side to side, the great fish can rake up sediments to find crabs or mollusks to eat, rip into large shoals of prey fish, strike out at enemies, and do battle with rivals. So any person who snares a sawfish is likely to regret it. Even specimens of moderate size have great strength and a terrible weapon at their disposal, and they make truly ferocious fighters when trying to break free from capture.

Size

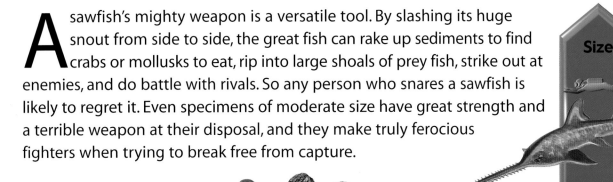

KEY DATA

LENGTH	Body up to 23ft (7m), including saw up to 5ft (1.8m) long
WEIGHT	Over 6.5 tons (2 tonnes)
PREY	Mainly fish and aquatic invertebrates, such as crabs, worms, and mollusks
WEAPONS & METHOD OF ATTACK	Long snout studded on both sides with 20 to 30 sharp, peglike "teeth"; uses its great speed and agility to plough into fish shoals and slash wounds with its deadly saw
LIFESPAN	Unknown

The six sawfish species inhabit most subtropical and tropical coastal waters and also swim upriver into freshwater habitats.

1 Two fishermen are hauling on a long net they've stretched across a river when they see that a sawfish has got entangled. The beast writhes in terror as it tries to escape the lethal mesh.

2 As the two men try to drag their oversize catch on board, the fish lashes to and fro. It slices into one man's leg, causing a gaping wound, before it manages to saw a hole in the net and make its escape.

Did You Know?

● The largetooth sawfish (*Pristis perotteti*) has now become firmly established inland in parts of its range. The population living in Lake Nicaragua, for example, seems to be completely landlocked and may even be a totally different species from the largetooth sawfish that live along the coasts of Central America.

● Like many sharks, sawfish give birth to litters of live young, and the body of a pregnant female caught off the coast of Sri Lanka contained 23 offspring. To make pregnancy and birth less hazardous for the mother, the teeth of baby sawfish are enclosed within a protective sheath, and their snouts remain soft and pliable until after they are born.

PIRANHA
Latin name: *Serrasalmus* species

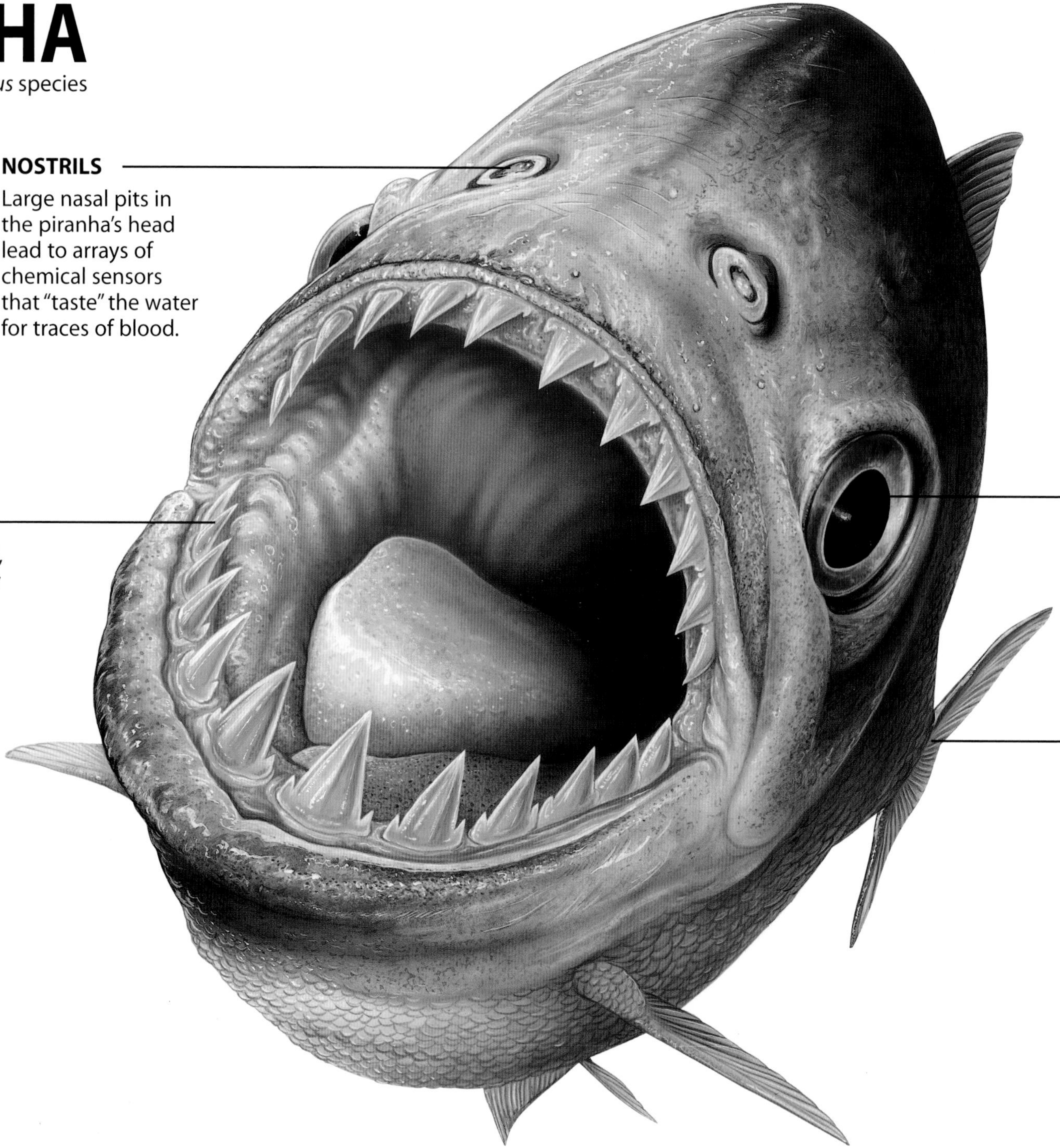

NOSTRILS

Large nasal pits in the piranha's head lead to arrays of chemical sensors that "taste" the water for traces of blood.

TEETH

Large and pointed, these have lethally sharp edges.

EYES

These are big and face slightly forward for range-finding binocular vision.

TAIL

Deep and muscular, the tail drives the piranha rapidly through the water when the fish charges into the attack.

Most of the time, piranhas content themselves with taking swift bites out of other fish and clearing up any carrion they come across. But the scent of fresh blood transforms them into vicious killers, with an ability to butcher animals that defies belief. Piranhas are most dangerous when trapped in pools of receding flood water. After days without food, the arrival of a wounded animal is an invitation for them to dine. Hearing its splashing, tasting its blood, they move swiftly in for the kill.

Size

KEY DATA

LENGTH	6–24in (15–60cm), depending on species; 12in (30cm) on average	The various species of piranha live in the river systems of tropical South America, including the Orinoco in Venezuela, the Amazon in Brazil, and the Paraná in Argentina. They are particularly common in the Amazon. Probably the largest (up to 24in/60cm long) and most dangerous species is *Serrasalmus piraya*, which is found in the Rio São Francisco in Brazil.
WEIGHT	Most species up to 4lb (2kg), but largest species more	
PREY	Mainly fish, including their own kind; occasionally birds and mammals	
WEAPONS	Razor-sharp, interlocking, triangular teeth	
TYPICAL ATTACK	Mass feeding frenzy	
LIFESPAN	Probably about 5 years	

1 Mauled by a jaguar, a capybara staggers into the water, dripping blood. Within seconds, dozens of piranhas arrive on the scene and start circling the dazed animal in the shallows. Suddenly, one darts in and sinks its teeth into the capybara. The fish spins around to gouge out a bloody mouthful, then retreats to swallow it.

2 Moments later, the water is a bloody whirlpool of flesh, fur, and fish, as one after the other the piranhas plunge in to attack. Struggling instinctively to keep its head above the surface and breathe to the last, the capybara prolongs its agony. The end is still swift, the fish reducing the creature to a skeleton in a matter of minutes.

Did You Know?

● Over 300 people may have been eaten by piranhas on 19 September 1981, when a boat sank at Óbidos on the Amazon in Brazil.

● Piranha schools often lurk beneath trees, occupied by nesting birds, to snap up young birds that fall into the water.

● In Brazil, when farmers drive cattle across rivers they may lose one animal each time to piranhas. It is said that some farmers sacrifice a weak or injured animal to make sure that the others cross safely.

● Native people in the Amazon Basin use piranha teeth in the home as cutting and slicing tools.

WELS CATFISH

Latin name: *Silurus glanis*

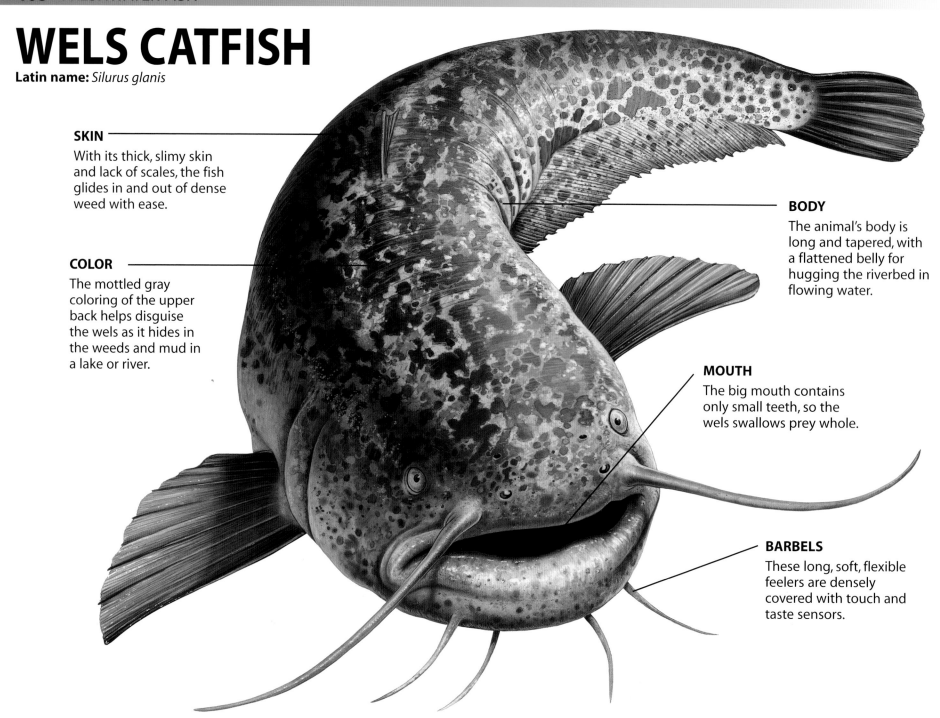

SKIN

With its thick, slimy skin and lack of scales, the fish glides in and out of dense weed with ease.

COLOR

The mottled gray coloring of the upper back helps disguise the wels as it hides in the weeds and mud in a lake or river.

BODY

The animal's body is long and tapered, with a flattened belly for hugging the riverbed in flowing water.

MOUTH

The big mouth contains only small teeth, so the wels swallows prey whole.

BARBELS

These long, soft, flexible feelers are densely covered with touch and taste sensors.

One of the biggest freshwater fish, this colossal beast is regarded by fishermen as a prize catch. It grows so vast by eating fish, frogs, and waterfowls—in fact, anything it can cram in its massive jaws. The wels catfish is perfectly suited to life in the murky, weed-strewn depths of rivers and lakes. The hunter's long feelers, or barbels, are better than eyes for navigating in the gloom and its strong sense of taste soon locates a juicy meal. Sneaking up on a victim from the shadowy depths, the wels catfish gets in position to launch a surprise attack.

Size

KEY DATA

LENGTH	Up to 16ft (5m)
WEIGHT	Up to 118lb (300kg)
WEAPONS	Vast mouth
DIET	Fish, waterbirds, frogs, small mammals, and carrion
LIFESPAN	Up to 30 years

The wels catfish is a native of eastern Europe, where it is widespread. It is found as far east as the Aral Sea, north to the Baltic, and around the Black and Caspian seas in the south. The wels has also been introduced (legally and illegally) into waterways in Portugal, Spain, England, France, and Germany.

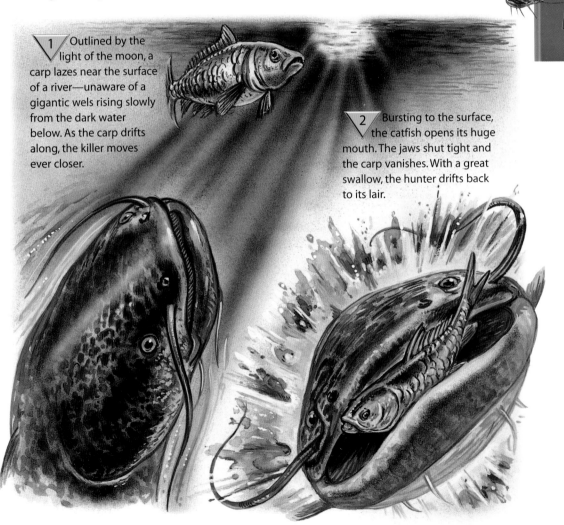

1 Outlined by the light of the moon, a carp lazes near the surface of a river—unaware of a gigantic wels rising slowly from the dark water below. As the carp drifts along, the killer moves ever closer.

2 Bursting to the surface, the catfish opens its huge mouth. The jaws shut tight and the carp vanishes. With a great swallow, the hunter drifts back to its lair.

Did You Know?

● The male wels is a devoted father. He makes a nest for the female's eggs by hollowing out a small depression on the bottom of the river or lake and filling it with water weed. After the female wels spawns in the nest, the male guards the heap of eggs until they hatch.

● The female lays up to half a million eggs at a time. Luckily, few of the offspring survive to adulthood, or the inland waterways would soon be overrun. The young catfish are eagerly hunted and eaten by other predatory fish, including older wels.

● Wels are often caught for food in eastern Europe, and in Hungary they are even raised on fish farms.

● The wels is such a voracious and indiscriminate feeder that fishermen have caught it using a bizarre range of foods to attract it, including offal, clotted pig's blood, and mince made from the rotting flesh of dead animals scraped off the roadside.

Jellyfish, Octopus, and Squid

*Of all the weird and wonderful sea creatures on Earth,
the jellyfish, octopus, and squid are, arguably, the
most peculiar.*

For one thing, they come in many unusual shapes. The Sea Anemone, for instance, has long tentacles that give it a pretty, flower-like appearance. The Giant Squid is all long, thick arms and a body that emerges from what looks like a headless fish. The Lion's Mane is the world's largest jellyfish with a diameter of more than 6ft 6in (2m) and a body shaped like an umbrella with up to 1000 tentacles dangling beneath it – each of them can be up to 115ft (35m) long. One of the best known and most deadly of jellyfish, the Portuguese Man o' War, floats along the surface of the sea or ocean on a bag full of gas But make no mistake about it— these strange features, however fascinating they may appear, are not for decoration. The Sea Anemone belies its outward beauty with the mass of stinging cells that lie along its tentacles. The Giant Squid's arms have double rows of suckers for grasping its prey. The tentacles of the Lion's Mane and the Portuguese Man o' War can deliver a ferocious, sometimes lethal, sting as they hang down, wafting in the water, waiting for potential victims to come near.

SEA ANEMONE

Latin name: Order *Actiniaria*

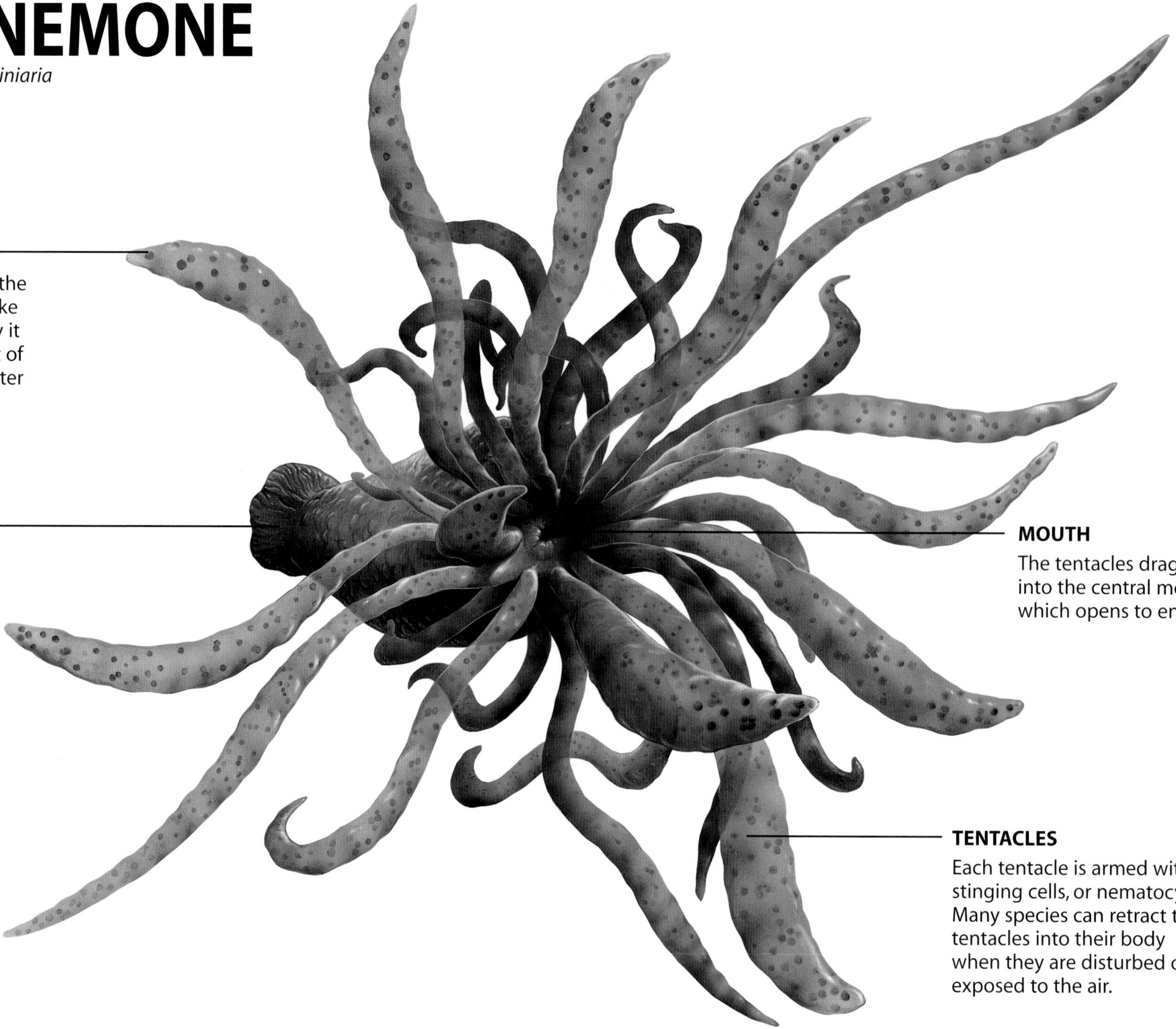

ADHESIVE DISK

The anemone grips the rock with a sucker-like disk, but if necessary it can move to get out of trouble or find a better feeding site.

BODY

The body is formed from outer and inner layers of cells, separated by jelly—just like the body of a jellyfish.

MOUTH

The tentacles drag prey into the central mouth, which opens to engulf it.

TENTACLES

Each tentacle is armed with stinging cells, or nematocysts. Many species can retract their tentacles into their body when they are disturbed or exposed to the air.

Sea anemones may look pretty and placid, but they can be surprisingly bad-tempered. They like their space, and if another anemone settles too close, there can be trouble. The occupier attacks the interloper with tentacles bearing extra-dense clusters of stinging cells until it creeps away. Stinging barbs at the ready, a sea anemone waits, anchored to a rock, for a victim to swim by and brush against its wafting tentacles. Hours of inactivity may pass, but a juicy shrimp or a plump little fish is well worth the wait.

Size

1 In the warm Red Sea, an anemone's tentacles attract a small fish as they wave like worms. Some touch the fish, triggering them to fire a fatal salvo of stings.

2 Paralyzed by the venomous stings, the fish is powerless to resist as the tentacles draw the creature toward the anemone's mouth. The fish disappears into the anemone's flexible body cavity.

3 The anemone's powerful digestive juices immediately get to work, dissolving the dying victim's flesh and guts. Later, the anemone spits out the indigestible remains of the fish, which drift away to be eaten by shrimp and crabs.

KEY DATA

SIZE	From ½in (1cm) to 3ft (1m) across, depending on species
PREY	Small fish, shrimp, worms, and planktonic animals
VENOM	Injected by stinging cells on tentacles
LIFESPAN	Some species 70 years plus

Sea anemones are found in all the seas and oceans of the world, mainly on rocks and reefs, though some live in deep waters. Most of the big, dangerous species live in the tropics.

Did You Know?

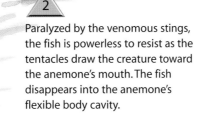

● All sea anemones can move around. Some creep along rock and coral on their sticky disks. Others turn upside-down and walk along on their tentacles. Some can even swim, by flexing their bodies and rapidly beating their tentacles.

● Beadlet anemones, found on tidal shores, are particularly aggressive to their neighbors. There are red and green types, and for some reason the red anemones always defeat the green ones.

● Anemones that live on tidal shores can retract their tentacles, contract into blobs of jelly, and secrete mucus, so they stay moist and can survive out of water for several hours at low tide.

● Some anemones reproduce by splitting in half, each half then living separately. In other species, there are males and females. In some, the eggs hatch inside the female, who then "gives birth" to baby anemones.

GIANT SQUID

Latin name: *Architeuthis dux*

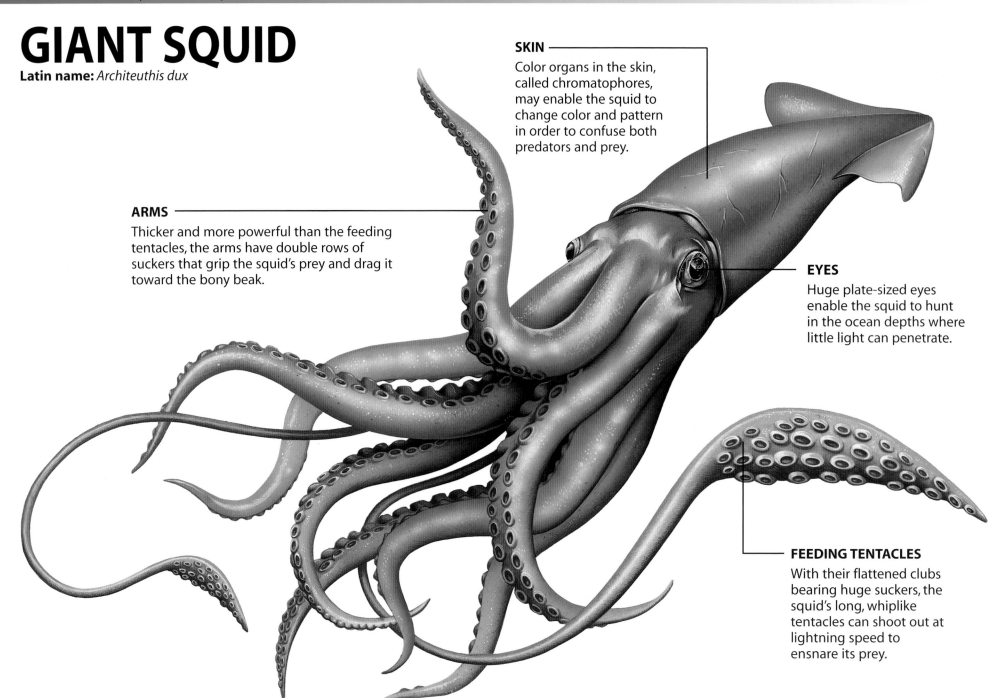

SKIN

Color organs in the skin, called chromatophores, may enable the squid to change color and pattern in order to confuse both predators and prey.

ARMS

Thicker and more powerful than the feeding tentacles, the arms have double rows of suckers that grip the squid's prey and drag it toward the bony beak.

EYES

Huge plate-sized eyes enable the squid to hunt in the ocean depths where little light can penetrate.

FEEDING TENTACLES

With their flattened clubs bearing huge suckers, the squid's long, whiplike tentacles can shoot out at lightning speed to ensnare its prey.

Seafarers have long told tales of huge serpents crushing ships, or of many-headed creatures with long curling tails. Judging by the drawings that were made in some accounts, they were probably describing giant squid. Serpent necks and heads may have been the squid's long feeding tentacles. A many-headed beast may have been a many-armed squid. The tail and fins of the giant squid might easily be mistaken for the rearing head of a sea serpent. An 18th-century Norwegian bishop described the monster called the Kraken as having a thick cylindrical body, a pointed head, trailing appendages, and large eyes, like pewter plate.

Size

KEY DATA

LENGTH	Probably 59ft (18m) or so
WEIGHT	Up to 3 tons (1 tonne)
LIMBS	8 arms, 2 tentacles
EYES	Up to 16in (40cm) in diameter
DEPTH OF ACTIVITY	1,650–4,920ft (500–1500m)
PREY	Other squid and fish
PREDATOR	Sperm whale
LIFESPAN	Unknown

The giant squid dwells in all the deepest oceans, but the largest concentrations have been found off the coasts of Norway, West and South Africa, New Zealand, Australia, Newfoundland, and the USA.

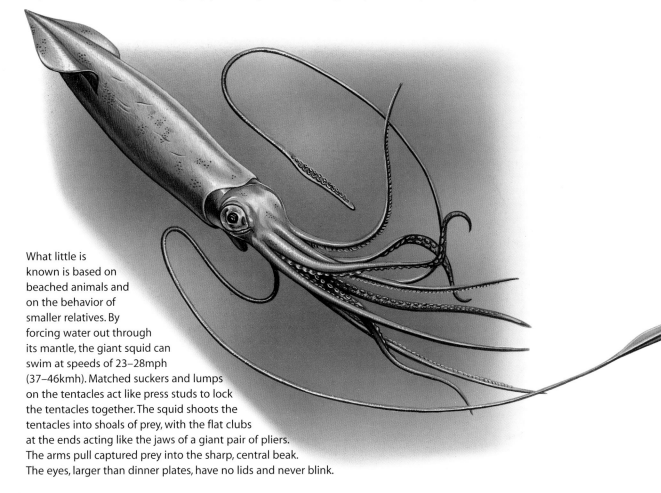

What little is known is based on beached animals and on the behavior of smaller relatives. By forcing water out through its mantle, the giant squid can swim at speeds of 23–28mph (37–46kmh). Matched suckers and lumps on the tentacles act like press studs to lock the tentacles together. The squid shoots the tentacles into shoals of prey, with the flat clubs at the ends acting like the jaws of a giant pair of pliers. The arms pull captured prey into the sharp, central beak. The eyes, larger than dinner plates, have no lids and never blink.

Did You Know?

● The giant squid has the largest eyes of any animal, and can detect tiny movements in conditions of deep-sea darkness, in which most creatures are blind.

● In the 1930s, a Norwegian ship was attacked three times by a giant squid that mistook it for a whale.

● The smallest giant squid ever discovered was 4in (10cm) long, newly hatched from an egg, found in 1981 in the nets of an Australian research ship at a depth of only 65ft (20m).

● The male giant squid injects his sperm into the skin of the female, where she stores it until she is ready to fertilize her millions of tiny eggs.

BOX JELLYFISH
Latin name: *Chironex, Chiropsalmus, Carukia* species

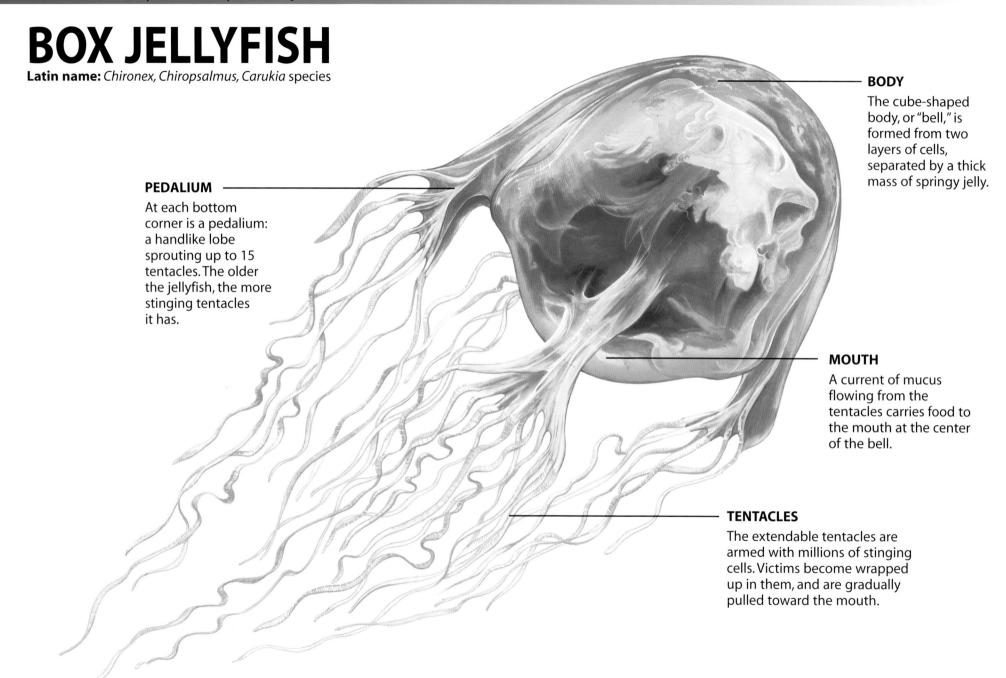

BODY

The cube-shaped body, or "bell," is formed from two layers of cells, separated by a thick mass of springy jelly.

PEDALIUM

At each bottom corner is a pedalium: a handlike lobe sprouting up to 15 tentacles. The older the jellyfish, the more stinging tentacles it has.

MOUTH

A current of mucus flowing from the tentacles carries food to the mouth at the center of the bell.

TENTACLES

The extendable tentacles are armed with millions of stinging cells. Victims become wrapped up in them, and are gradually pulled toward the mouth.

Most jellyfish are circular, but box jellyfish have bodies like rounded cubes of jello. Tentacles loaded with stinging cells trail up to 9ft (3m) in the water, and some species are armed with a potent venom that can easily kill a person. Box jellyfish are often found in swarms and move faster than a person can wade, which makes them a real menace. What's more, the whole creature is transparent, so for years no one knew what it was that sent swimmers screaming in agony from the water, clawing at the clinging threads that burned their skin.

Size

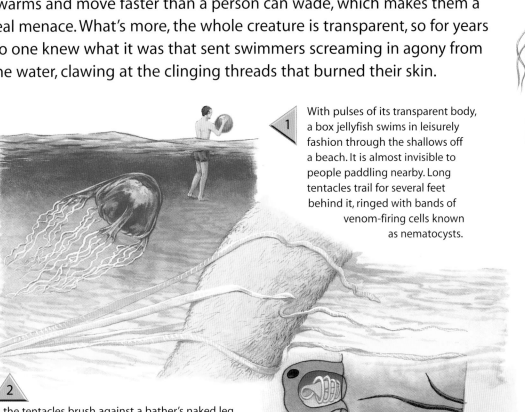

1 With pulses of its transparent body, a box jellyfish swims in leisurely fashion through the shallows off a beach. It is almost invisible to people paddling nearby. Long tentacles trail for several feet behind it, ringed with bands of venom-firing cells known as nematocysts.

2 As the tentacles brush against a bather's naked leg, they wrap around the exposed limb. Jumping back in alarm, the bather becomes entangled further, and screams in pain as the tentacles start to burn his skin.

3 The burning is caused by venom from microscopic harpoons in the nematocysts. Long, needle-pointed threads are stored inside-out in pressurized capsules with hair-trigger lids, and shoot the right way out at the lightest touch. The threads have venomous tips and barbs that catch in the bather's skin. And as the agonized victim rubs his leg, he causes still more cells to inject him.

KEY DATA

BODY WIDTH	Up to 6in (15cm) (*Chironex fleckeri*)
TENTACLE LENGTH	Up to 9 ft (3m) each, 330 ft (100m) total
DIET	Shrimp and small fish
VENOM	Injected by nematocysts; can kill in under 5 minutes

Box jellyfish are found worldwide, but the most dangerous ones live in the shallow coastal waters of northern Australia and Southeast Asia. Species include the Chironex, Chiropsalmus, and Carukia box jellyfish.

Did You Know?

● For some reason, box jellyfish cannot sting through nylon tights, so lifeguards used to wear them for safety before they had special protective suits.

● Box jellyfish are attracted to light, and many people are stung at night as they swim near illuminated boats or harbors.

● If a box jellyfish loses some tentacles, it grows some more.

● Once a nematocyst has fired, it cannot be recoiled. The cell must be replaced, which takes about two days.

● The astounding potency of box jellyfish stings is probably a defense against big fish that become tangled in the tentacles. Large animals must be disabled quickly, before they damage the jellyfish's soft body.

● Amazingly, hawksbill turtles manage to eat box jellyfish, and seem to be immune to their stings.

SEA NETTLE

Latin name: *Chrysaora* species

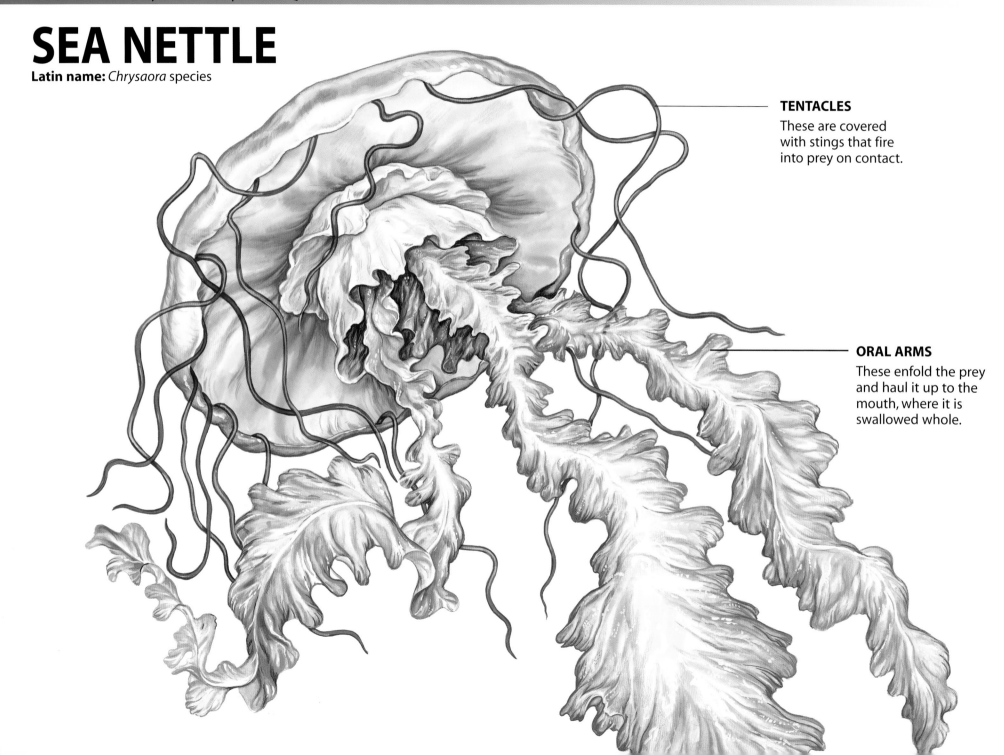

TENTACLES

These are covered with stings that fire into prey on contact.

ORAL ARMS

These enfold the prey and haul it up to the mouth, where it is swallowed whole.

A sea nettle has a bell-shaped body with 24 long, stinging tentacles. The mouth on the underside has four ribbon-like oral arms. The creature moves by contracting muscles in its body, which squeezes the jello-like tissue, forcing water out so pushing it along. Always on the move, the sea nettle trails tentacles with vast numbers of nematocysts—cells containing a coiled barb. Triggered by touch, or chemicals in the water, each fires a venomous harpoon into the target. The paralyzed prey is helpless as the oral arms haul the victim up to the mouth.

Size

1 ▸ Two teenagers paddle out into the sea in a small, rubber dingy. They dare each other to see who can remain standing the longest. As they sway, trying to keep their balance, one topples into the sea.

2 ▸ Unseen by the boys, a swarm of sea nettles lurks just below them— long tentacles primed and ready. The boy splashes right into the middle of the swarm, triggering the release of thousands of stinging barbs into his tender flesh.

KEY DATA

SIZE	Bell up to 3ft (1m)	
PREY	Plankton, fish, roe, and other jellyfish	
WEAPONS	Touch-activated stinging cells on tentacles	The east coast sea nettle (*Chrysaora quinquecirrha*) ranges along the Atlantic coast of North America from Massachusetts to Mexico and the Caribbean. Other species, including its bigger cousin, the west coast sea nettle (*C. flucescens*), inhabit Pacific coastal waters.
LIFESPAN	Unknown	

Did You Know?

● Sea nettles get their name from the European stinging nettle, a plant with tiny spines on the leaves that causes a painful rash. Early English colonists of the USA gave the name to the swarming, local jellyfish.

● Unlike most other jellyfish, sea nettles thrive in sea water with a low salt content, such as that found in bays and river estuaries. Sea turtles and predatory sea fish keep out of these waters, and few other jellyfish live there to compete for food.

● Sea nettles are useful to the oyster industry because they gobble up the comb jellies that otherwise feed on the oyster's free-swimming larvae. Sea nettles engulf oyster larvae, but then spit them out again, undigested and unharmed.

● On its travels through the ocean, the sea nettle sometimes picks up a hitchhiker in the form of a young cancer crab, which hides inside the bell of the jellyfish.

LION'S MANE

Latin name: *Cyanea capillata*

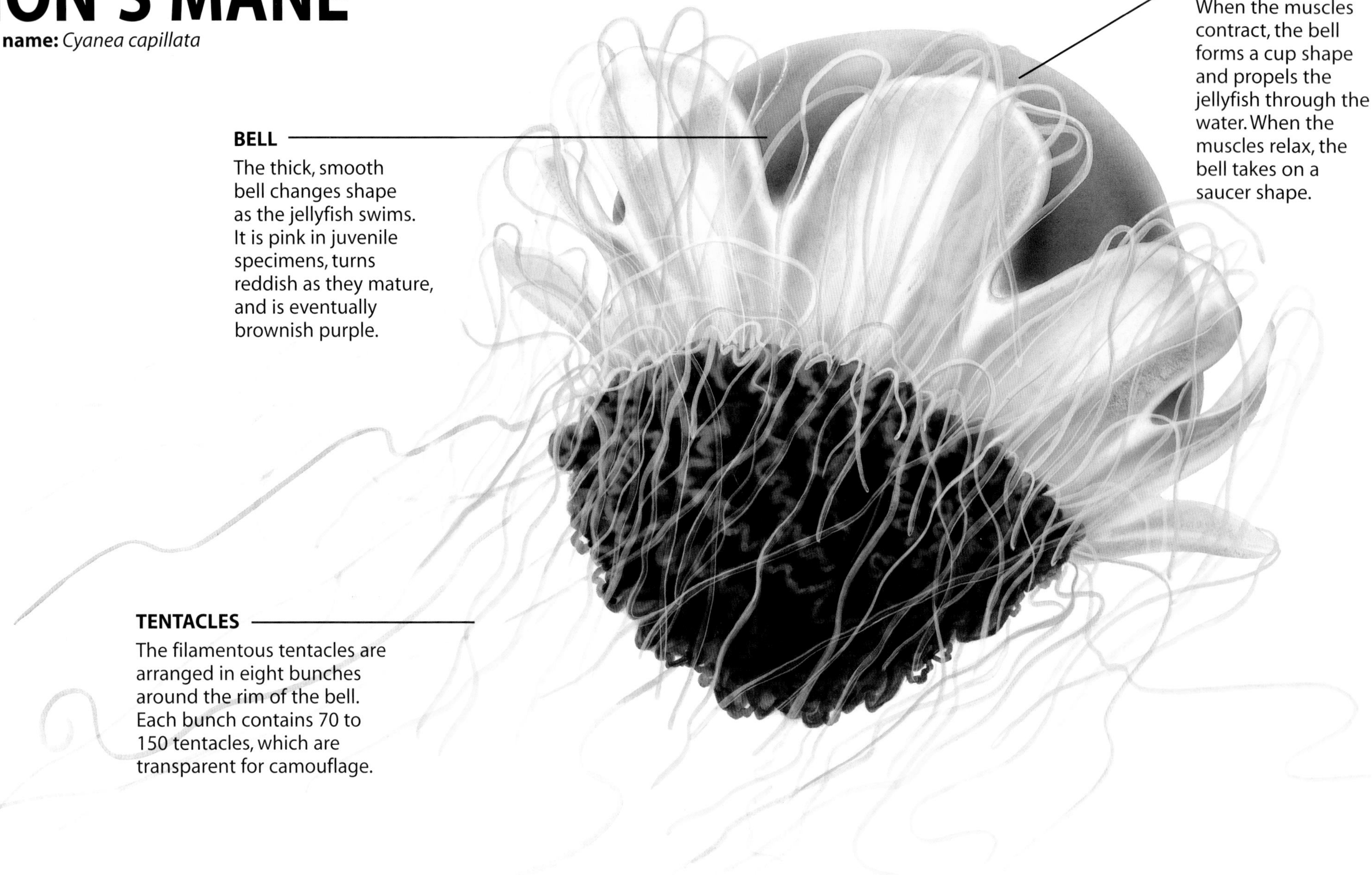

BELL

The thick, smooth bell changes shape as the jellyfish swims. It is pink in juvenile specimens, turns reddish as they mature, and is eventually brownish purple.

MUSCLES

When the muscles contract, the bell forms a cup shape and propels the jellyfish through the water. When the muscles relax, the bell takes on a saucer shape.

TENTACLES

The filamentous tentacles are arranged in eight bunches around the rim of the bell. Each bunch contains 70 to 150 tentacles, which are transparent for camouflage.

With hundreds of deadly tentacles dangling beneath its umbrella-like body, the lion's mane jellyfish can sting even when dead if its tentacles are moist. The lion's mane is one of the world's biggest jellyfish, with a fiery and ferocious sting. Luckily, this toxic drifter lives offshore, but large numbers sometimes invade the shallows, stinging unwary bathers and, on occasions, taking lives.

Size

KEY DATA

DIAMETER	12in (30cm) to over (7ft) 2m	
TENTACLES	Up to 1000 —they can be up to 114ft (35m) long	
PREY	Small fish and other jellyfish	
WEAPONS	Numerous stinging cells	
LIFESPAN	Unknown	

The lion's mane jellyfish drifts in the northern waters of both the Atlantic and Pacific oceans, as well as in their neighboring seas.

1 A boy paddles in the surf on a quiet beach, unaware of a dead lion's mane jellyfish lying in his path. As he stumbles across it, its trailing tentacles sting one of his feet.

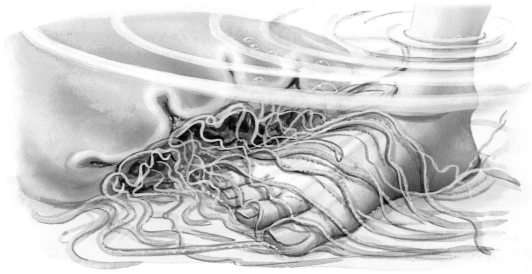

2 The boy cries out as pain sears through his foot, and the dead jellyfish continues to sting him as he struggles to shake off the tangle of tentacles. His family hear his agonized screams and run to his aid. This boy will certainly watch his step in the future when walking in the surf.

Did You Know?

● Like a number of jellyfish and other marine creatures, the lion's mane jellyfish is capable of glowing in the dark, producing its own natural bioluminescence.

● Some juvenile fish develop a coating of mucus that makes them immune to the venom of the lion's mane jellyfish. Opportunistic young cod, haddock, whiting, and horse-mackerel sometimes take shelter in its curtain of tentacles, traveling with the jellyfish for hundreds of miles.

● In 1865, the largest recorded specimen of lion's mane jellyfish washed up on shore in Massachusetts Bay in the USA. Its bell was 7ft 6in (2.3m) wide and the longest of its tentacles stretched out to more than 118ft (36m).

● No other species of jellyfish has been known to attain such an enormous size. By contrast, the smallest species of jellyfish in the oceans has a bell diameter of less than ¾in (2cm) when fully grown.

GIANT OCTOPUS

Latin name: *Enteroctopus dofleini*

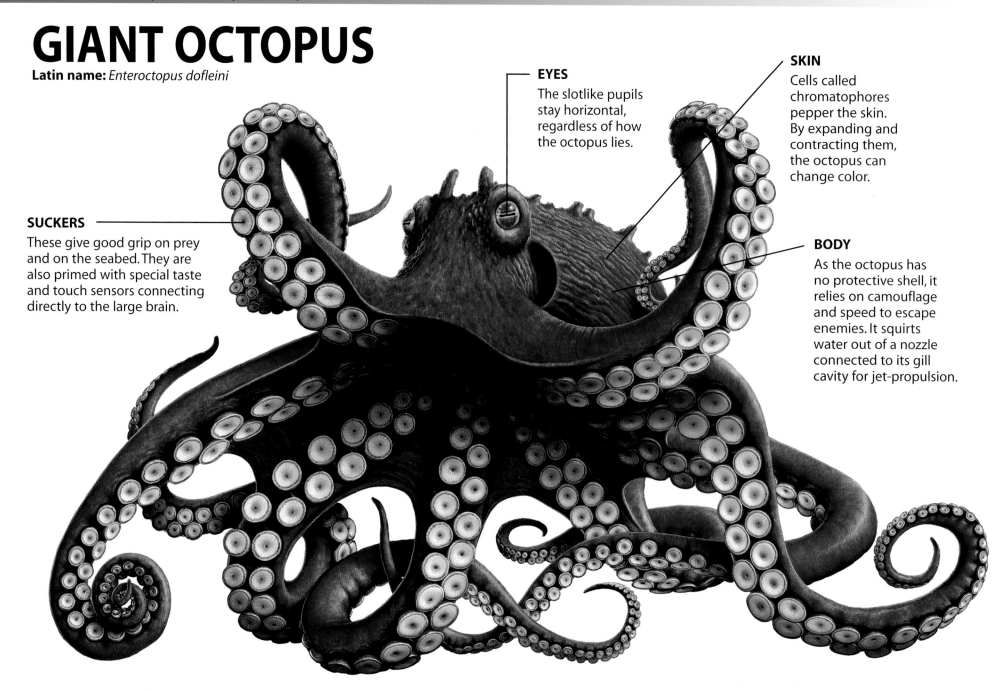

EYES
The slotlike pupils
stay horizontal,
regardless of how
the octopus lies.

SKIN
Cells called
chromatophores
pepper the skin.
By expanding and
contracting them,
the octopus can
change color.

SUCKERS
These give good grip on prey
and on the seabed. They are
also primed with special taste
and touch sensors connecting
directly to the large brain.

BODY
As the octopus has
no protective shell, it
relies on camouflage
and speed to escape
enemies. It squirts
water out of a nozzle
connected to its gill
cavity for jet-propulsion.

A mighty mollusk, the Pacific giant octopus is brainier than any fish or reptile on the planet—despite being a distant relative of garden slugs and snails. It is not a creature to tangle with lightly. It has a maximum tentacle span of 23ft (7m) or more and over 2000 strong suckers. Intelligent and inquisitive, the giant octopus takes a keen interest in everything that goes on around its den.

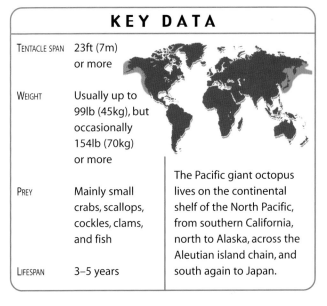

SIZE

KEY DATA

TENTACLE SPAN	23ft (7m) or more
WEIGHT	Usually up to 99lb (45kg), but occasionally 154lb (70kg) or more
PREY	Mainly small crabs, scallops, cockles, clams, and fish
LIFESPAN	3–5 years

The Pacific giant octopus lives on the continental shelf of the North Pacific, from southern California, north to Alaska, across the Aleutian island chain, and south again to Japan.

Emerging stealthily from its lair under a boulder, a giant Pacific octopus extends a long tentacle and coils it around the leg of a diver. Understandably, the diver's instant reaction is to panic. But the octopus is merely being curious. Having sampled the peculiar taste of the wet suit with its suckers, the gentle giant quickly releases its grip and slips out of sight.

Did You Know?

● Despite its size, the Pacific giant octopus has enemies. Seals, big fish, and sea otters all relish raw octopus and readily attack the Pacific giant. A study found that up to half the Pacific giant octopus living off the coast of Alaska bear battle scars. Some even lose tentacles in attacks, but these eventually grow back.

● The Pacific giant octopus has a big appetite, eating as many as eight 2–4in (5–10cm) crabs every night—adding nearly two percent to its weight each day. From tipping the scales at only 1–2lb (0.5–1kg) at a year old, it swells to 33lb (15kg) by the time it is three.

● There are fairly reliable records of Pacific giant octopus weighing more than 297lb (135kg)—and one that weighed more than 397lb (180kg)!

● The female lays up to 100,000 eggs. She then guards, aerates, and cleans them, without eating, until they all hatch—up to seven months later. She then dies of starvation.

BLUE-RINGED OCTOPUS

Latin name: *Hapalochlaena spp.*

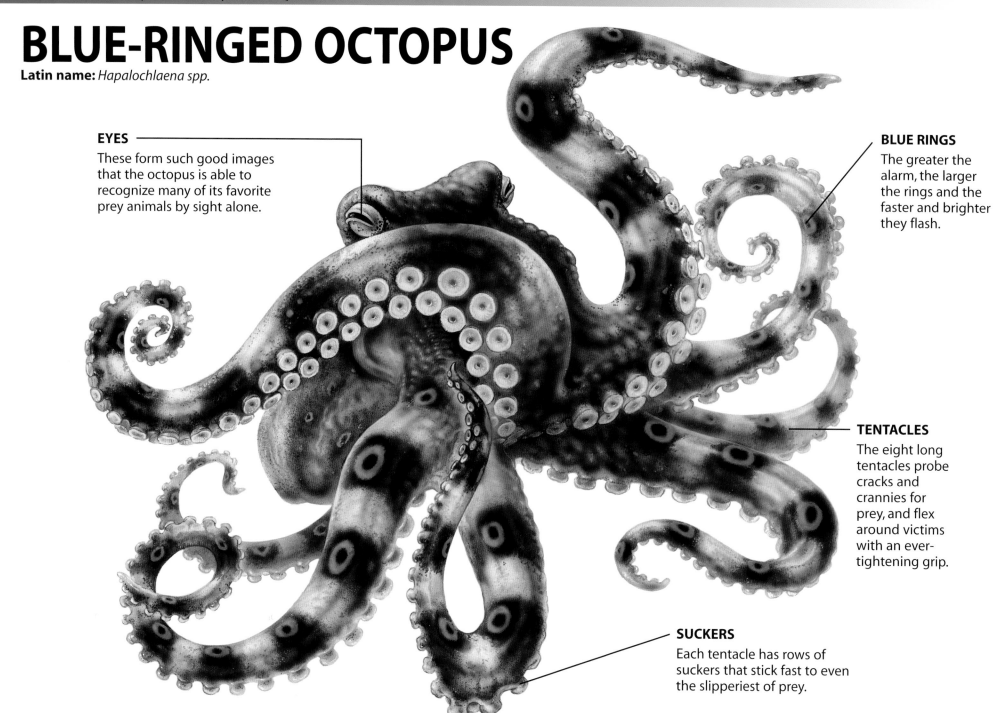

EYES
These form such good images that the octopus is able to recognize many of its favorite prey animals by sight alone.

BLUE RINGS
The greater the alarm, the larger the rings and the faster and brighter they flash.

TENTACLES
The eight long tentacles probe cracks and crannies for prey, and flex around victims with an ever-tightening grip.

SUCKERS
Each tentacle has rows of suckers that stick fast to even the slipperiest of prey.

When the blue-ringed octopus is excited, its beautiful colors flash extra-bright. Energy crackling through its network of nerves triggers a reaction in color cells in its skin. While some of the darker cells make smaller dots of color, the bright blue ones enlarge—to dazzling effect. The octopus is lethal, but not every predator on the reef knows it, so its bright colors act as a warning to a potential enemy.

Size

1 ▽ A blue-ringed octopus emerges from its lair to search for food away from the reef. In the open water, it is surprised by a hungry and inquisitive young coral trout. As the fish moves within reach of its tentacles, the octopus rapidly flashes its vivid blue rings. But the fish is too inexperienced to recognize the warning signs.

2 ▽ Not realizing the terrible risk it is taking, the coral trout darts in to attack. The octopus fights back, and within seconds sinks its sharp beak into the top of its opponent's head.

The bite delivers a massive dose of venom, which courses through the fish's body, seizing up its muscles. Racked by spasms, the fish drifts away to die—while the octopus makes good its escape.

3 ▽

KEY DATA

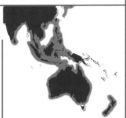

LENGTH	*Hapalochlaena maculosa* up to 41/2 in (12cm); *H. lunulata* up to 8in (20cm)
HABITAT	Rockpools and coral reefs
DIET	Shellfish, small fish, crabs, and other crustaceans
TYPICAL ATTACK	Single bite
VENOM	Contains a paralyzing toxin called tetrodotoxin (TTX); fatal in minutes if victim receives no medical help
LIFESPAN	Probably 2 years

There are two species of blue-ringed octopus. *Hapalochlaena maculosa* lives in warm shallow water off the southern coast of Australia. *H. lunulata* occurs in the tropical shallows of the Indo-Pacific, from northern Australia to southern Japan. It is especially common on coral reefs.

Did You Know?

● If a blue-ringed octopus loses one of its tentacles in a battle with a predator, it simply grows another.

● After a female blue-ringed octopus lays her eggs, she cradles them in her tentacles to protect them until they hatch.

● The blue-ringed octopus can live a surprisingly long time out of water. Captive specimens have even been known to creep out of their tanks in search of food.

● A baby blue-ringed octopus evades predators by squirting black ink into the water. As its venom glands and blue rings develop, its ink sacs shrivel away.

OPALESCENT SQUID

Latin name: *Loligo opalescens*

EYES

The huge eyes of the squid have thick optic nerves that provide excellent vision. Each eye is covered by a transparent protective membrane that protects the organ from damage during struggles.

SKIN

This houses a layer of cells called chromatophores; by expanding or contracting this layer, the squid creates rapid changes of color.

TENTACLES

In addition to the two feeding tentacles, the squid has eight, shorter sucker-covered ones that it uses to pull prey toward the mouth, with a venom-laden horny beak, located at their base.

FEEDING TENTACLES

The squid has two long feeding tentacles that it shoots out to grab prey.

SUCKERS

Each tentacle is armed with powerful suckers that grip the squid's slippery victims.

A clever predator that communicates with others of its kind by showing luminous, changing patterns across its skin, the opalescent squid tracks prey with eyes like two huge headlamps, stalking its quarry through the ocean depths. If the crafty killer is spotted, it has another tactic: it produces a mesmerizing display of flashing colors to lure victims to their doom. A big, juicy fish is bound to attract a hungry opalescent squid. With jet force to shoot itself forward, powerful suckers to fasten onto the unsuspecting victim, and surprise on its side, the assassin can tackle prey much larger than itself.

Size

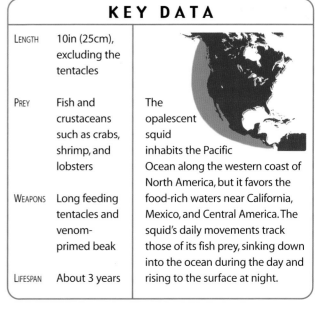

KEY DATA

LENGTH	10in (25cm), excluding the tentacles		
PREY	Fish and crustaceans such as crabs, shrimp, and lobsters	The opalescent squid inhabits the Pacific Ocean along the western coast of North America, but it favors the food-rich waters near California, Mexico, and Central America. The squid's daily movements track those of its fish prey, sinking down into the ocean during the day and rising to the surface at night.	
WEAPONS	Long feeding tentacles and venom-primed beak		
LIFESPAN	About 3 years		

1 A squid spots a plump fish and lines itself up to attack. Blasting a jet of water behind it, the killer hurtles toward its target. Terrified, the fish tries to makes its escape, but it's now in range of the killer's long feeding tentacles.

2 The predator shoots out the long feeding tentacles, locking onto the fleeing prey and stopping it in its tracks, then coils more tentacles around it. The fish struggles frantically, but the attacker holds on tight and sinks a brutally sharp beak into the victim's flesh. As the squid's paralyzing venom takes effect, the hunter prepares for a feast.

Did You Know?

● The opalescent squid can jet off in any direction by changing the angle of its mantle. When fleeing a hungry blue shark, the squid often rockets straight out of the water.

● The opalescent squid is a highly sophisticated animal, but some of its relatives are much more primitive. The squid is a type of mollusk—a group of over 100,000 species that includes the lowly slug and snail.

● After growing and feeding for about three years, opalescent squid gather in huge schools for a final, spectacular mating ritual. By the end of it, the squid are so exhausted that they drift away and die.

● The opalescent squid's venom is laced with neurotoxins that attack a victim's nervous system, leaving it paralyzed. Squid aren't deadly to humans, but some mollusks are. The geographer cone shell (*Conus geographus*) injects toxins that kill up to a fifth of its human victims.

NAUTILUS

Latin name: *Nautilus* species

HOOD
The nautilus can retreat into its shell and shut the hood like a trapdoor.

SHELL
The open end houses the body; other chambers behind it contain gas and seawater for adjusting buoyancy.

TENTACLES
There may be up to 90 tentacles. The nautilus can extend them to grab live prey, gather carrion, or cling to a support such as the seabed.

EYE
The big eyes probably only work well in bright light.

FUNNEL
This flexible tube pokes out from among the tentacles. It squirts water out of the mantle to thrust the nautilus along.

The nautilus is one of the cephalopods, a group of mollusks that includes the squid, cuttlefish, and octopus. Cephalopods find prey by eye and scent, and catch it with long, sensitive tentacles. They breathe by drawing oxygen-rich water into a gill cavity and then blowing it out through a funnel. By blowing extra-hard, they can escape their enemies by jet propulsion. The nautilus is not streamlined like a squid, so it moves only slowly. It does have its shell, though, and if it is attacked it just pulls in its tentacles, closes its protective hood, and sits it out.

Size

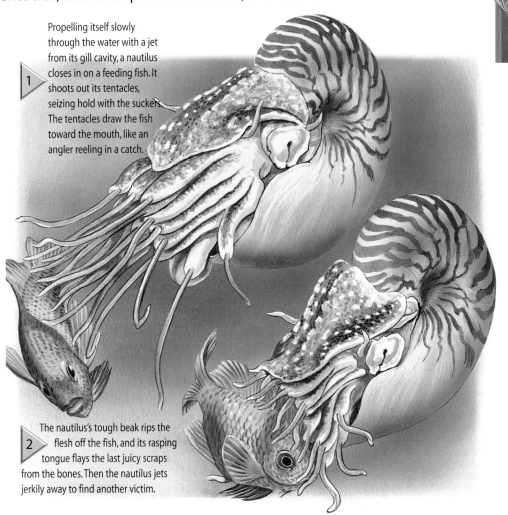

1 Propelling itself slowly through the water with a jet from its gill cavity, a nautilus closes in on a feeding fish. It shoots out its tentacles, seizing hold with the suckers. The tentacles draw the fish toward the mouth, like an angler reeling in a catch.

2 The nautilus's tough beak rips the flesh off the fish, and its rasping tongue flays the last juicy scraps from the bones. Then the nautilus jets jerkily away to find another victim.

KEY DATA

SHELL SIZE	Up to 10in (25cm) across, depending on species	
MOVEMENT	By jet propulsion and controlled buoyancy	
PREY	Crabs, shrimp, small fish, and carrion	
LIFESPAN	Unknown	

The five surviving species of nautilus live in the coral seas of the Indian and Pacific oceans, from the Philippines in the north, south as far as Australia's Great Barrier Reef. Nautilus normally feed in deep water near the reefs, but migrate into shallow water to breed.

Did You Know?

● An ancestor of the nautilus was Endoceras, which lived around 450 million years ago. Its shell was almost straight, not spiraling, and reached up to 12ft (3.6m) in length.

● Nautilus have been tracked diving to a depth of 1800ft (550m). Normally, water pressure would crush the shell at any depth greater than 1150ft (350m), but the buoyancy gases inside the shell stop it from imploding.

● Fossil remains of nautilus-like animals have been found in rocks that are over 500 million years old.

● As it grows, a nautilus adds new chambers to the mouth of its shell. Periodically, it eases forward from a cramped old chamber to occupy the newest one. A fully grown adult may have 30 or more chambers.

● Pacific fishers catch nautilus in bamboo traps. They boil up the animals' flesh to make soup and sell the attractive shells to collectors.

PORTUGUESE MAN-O-WAR
Latin name: *Physalia* species

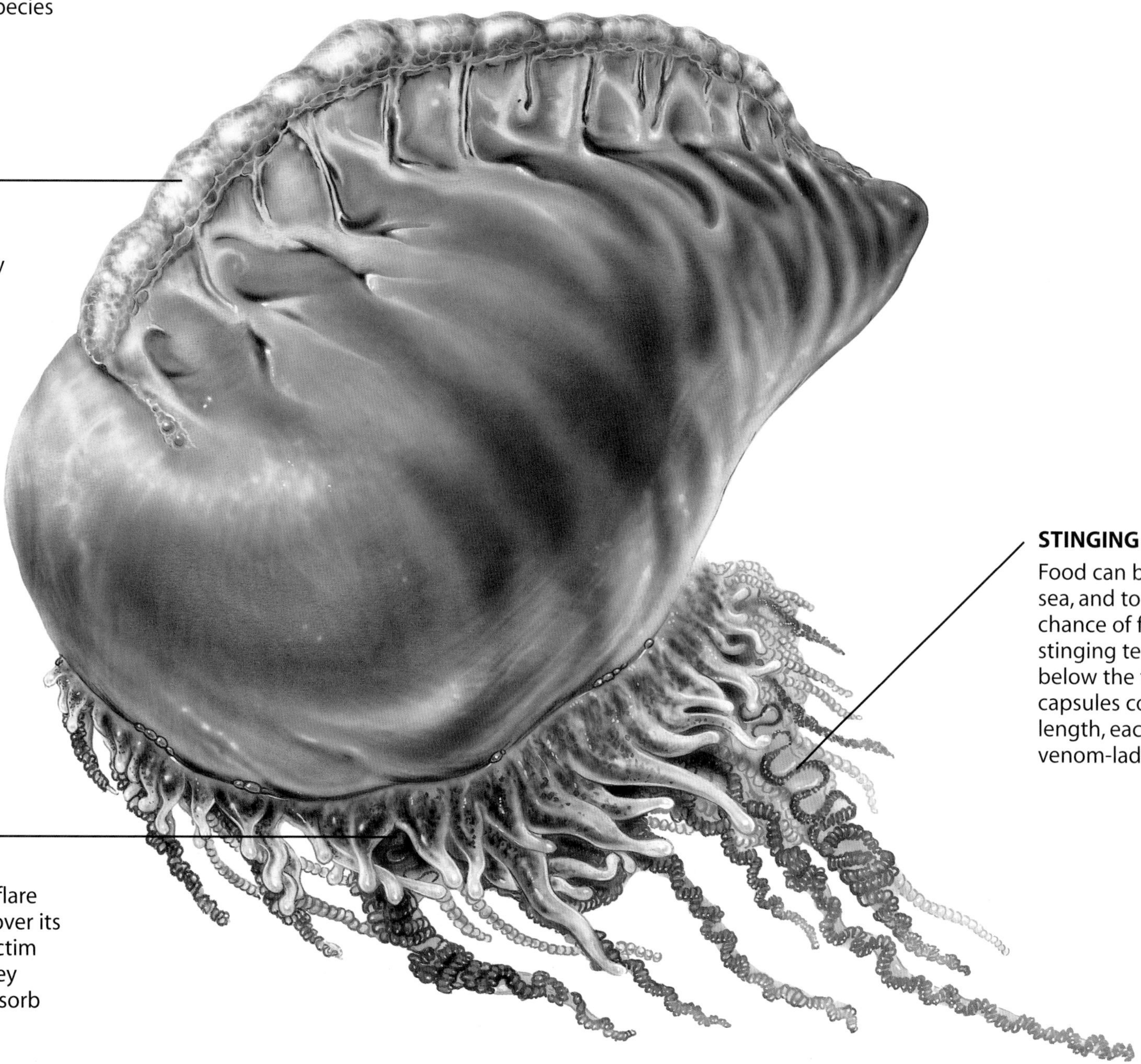

CRESTED FLOAT

Gases secreted by a special gland inflate the float, which is topped by a pink-tinged crest that acts as a sail.

STINGING TENTACLES

Food can be scarce out at sea, and to increase the chance of finding prey, the stinging tentacles extend far below the float. Microscopic capsules cover their entire length, each containing a venom-laden harpoon.

FEEDING BODIES

As prey is reeled in, the tubular feeding bodies flare wide open and spread over its surface. Covering the victim with digestive juices, they dissolve its flesh and absorb the nutrients.

As it sails across the ocean buoyed up by its gas-filled float, the Portuguese man-o-war trails its deadly tentacles far below, every foot armed with millions of venom-loaded stinging cells. It might not have a brain and it cannot actively swim, but the man-o-war is a competent killer. As fish and shrimp blunder into its long, stinging snare, it reels them in, smothers them in digestive juices, and devours them. A portuguese man-o-war looks harmless from above, and can be missed among the waves, but below the surface it's another story...

Size

KEY DATA

FLOAT LENGTH	Up to 12in (30cm)	
TENTACLE LENGTH	Usually about 39ft (12m), but can be up to 164ft (50m)	
PREY	Fish and crustaceans	Portuguese men-o-war drift over all the warmer oceans of the world, driven by winds and currents. Occasionally they are swept inshore by storms and are stranded on exposed beaches.
VENOM	Injected by special cells on the stinging tentacles	

1

In a shallow tropical sea, an amateur snorkeler anchors near a coral reef and climbs eagerly into the water. In his haste, he fails to spot the man-o-war's small float bobbing in the distance.

2

As he swims toward the reef, he brushes into the man-o-war's long, trailing tentacles, which contract and coil around him. Writhing in pain, he tries to struggle free, but only succeeds in triggering more stinging cells.

Did You Know?

● Although the man-o-war's main victims are small fish and shrimp, it can also kill and devour larger, more powerful fish such as herrings.

● When it gets hot, the man-o-war's float is deflated every few minutes. Leaning first one way and then the other, it dips each side into the water to stop itself from drying out.

● The man-o-war is similar in shape to the hats worn by medieval Portuguese sailors, which is how it got its name. In some parts of the world it is known as a bluebottle.

● Portuguese men-o-war often drift across the oceans in swarms containing thousands of individuals.

● Some fish are almost immune to the man-o-war's stinging cells, and one of these is the bluebottlefish (*Nomeus gronovi*), which lives among the man-o-war's tentacles. It even feeds on the tentacles, which simply grow again as it nibbles them away.

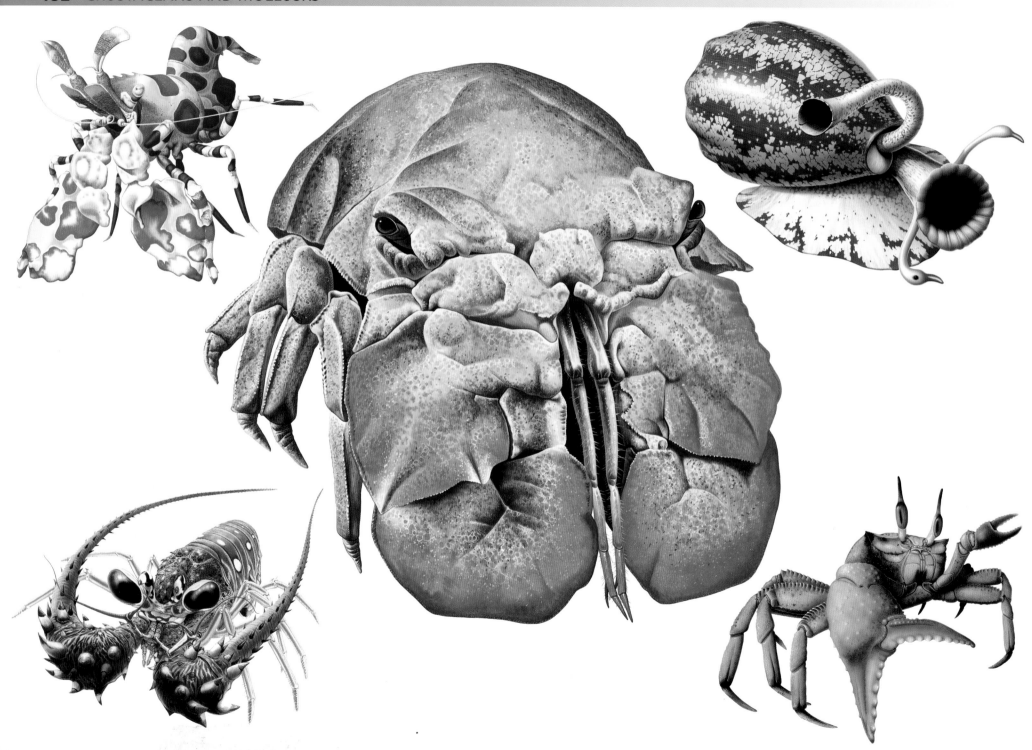

Crustaceans and Mollusks

*Although not totally foolproof against attack, the hard shells
that armor the soft bodies of crustaceans and mollusks are
a challenge for creatures seeking to make a meal of them.*

It takes very sharp teeth and a mighty bite to crush through the shells. So this armor gives protection against many sea creatures that lack the weapons to tackle it. But when crustaceans or mollusks turn predator, they can be highly dangerous opponents. The Pistol Shrimp is only 2in (5cm) long, but it has a very large claw with a huge muscle that shoots out a shock wave which knocks out its prey with the force of a battering ram. The Horseshoe Crab, which is basically a heavily armored spider, feeds on other shellfish, crushing their armor with its powerful hind legs. The arrow crab prolongs the agony for its prey by eating it piece by piece while it is still alive. Some crustaceans have unusual, even weird, habits. The Hermit Crab, for instance, is a "squatter": it searches the seabed for empty shells vacated by other sea creatures and just moves in. The Cuttlefish mollusk makes instant orphans of its own offspring by promptly dying after laying its eggs. The Water Scorpion makes soup of the innards of its prey by injecting it with toxic saliva.

PISTOL SHRIMP

Latin name: *Alpheus* species

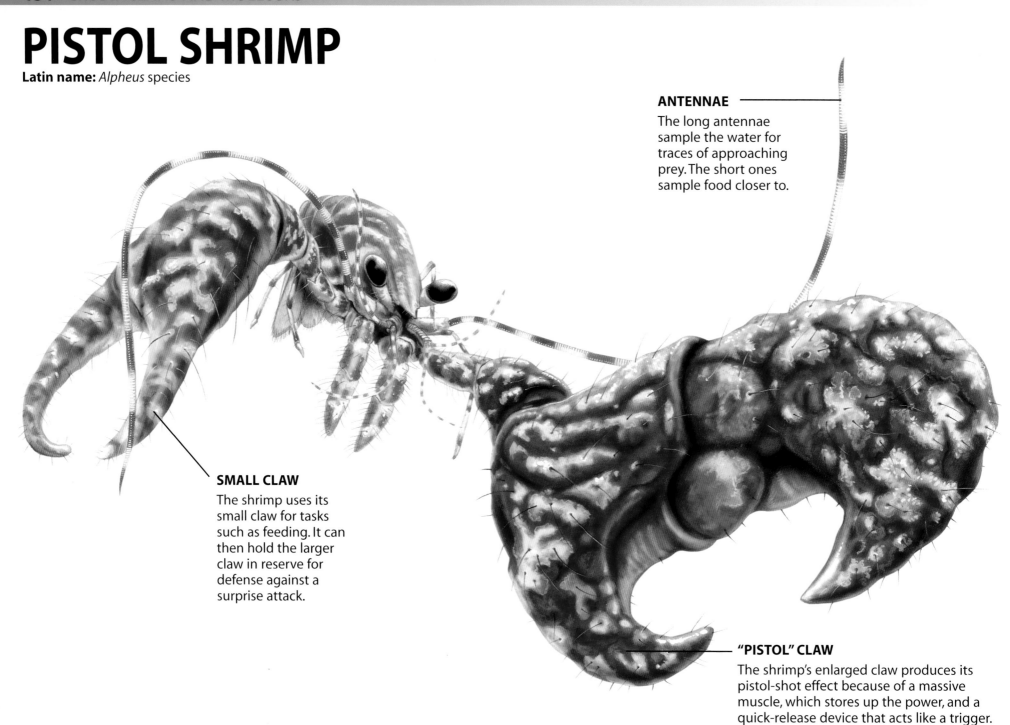

ANTENNAE
The long antennae sample the water for traces of approaching prey. The short ones sample food closer to.

SMALL CLAW
The shrimp uses its small claw for tasks such as feeding. It can then hold the larger claw in reserve for defense against a surprise attack.

"PISTOL" CLAW
The shrimp's enlarged claw produces its pistol-shot effect because of a massive muscle, which stores up the power, and a quick-release device that acts like a trigger.

Meet the fastest claw in the West! Any animal facing this sharpshootin' shrimp is in for a shock. A blast from the pistol-packing critter can send an enemy reeling. The fast-shooting pistol shrimp uses a specially modified claw to produce a loud shock wave powerful enough to stun any small animal that strays into range. As sound waves travel four times faster through water than air, a sudden loud noise in water creates a shock wave that smashes into obstacles like a battering ram.

Actual Size

1 A fish approaches the shrimp warily—pausing just outside grabbing range, unaware it is still at risk. Suddenly the shrimp's claw snaps shut, sending a shock wave through the water and into the fish.

2 Racing over the seabed, the pistol shrimp grabs its prey before the stunned fish has a chance to recover. The shrimp grips the animal with the smaller of its two claws and fires into the fish once more, this time at point-blank range, to keep it stunned. The shrimp then drags its victim back to its burrow to rip it apart and eat at leisure.

KEY DATA

LENGTH	Up to 2in (5cm)
LIFESTYLE	Burrowing ambush-predator
PREY	Mainly small shrimp, fish, and crabs
WEAPON	Stun-gun claw
ATTACK	Stuns victims that come within range
BREEDING	Produces millions of eggs
WATER DEPTH	Down to 65ft (20m)
LIFESPAN	Unknown

The various species of pistol shrimp live in warm, shallow seas, from the Caribbean to the Pacific Ocean. They mainly inhabit coral reefs, the sandy beds of lagoons, and rubble on rocky shores.

Did You Know?

● The pistol shrimp's fire-power is so punishing that a single blast from one has been known to crack the shell of a small crab. Captive pistol shrimps have even shattered the glass sides of their tanks.

● In most species of pistol shrimp, males and females pair for life, for mutual support and protection.

● The pistol shrimp isn't the only noisy crustacean living around coral reefs. The mantis shrimp makes a loud crack when it strikes out at prey or predators. The pantonine shrimp produces a rapid series of loud clicks by snapping its claws one at a time. It may do this to frighten away predators.

CONE SHELL

Latin name: *Conus* species

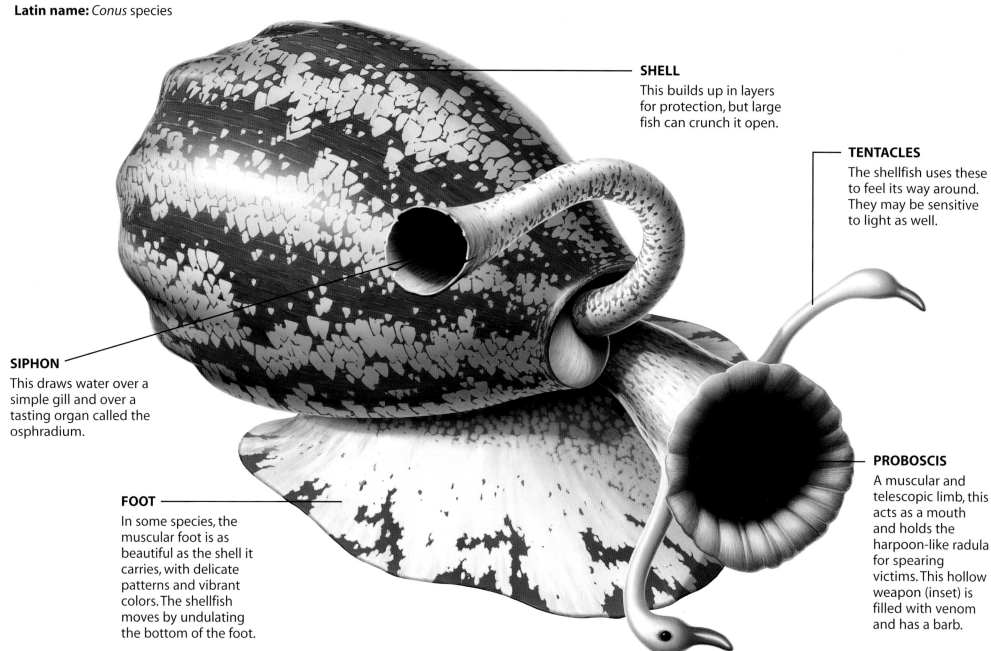

SHELL
This builds up in layers for protection, but large fish can crunch it open.

TENTACLES
The shellfish uses these to feel its way around. They may be sensitive to light as well.

SIPHON
This draws water over a simple gill and over a tasting organ called the osphradium.

PROBOSCIS
A muscular and telescopic limb, this acts as a mouth and holds the harpoon-like radula for spearing victims. This hollow weapon (inset) is filled with venom and has a barb.

FOOT
In some species, the muscular foot is as beautiful as the shell it carries, with delicate patterns and vibrant colors. The shellfish moves by undulating the bottom of the foot.

Collectors around the world avidly search shallows and coral reefs for rare cone shells. But when they pick up prize live specimens with their bare hands, they are dicing with a swift but agonizing death. Silent assassins of the sea, cone shells are endlessly patient, unnervingly stealthy, and unfailingly accurate killers. They spend the day buried in the sand or hiding in coral crevices, but as night falls they switch to predator mode.

Size

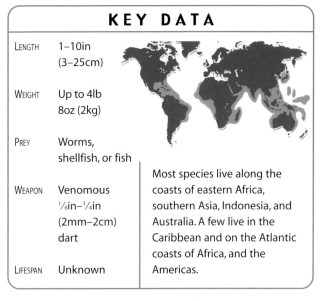

KEY DATA

LENGTH	1–10in (3–25cm)
WEIGHT	Up to 4lb 8oz (2kg)
PREY	Worms, shellfish, or fish
WEAPON	Venomous $\frac{1}{8}$in–$\frac{3}{4}$in (2mm–2cm) dart
LIFESPAN	Unknown

Most species live along the coasts of eastern Africa, southern Asia, Indonesia, and Australia. A few live in the Caribbean and on the Atlantic coasts of Africa, and the Americas.

1 Tasting the water with its siphon, a cone shell traces the scent of a small fish. Going to battle stations, the shellfish inches toward its prey—which isn't alarmed, fearing only big, fast fish.

2 Slowly, like the muzzle of a gun, the shell's proboscis emerges, gripping a venomous harpoon. Suddenly, the proboscis shoots out and rams the harpoon deep into the fish.

3 The fish struggles briefly but succumbs quickly to the paralyzing venom. The cone shell's proboscis then expands and slowly but surely draws in and engulfs the fish whole. The fish will take several days to digest, but will keep the cone shell going through the many nights it fails to catch such a prize meal.

Did You Know?

● There are about 400 species of cone shell, 90 percent of which hunt only shellfish and worms. The 40 or so species that hunt fish have the fastest-acting and most virulent venom, and are the most dangerous.

● A cone shell that eats worms harpoons them inside their burrows. Divers report watching almost interminable tugs of war, as a cone shell slowly draws its victim out of its hideaway like a blackbird pulling an earthworm from a lawn.

● The colors and patterns that adorn cone shells are unique in each species and often give a species its name. The geographer cone shell has a maplike pattern, the textile cone shell has one like woven cloth.

● As a cone shell matures, it may coat its shell in rough debris to hide its conspicuous colors and blend in with the seabed. Collectors must then break off the dowdy covering to expose the beauty beneath.

HORSESHOE CRAB

Latin name: Family *Limulidae*

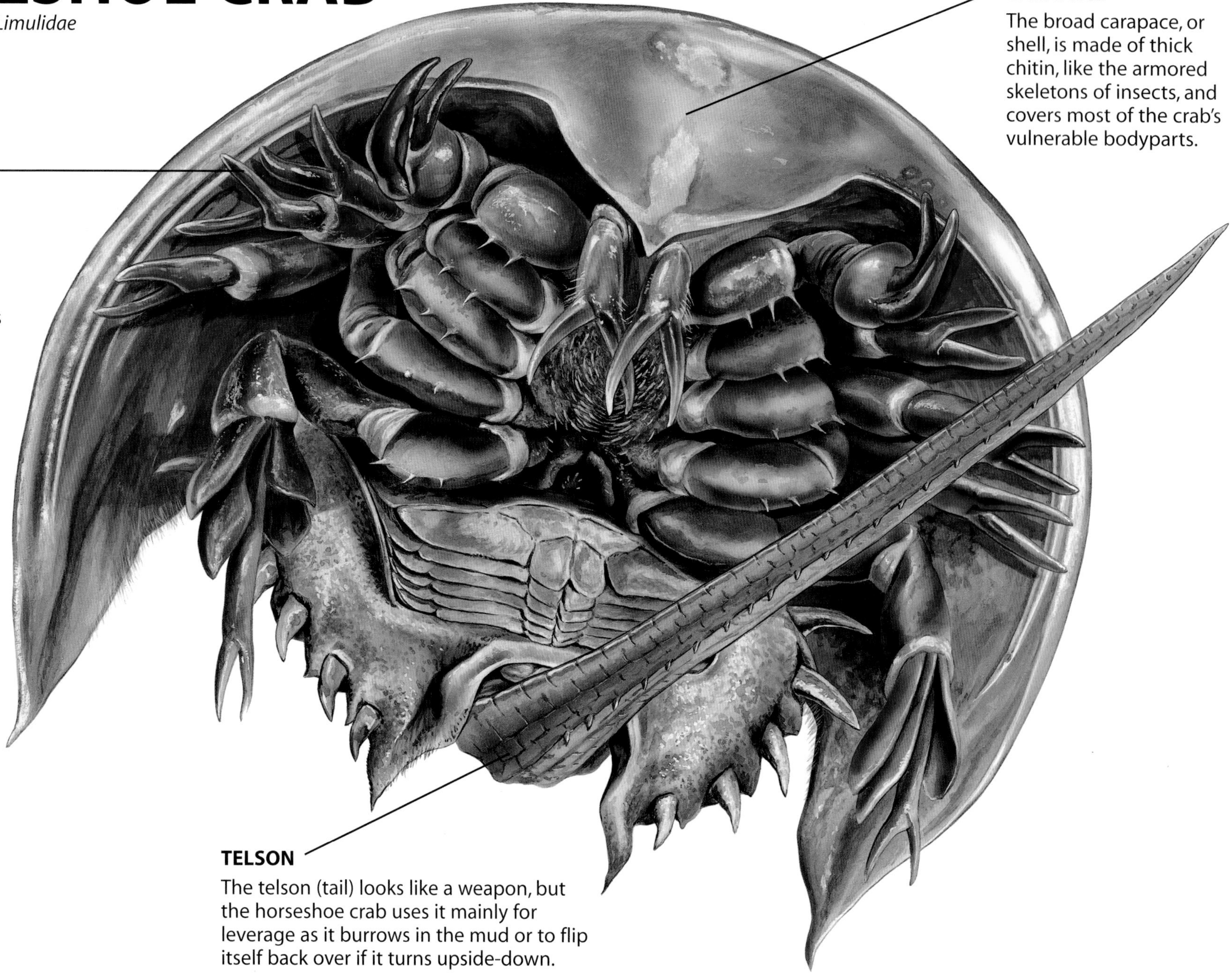

CARAPACE

The broad carapace, or shell, is made of thick chitin, like the armored skeletons of insects, and covers most of the crab's vulnerable bodyparts.

LEGS

The horseshoe crab has five pairs of walking legs, each with pincer-like feet. The hindmost pair have whorls of spines for shifting sand, and enlarged bases for crushing shells.

TELSON

The telson (tail) looks like a weapon, but the horseshoe crab uses it mainly for leverage as it burrows in the mud or to flip itself back over if it turns upside-down.

At rest, this strange sea creature could be mistaken for a shiny stone. And when it moves, it looks more like a weird wind-up toy, trundling along with its legs completely hidden from view under its domed shell. You might not think so to look at it, but a horseshoe crab is basically a spider in heavy armor, with most of its bodyparts hidden under its shell. Its body is specially adapted for life in the sea, but a few spidery features still remain. It feeds mainly on shellfish, digging them out and crushing them with its strong hindlegs.

Size

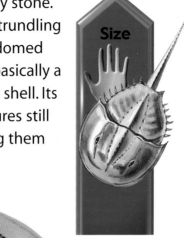

KEY DATA

LENGTH	Up to 24in (60cm) (*Limulus polyphemus*)	
SEXUAL MATURITY	9–12 years	
DIET	Marine worms, shellfish, algae, and carrion	The American horseshoe crab lives off the Atlantic and Gulf coasts of North Amex, the coasts of southern and eastern Asia, from India and east to Indonesia, the Philippines, and Japan.
LIFESPAN	Up to 19 years	

1 The horseshoe crab's shell is split into two parts, connected by a hinge joint (1). The front section corresponds to a spider's cephalothorax (combined head and thorax), the rear section to a spider's abdomen. The crab has a compound eye (2) on each side to register movement, as well as two simple eyes (3) at the front, which are sensitive to ultraviolet light.

2 The hind section of the shell hides the crab's gill plates (1), each containing up to 200 delicate membranes for extracting oxygen from the water. The crab's mouth (2) lies at the heart of the front section. In front of it are two chelicerae (3), but these look more like legs than the fangs of a true spider.

Did You Know?

● A horseshoe crab has no way of cleaning its shell, so when a mature crab stops molting, it may become encrusted with algae, tubeworms, barnacles, and small mollusks.

● When Native Americans went fishing, they used the spiked tails of horseshoe crabs as spearheads.

● Although horseshoe crabs are marine animals, one Indian species occasionally travels upriver and has been found 90 miles (145km) from the sea.

● Young horseshoe crabs can swim upside-down by fanning out their gill plates and using them as paddles.

● Newly hatched horseshoe crabs look like small trilobites —ancient marine animals that became extinct more than 200 million years ago—although they aren't closely related.

● Before food enters the crab's stomach, it is ground up in a special muscular sac known as a gizzard.

HERMIT CRAB
Latin name: Family *Paguridae*

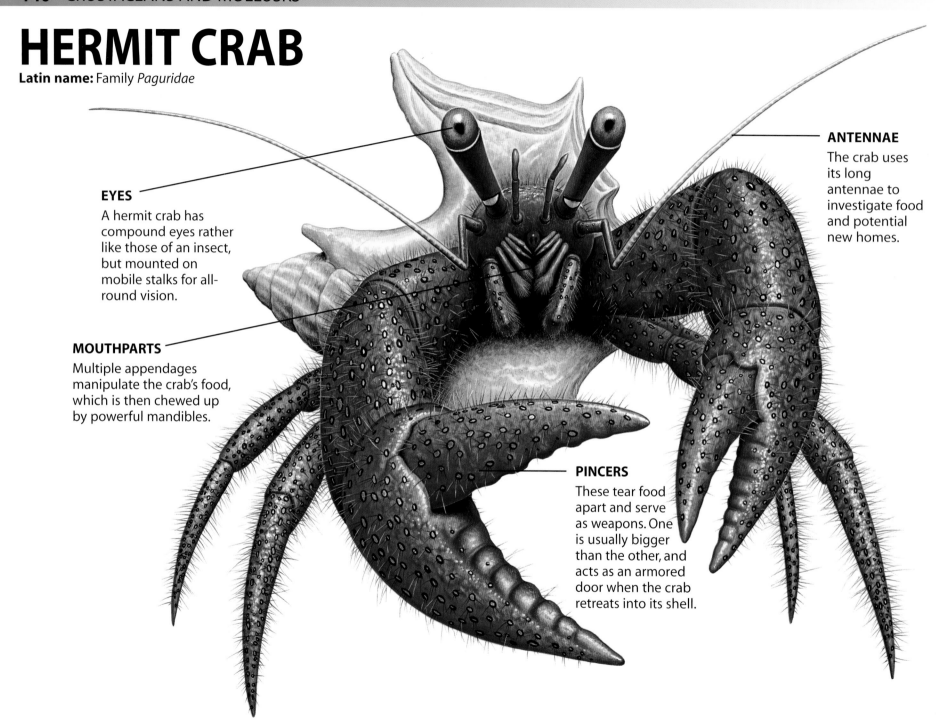

EYES

A hermit crab has compound eyes rather like those of an insect, but mounted on mobile stalks for all-round vision.

MOUTHPARTS

Multiple appendages manipulate the crab's food, which is then chewed up by powerful mandibles.

ANTENNAE

The crab uses its long antennae to investigate food and potential new homes.

PINCERS

These tear food apart and serve as weapons. One is usually bigger than the other, and acts as an armored door when the crab retreats into its shell.

A hermit crab makes its home in an empty shell. The weight of the shell keeping the crab on the seabed, where it roams in search of tasty scraps. Finding a crushed mollusk or rotting fish, it rips off bits with its pincers and passes them to its mouthparts. When a hermit crab outgrows its shell, it looks for a bigger home. But finding a new home isn't always easy, and if a badly housed hermit crab spots another with a shell that is too big for it, there might be a fight for ownership.

Size

KEY DATA

LENGTH	Up to 12in (30cm)
LIFESTYLE	Seabed scavenger
DIET	Any animal or plant matter
DEFENSES	Powerful pincers and protective shell
LIFESPAN	Depends on shell availability

Paguridae hermit crabs live in all the seas and oceans of the world, from the seashore to the deep sea. The land hermit crabs belong to a separate family.

1. After hunting in vain for another home, a cramped hermit crab finds a shell that is exactly the right size—unfortunately with another hermit crab in residence. Undeterred, it attacks the owner, until the other flees the vicious onslaught.

2. As the victor settles into its roomy new home, the evicted crab is left without a shell, its soft abdomen exposed. With no suitable alternatives in sight, it makes an easy target, and is rapidly attacked by a hungry fish.

Did You Know?

● Shells with right-handed spirals are more common, so a hermit crab's tail twists to the right. But some hermit crabs are found jammed uncomfortably in left-handed shells.

● In areas where there are no big sea snails, hermit crabs never get the chance to grow to their full size. When lack of space forces them out of their existing shells, they can't find new ones and are killed by predators.

● A female hermit crab carries her eggs inside her shell until they hatch into tiny larvae, which then drift in the ocean until they are ready to find miniature shells of their own.

● The enormous, coconut-eating robber crab is a type of land hermit crab, although it doesn't live in a shell—but it probably couldn't find one big enough even if it wanted to.

● Pagurrita crabs are specialized hermit crabs that live inside tiny tubes in dense growths of coral.

SLIPPER LOBSTER

Latin name: Family *Scyllaridae*

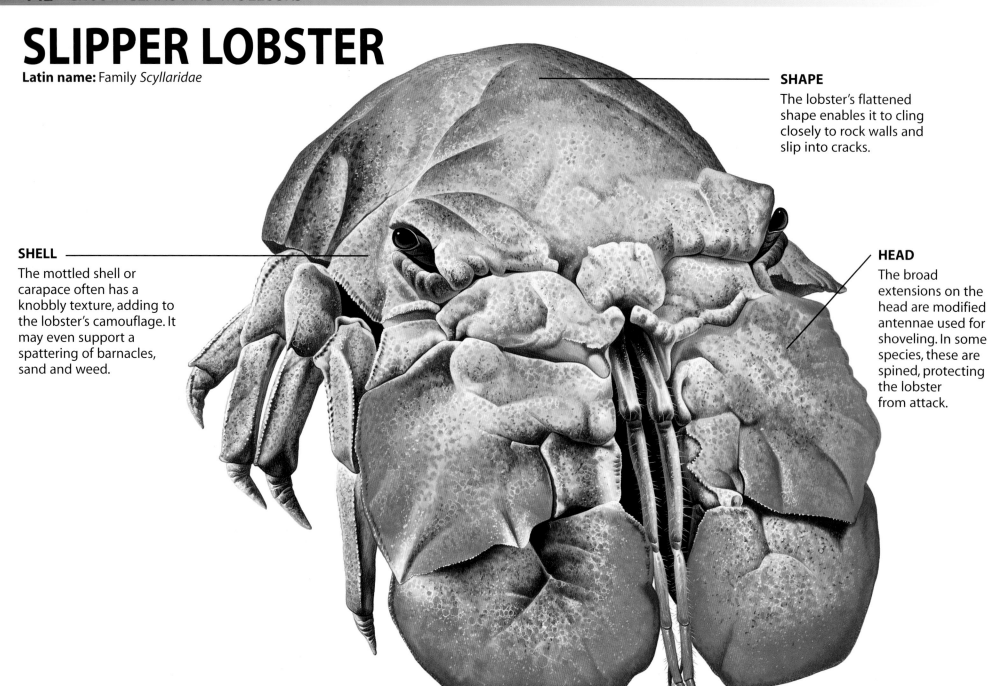

SHAPE

The lobster's flattened shape enables it to cling closely to rock walls and slip into cracks.

SHELL

The mottled shell or carapace often has a knobbly texture, adding to the lobster's camouflage. It may even support a spattering of barnacles, sand and weed.

HEAD

The broad extensions on the head are modified antennae used for shoveling. In some species, these are spined, protecting the lobster from attack.

W ith its broad, flattened body, rough shell, and huge, shovel-like antennae, this peculiar, pincerless lobster looks more like a sunken bedroom slipper or a Spanish dancer's colorful skirt. When it comes to food, most slipper lobsters aren't choosy, and will happily feed on dead sea creatures. But they don't like sharing, so if two individuals chance upon the same carcass, it soon becomes a free-for-all.

Size

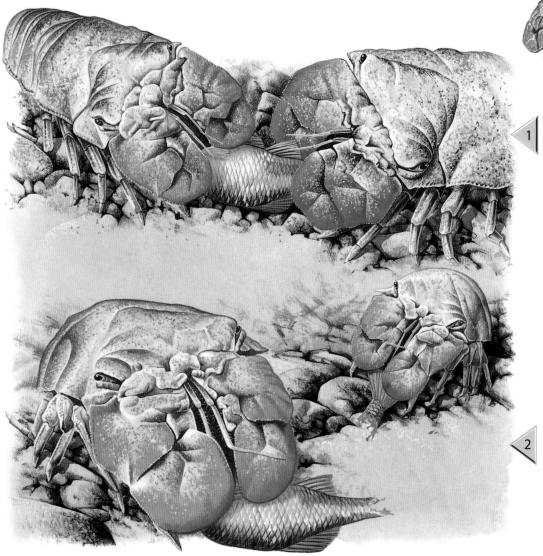

KEY DATA

LENGTH	6–20in (15–50cm)
WEIGHT	Up to 4–5lb (2kg)
DIET	Some eat algae and sea plants; some eat mollusks, worms, other crustaceans, and carrion
SPECIES	About 70

Slipper lobsters live in warm coastal waters at depths of 16–1968ft (5–600m). Habitats include mud, sand, or rocky bottoms, seagrass beds, and coral reefs.

1 Attracted by a fetid fish carcass at the border of their territories, two slipper lobsters scuttle over, eager for a feed. The two have little in the way of weapons, so their dispute soon turns into a strenuous tug of war, as each cantankerous crustacean tries to claim the prize.

2 With a mighty rip, the stinking fish suddenly tears in two, leaving one lucky lobster with the lion's share. The other poor creature has to make do with the tail and a few scraps.

Did You Know?

● A slipper lobster's fertilized eggs look like clusters of tiny berries—so a female carrying eggs on her legs is known as a "berried" female.

● Some slipper lobster larvae hitch a lift on the umbrellas of passing jellyfish, holding fast with tiny hooks at the tips of their spindly legs.

● Slipper lobsters known as the Balmain bug (*Ibacus peronii*) and the deep-water bug (*Ibacus alticrenatus*) are popular "tucker" in Australia.

● If a predator twists a lobster's leg, it snaps off at a special "break point," enabling the lobster to shed its leg and scuttle off to safety. A new limb starts growing straight away.

● Like most crustaceans, a lobster must shed its exoskeleton as it grows. The old one splits and the lobster wriggles out, taking in water to enlarge its body. After its new shell hardens, it expels the water again, leaving space for its body to grow.

CUTTLEFISH

Latin name: Family *Sepiidae*

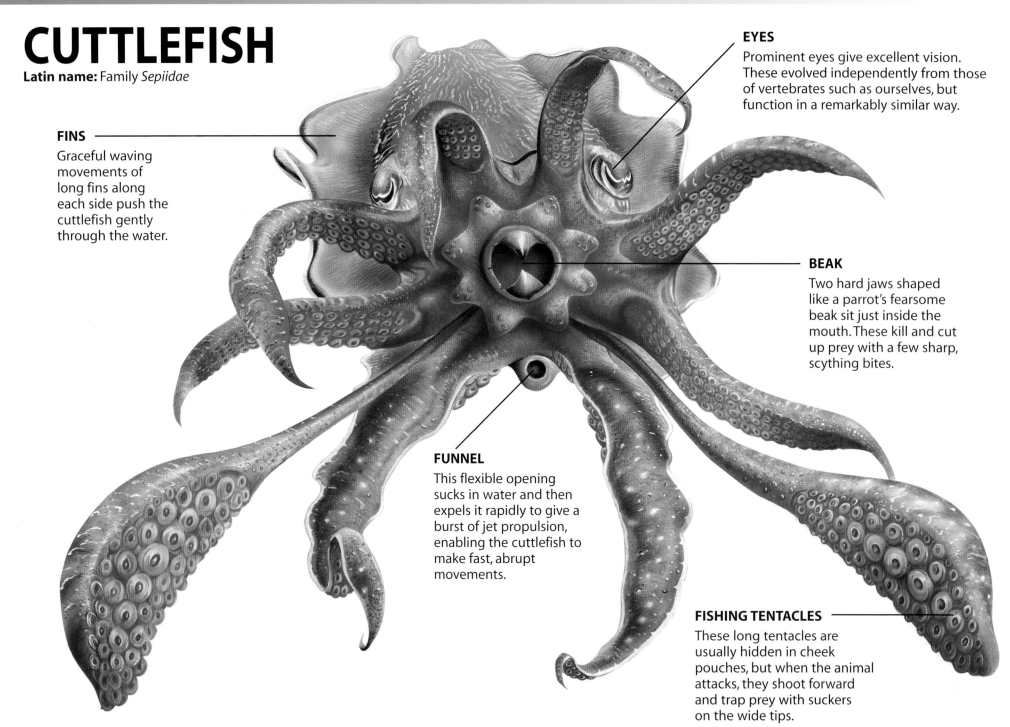

EYES

Prominent eyes give excellent vision. These evolved independently from those of vertebrates such as ourselves, but function in a remarkably similar way.

FINS

Graceful waving movements of long fins along each side push the cuttlefish gently through the water.

BEAK

Two hard jaws shaped like a parrot's fearsome beak sit just inside the mouth. These kill and cut up prey with a few sharp, scything bites.

FUNNEL

This flexible opening sucks in water and then expels it rapidly to give a burst of jet propulsion, enabling the cuttlefish to make fast, abrupt movements.

FISHING TENTACLES

These long tentacles are usually hidden in cheek pouches, but when the animal attacks, they shoot forward and trap prey with suckers on the wide tips.

After launching a lightning assault, this gently floating hunter drags prey into its jaws and kills them with a few bites of its chitinous beak, then pulls chunks of flesh into its gullet with a rasping tongue that probes to and fro in its mouth. The cuttlefish is so adept at bodily disguise that it can make itself resemble all kinds of inert objects, often using its tentacles to obscure its body shape or waving them in an enticing manner to lure curious prey within its grasp.

Size

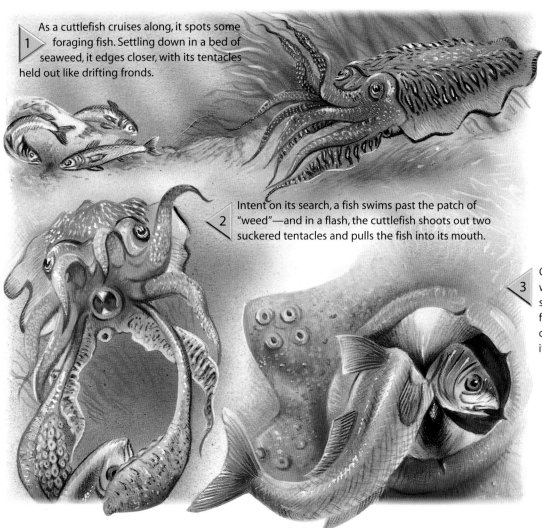

1 ▷ As a cuttlefish cruises along, it spots some foraging fish. Settling down in a bed of seaweed, it edges closer, with its tentacles held out like drifting fronds.

2 Intent on its search, a fish swims past the patch of "weed"—and in a flash, the cuttlefish shoots out two suckered tentacles and pulls the fish into its mouth.

3 Chopping down with its beak and squirting venom from its mouth, the cuttlefish subdues its wriggling prey.

KEY DATA

LENGTH	¾–20in (2–50cm)
WEIGHT	Up to 26lb (12kg)
PREY	Worms, shelled mollusks, shrimp, crabs, and fish
WEAPONS	Tentacles, beak, venom glands, and rasping tongue

More than 100 species of cuttlefish go serenely about their killing business throughout the seas and oceans of the world, blending to match any background—be it a sandy seabed, a patch of seaweed, a rock-face, or a head of coral.

Did You Know?

● Dramatic color and pattern changes also play an important part in cuttlefish courtship displays—with an amorous male often trying out a series of different "looks" in his efforts to win over a female.

● Cuttlefish, squid, and octopus show far more complex behavior than other mollusks such as snails and slugs, so it's no surprise to find they have an enlarged brain. In the cuttlefish, this is ring-shaped and lies just behind the eyes inside a protective "box" of gristly cartilage.

● Hordes of dead cuttlefish regularly wash ashore in some parts of the world. These are adults that congregate along the coast to breed, then die soon after egg-laying.

● A fleeing cuttlefish can shoot inky pigment into the water from a special sac in its body. The billowing cloud obscures its dash and, hopefully, confuses a predator long enough for the cuttlefish to make its escape.

HARLEQUIN SHRIMP

Latin name: *Hymenocera picta*

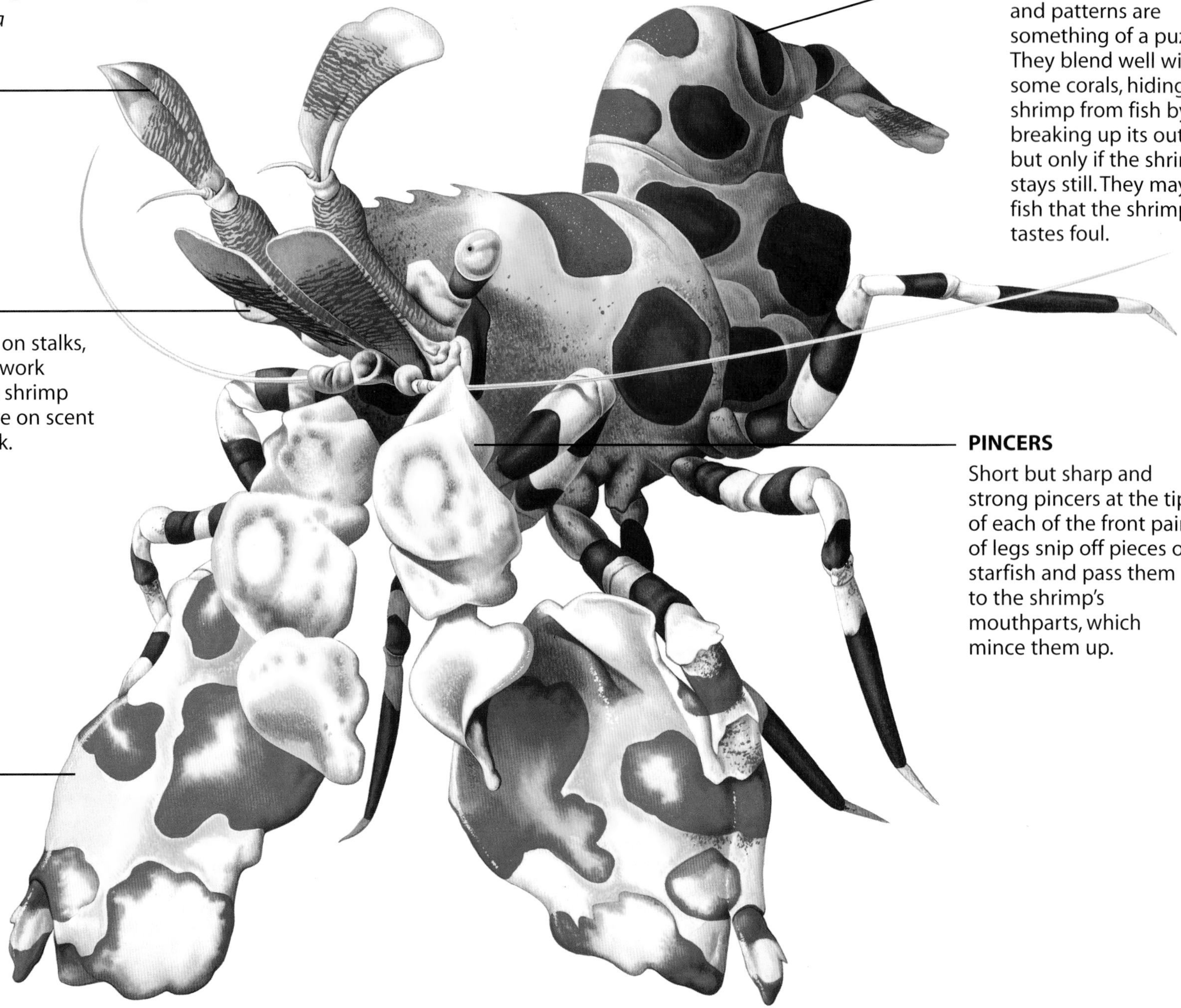

MARKINGS

The spectacular colors and patterns are something of a puzzle. They blend well with some corals, hiding the shrimp from fish by breaking up its outline—but only if the shrimp stays still. They may fool fish that the shrimp tastes foul.

ANTENNAE

The sensitive, leaf-shaped antennae detect faint scents in the water, leading the shrimp to prey or a partner.

EYES

These are on stalks, but don't work well—the shrimp relies more on scent in the dark.

PINCERS

Short but sharp and strong pincers at the tip of each of the front pair of legs snip off pieces of starfish and pass them to the shrimp's mouthparts, which mince them up.

CLAWS

The shrimp's massive claws are probably just for show, to impress mates or scare away enemies.

Little is known about the mysterious, and bizarrely colorful, harlequin shrimp, for it hides out of sight by day and few have been spotted let alone studied. But piecing together what little information there is, produces a picture of a quite remarkable crustacean. A starfish has a thick, knobbly topside to protect it from many predators, but is no defence against the harlequin shrimp, which simply turns it upside down to expose its soft and succulent underside. Then it slowly eats it, one arm after another.

Size

KEY DATA

LENGTH	2–21/2in (5–6cm)	
HABITAT	Coral reefs and rocky shores down to about 30ft (10m)	
PREY	Starfish	
WEAPONS	Sharp, strong nippers	
LIFESPAN	Unknown	

The Harlequin shrimp is found on coral reefs and rocky coasts in the warm tropical waters of the Indian and western Pacific oceans, as far afield as the Maldives (off southern India), the Great Barrier Reef (off northeastern Australia), and Hawaii.

1 A hungry harlequin shrimp returns triumphantly to its hidey-hole, hauling the spoils of a successful hunting trip behind it: a fresh, plump starfish. Back in the safety of its home, the shrimp grabs hold of the starfish and gradually levers the hapless creature up and over, like a judo throw in slow motion.

2 The shrimp pins down the tip of one of its victim's arms with its massive claws. There's only one place the starfish is going now: into the shrimp's digestive tract—one tiny snipped-off piece at a time.

Did You Know?

● The harlequin shrimp gets its name from a character in Italian comic plays, who first appeared in the mid-16th century. Like the shrimp, he wore a colorful outfit. Other common names for the harlequin shrimp include the clown, painted, and dancing shrimp.

● The harlequin shrimp's exquisite bold coloring makes it a popular aquarium pet with some enthusiasts—if rather an expensive one to buy and keep. It is happiest in male–female pairs, and can be fed only on starfish, fresh or frozen.

● A shrimp must molt its hard exoskeleton occasionally as it grows. It doesn't eat for two days before it does this, so its body shrinks free of the shell. It then swells itself with water to split the old coat away. A new shell then grows, but until it hardens over a few days the shrimp is defenseless. So, shrimp often molt at New Moon, when there is no moonlight to help predators find them.

SPIDER CRAB

Latin name: *Majidae* species

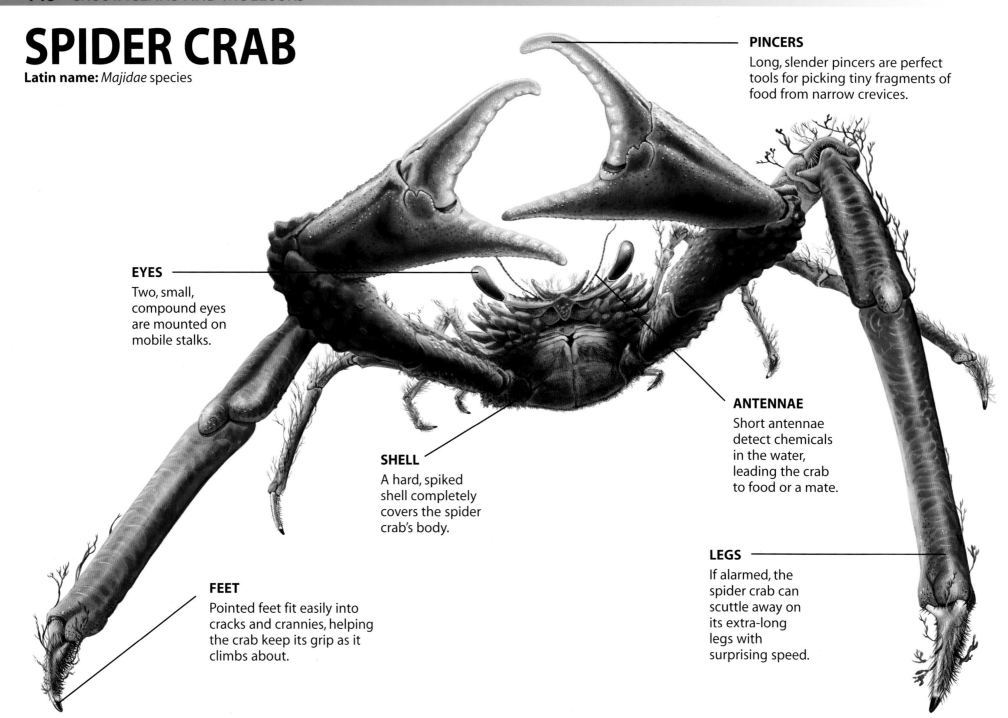

PINCERS
Long, slender pincers are perfect tools for picking tiny fragments of food from narrow crevices.

EYES
Two, small, compound eyes are mounted on mobile stalks.

ANTENNAE
Short antennae detect chemicals in the water, leading the crab to food or a mate.

SHELL
A hard, spiked shell completely covers the spider crab's body.

FEET
Pointed feet fit easily into cracks and crannies, helping the crab keep its grip as it climbs about.

LEGS
If alarmed, the spider crab can scuttle away on its extra-long legs with surprising speed.

Scuttling sideways over the seabed on stiltlike legs, a spider crab looks like some weird Martian probe on a mission. Its two pointed claws work like mechanical grabs to pluck tasty morsels and pass them to the array of mouthparts. They use their neat, narrow pincers to pick rotting flesh from the remains of the dead on the seabed. Spider crabs do not have an internal skeleton, but like all crabs—and insects, too—they have a tough casing, or exoskeleton, over the entire body that protects the soft innards.

Size

A giant spider crab is so big that if it ever took a beach stroll it could, in theory, tiptoe over a camper van. Luckily for us, it stays underwater.

Deep-sea water pressure is high, but a layer of tough chitin keeps the shell from caving in. The leg joints are hinged to move in one plane only: sideways. Their smooth surfaces of gristle keep friction low. Two muscles inside each leg section attach to rods in the next section. One muscle pulls to bend the joint; the other flexes it again.

KEY DATA

BODY	Up to 18in (45cm) long	
LEGSPAN	Up to 26ft (8m)	
PREY	Algae and sponges, small marine animals, and carrion	
HABITAT	Sea floor	
LIFESPAN	Unknown	

Spider crabs are found in all the oceans and seas, except for the freezing waters in the polar regions. They are most common in shallow waters, where there is plenty of food and shelter.

Did You Know?

● An immature spider crab can grow only by molting its hard outer skeleton. The old skeleton is cast off to reveal a soft replacement underneath, which the crab inflates to a larger size before it hardens.

● If a spider crab loses a leg in an accident, it grows a new one, which gets longer every time it molts.

● Certain species of spider crab protect themselves by resting next to snakelock anemones, and seem immune to their stings. By sitting with the back of its shell against the anemone's central column, a crab is almost completely hidden from view by the overhanging tentacles.

● Sometimes spider crabs become stranded in rockpools on tidal shores, and they cannot survive out of water.

● One type of spider crab feeds on plankton. It hangs from weeds by its hindlegs and sweeps the water with its claws to scoop up morsels.

WATER SCORPION

Latin name: *Nepidae* species

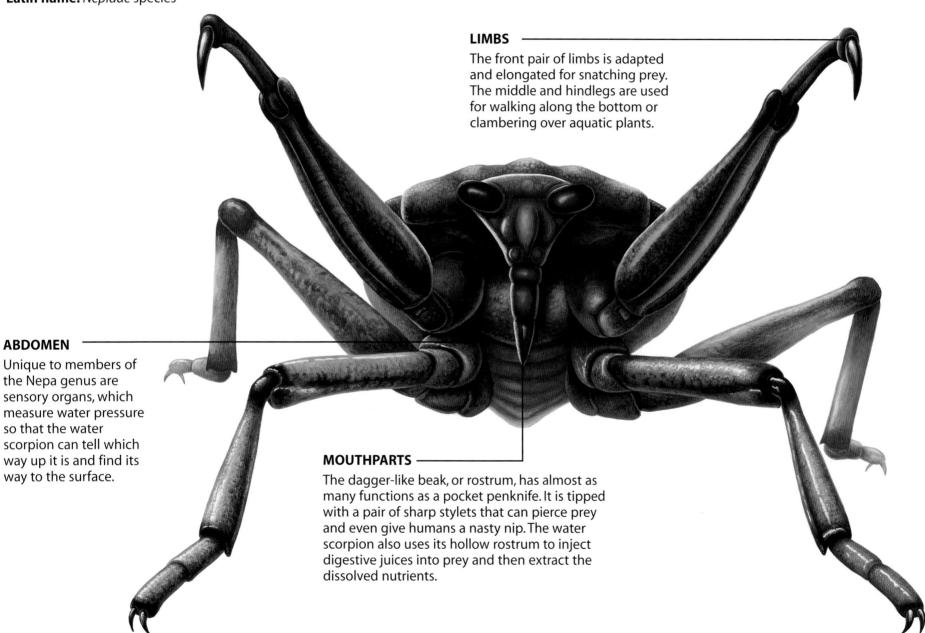

LIMBS

The front pair of limbs is adapted and elongated for snatching prey. The middle and hindlegs are used for walking along the bottom or clambering over aquatic plants.

ABDOMEN

Unique to members of the Nepa genus are sensory organs, which measure water pressure so that the water scorpion can tell which way up it is and find its way to the surface.

MOUTHPARTS

The dagger-like beak, or rostrum, has almost as many functions as a pocket penknife. It is tipped with a pair of sharp stylets that can pierce prey and even give humans a nasty nip. The water scorpion also uses its hollow rostrum to inject digestive juices into prey and then extract the dissolved nutrients.

Cloaked in its dull brown armor, the water scorpion loiters in ponds and ditches. It is only when it strikes that it shows the strength of its grabbing pincers, overpowering prey in seconds. So devastating is its ambush, the water scorpion can even catch speedy fish. Thanks to its muddy camouflage and extra-long breathing tube, it need not give away its whereabouts, and is always ready to attack with deadly speed.

Actual size

1 Clinging upside-down to the pond vegetation, a water scorpion thrusts its long breathing tube up toward the air. The rigid tube pierces the surface film of the water, and air flows into the cavity beneath the bug's carapace. The bug then clambers over the pond weeds into a concealed position and waits in ambush for prey.

2 As soon as a small fish swims within range, the water scorpion strikes as quick as a flash. It grabs the fish in the firm grip of its scythelike forelegs and pulls it in toward its stabbing jaws.

3 The water scorpion devours its helpless prey, tearing at the fish's flesh with the sharp stylets (tips) of its rostrum. It then injects a deadly dose of venomous saliva, which turns the fish's innards to a runny soup. The water scorpion uses its rostrum to suck up the fish juices.

Did You Know?

● The water scorpion can actually hang by its siphon from the surface film of the water.

● If disturbed, this inconspicuous little bug may play dead until danger has passed.

● Although it is classed as a non-swimmer, the water scorpion can scull across the water by moving its forelegs up and down and kicking with its middle and hindlegs.

● The female water scorpion uses her breathing tube for laying eggs. The eggs are shaped rather like a tiny jellyfish. Each has seven long, dangling projections by which it is attached to water plants.

GHOST CRAB

Latin name: *Ocypode* species

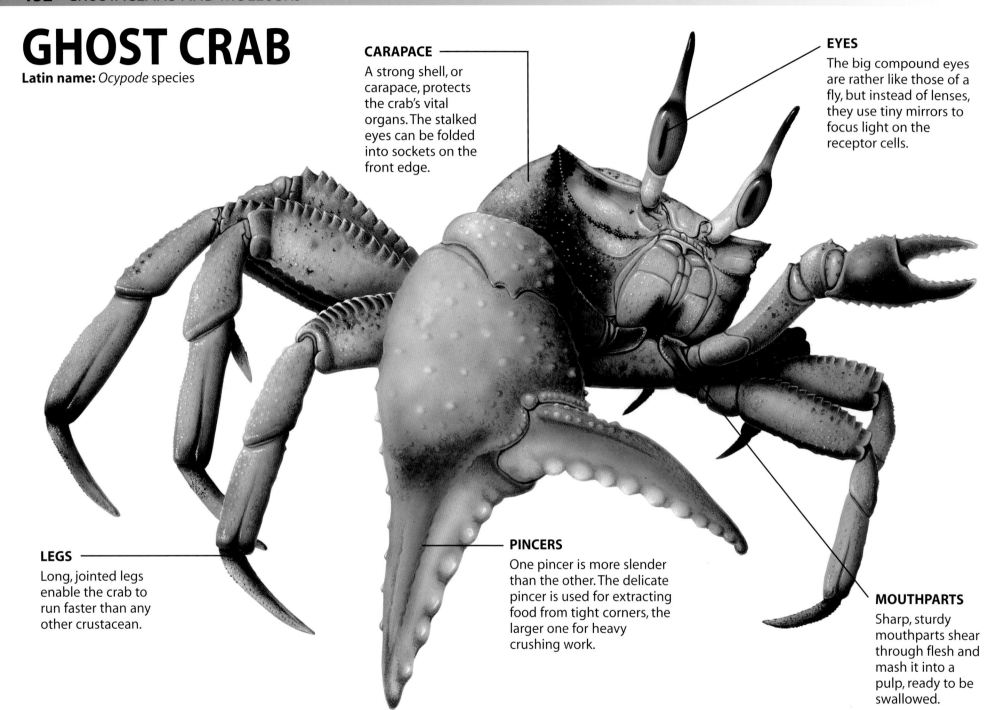

CARAPACE
A strong shell, or carapace, protects the crab's vital organs. The stalked eyes can be folded into sockets on the front edge.

EYES
The big compound eyes are rather like those of a fly, but instead of lenses, they use tiny mirrors to focus light on the receptor cells.

LEGS
Long, jointed legs enable the crab to run faster than any other crustacean.

PINCERS
One pincer is more slender than the other. The delicate pincer is used for extracting food from tight corners, the larger one for heavy crushing work.

MOUTHPARTS
Sharp, sturdy mouthparts shear through flesh and mash it into a pulp, ready to be swallowed.

As the sea rises and floods the shore, the ghost crab sits tight in its damp burrow, often more than 3ft (1m) below the surface. Once the water ebbs away again, it emerges to feast on the latest crop of delicacies delivered by the tide, although it avoids broad daylight, as the sun's heat can be fatal. Its hinged pincers and strong jaws make short work of anything from armored lobsters to venomous jellyfish.

Size

1 ▷ A ghost crab emerges from its burrow to sift through the scattered debris heaped along the tideline. Carefully picking tasty tidbits from the rubbish with its pincers, it slices up each morsel with scissor-sharp mouthparts.

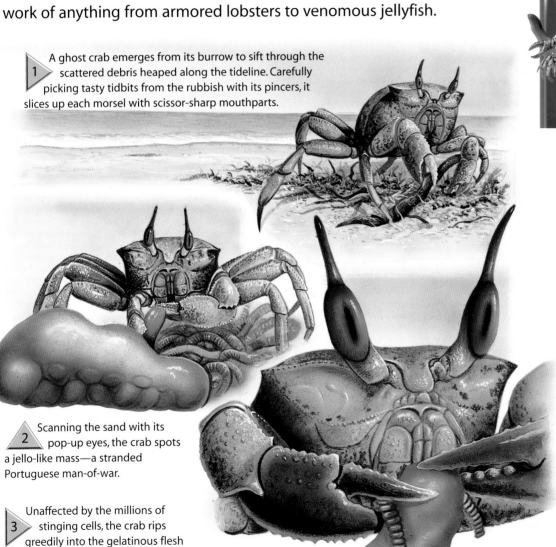

2 ▷ Scanning the sand with its pop-up eyes, the crab spots a jello-like mass—a stranded Portuguese man-of-war.

3 ▷ Unaffected by the millions of stinging cells, the crab rips greedily into the gelatinous flesh with its powerful pincers.

KEY DATA

SIZE	Shell up to 21/2in (6cm) wide, depending on species
DIET	Carrion, small animals, and some plant material
WEAPONS	Two strong pincers
LIFESPAN	Unknown

Ghost crabs live on tropical and subtropical shores around the world, and are found wherever there are suitable tidal beaches with sand or mud in which they can dig their burrows.

Did You Know?

● When the ghost crab is deep in its burrow, it sometimes makes a rasping chirrup by rubbing its legs together like a cricket. This may be a way of claiming the burrow as its territory, warning off rival crabs.

● The ghost crab isn't fussy what it eats, devouring everything from freshly hatched turtles to the rotting flesh of dead fish or drowned birds.

● In mangrove swamps, ghost crabs sometimes climb into the branches of trees to hunt insects hiding among the leaves. They also lurk near the water, snatching up small fish as they feed at the edge of the rising tide.

● If threatened, a ghost crab scuttles off at an impressive rate, reaching speeds of more than 6ft (2m) per second.

● In colder months, the ghost crab plugs the entrance to its burrow with sand and remains dormant.

SPINY LOBSTER

Latin name: *Panulirus* species

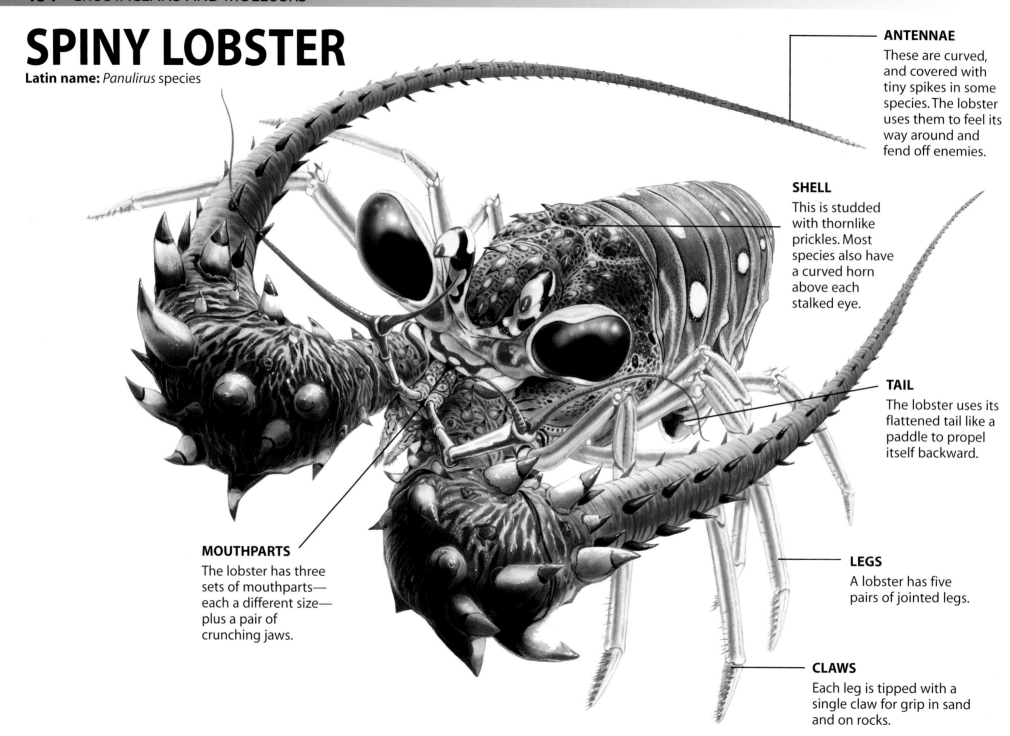

ANTENNAE
These are curved, and covered with tiny spikes in some species. The lobster uses them to feel its way around and fend off enemies.

SHELL
This is studded with thornlike prickles. Most species also have a curved horn above each stalked eye.

TAIL
The lobster uses its flattened tail like a paddle to propel itself backward.

MOUTHPARTS
The lobster has three sets of mouthparts—each a different size—plus a pair of crunching jaws.

LEGS
A lobster has five pairs of jointed legs.

CLAWS
Each leg is tipped with a single claw for grip in sand and on rocks.

A spiny lobster's outrageous-looking, thorny armor may seem a bit over the top, but this bristle-clad crustacean has many enemies in its underwater world. Plenty of fish enjoy the delicious taste of fresh lobster meat just as much as we do. When it comes to finding food, any fatally wounded creature is fair game for the spiny lobster, even the rotting or bleeding remains of its own kind. As night falls, it crawls out of its crevice and feels its way across the ocean floor, carefully "tasting" the water as it goes. Sooner or later, it homes in on a promising scent trail.

Size

KEY DATA

LENGTH	Body up to 20in (50cm); antennae up to 24in (60cm)
WEIGHT	Usually up to 17lb (8kg), but many are caught before reaching this size; one caught off California weighed 32lb (14.4kg)
DIET	Live prey consists mostly of slow-moving animals such as shellfish, starfish, and crabs. Also scavenges on dead and dying creatures
LIFESPAN	Unknown, but may be 50 years or more for ones that avoid being eaten by fish or caught in pots

The spiny lobster inhabits shallow rocky areas and coral reefs in the Pacific, Atlantic, and Indian oceans. It is found on both coasts of the Americas, all around Africa and India, and throughout southeastern Asia.

1 A spiny lobster working its way across the sand picks up the smell of blood and follows it to its source: another spiny lobster, lying on its back and feebly wiggling the raw stumps of its legs—the victim of a savage attack by a big fish.

2 Its antennae waving on constant alert for danger, the spiny lobster looms over its stricken relative and sets to work with its multiple mouthparts. The largest parts rip into the flesh, gouging out small chunks and tearing off long strips. Smaller ones manipulate the bite-size morsels into the lobster's crunching jaws. The victim is eaten slowly alive, but eventually its feeble twitching ceases altogether. A short while later, nothing is left of its carcass but an empty shell.

Did You Know?

● At the base of each antenna, the spiny lobster has a flap that it can rub back and forth on a smooth ridge to produce a rasping sound. It makes this sound when it feels threatened, to scare away predators. Members of a line may also use it to communicate with each other on their migration marches, to help to keep the train together.

● A migrating column of spiny lobsters can be up to 60 individuals strong and may travel up to 62 miles (100km) in a week, covering 9 miles (15km) each day.

● The spiny lobster occasionally moves into deep water far below the crest of a reef. It has been seen at depths of more than 330ft (100m).

ARROW CRAB

Latin name: *Stenorhynchus* species

ROSTRUM

This is the barbed, pointed beak that juts out at the front of the shell. It is more prominent than that of other spider crabs and is used to spear its victims.

MANDIBLES

These specialized jaws chew up the crab's food, once the pincers have torn the prey into bite-size lumps.

CARAPACE

This is the upper surface of the shell. The crab must shed its carapace regularly before it can grow.

EYES

The eyes stick out from the side of the head for better visibility. The arrow crab has better eyesight than most crabs.

PINCERS

The powerful pincers are a pair of modified legs. They are used to tear the food into chunks.

LEGS

The long, thin legs are made of a tough material called chitin and studded with sharp spines.

Like a spider, this reef-dweller has a taste for live prey and will add any small sea creature to its menu. It is happy to scavenge pieces of dead sea animal for its meals, but given the chance, this crustacean is an aggressive predator, catching a victim with its sharp snout and spiny legs. The prey is slowly eaten alive, snipped into bite-size pieces by razor-like pincers.

actual Size

KEY DATA

SIZE	Body 1¼in (3cm) long, ½in (1cm) wide
LEGSPAN	Up to 3in (7cm)
DIET	Mainly carrion, fish, shrimp, and other invertebrates
WEAPONS	Beaklike rostrum, spiny legs
LIFESPAN	Unknown

The arrow crab inhabits shallow tropical waters including the Caribbean, western Atlantic, eastern Pacific seaboard, the Indo-Pacific region, and eastern Africa.

2 The next time the crab goes hunting, it uses a different technique, grabbing a small reef fish with its legs. The leg spines stop the fish escaping as the pincers get to work once more.

1 With split-second timing, an arrow crab spears a small juvenile coral reef fish on the tip of its long rostrum. The fish struggles, but the pincers are soon at work snipping the fish into edible chunks.

Did You Know?

● In the United States, arrow crabs are sold in pet stores to aquarium owners who want to add extra interest to their fish tanks. However, anyone who is unaware of the arrow crab's awesome hunting skills may be surprised to find that their exotic fish suddenly go missing.

● Female arrow crabs give birth to up to 5 million offspring. Luckily for the small fish that inhabit the same waters, only 20 or 30 of these ever survive to become full-size adults.

● Arrow crabs hatch out into tiny, free-swimming, shrimplike larvae that live near the surface and feed on plankton. They then go through a series of molts, shedding their "skins" and becoming more crablike.

● If an arrow crab loses a leg to an enemy, a small replacement limb forms the next time the animal sheds its shell. It may take seven or eight molts to repair a damaged limb or to grow a new one to full size.

Mammals, Reptiles, and Other Monsters

Some creatures in this category are masters of camouflage.
The ferocious American Alligator, for example, disguises itself
as a harmless log floating in the swamps where it lives.

The South American Matamata does it the leisurely way. It sits motionless beneath the water's surface, letting algae accumulate on its back, thus building up camouflage. The Sea Cucumber looks like a fat version of the tubular salad vegetable, but that is just its way of fooling anyone who approaches it. Swimmers or fish who touch a sea cucumber get a nasty surprise when it shoots out toxic filaments that deliver a vicious sting. This category also includes several creatures that work hard for their food, while others laze around waiting for food to come to them. The Saltwater Crocodile, for example, is feared for its rightful reputation as a man-eater. It will launch an attack on anything within its striking distance, whether it is a fish, a bird, a water buffalo or even a human being. The Snapping Turtle, on the other hand, lurks at the bottom of a pond. Being a slow swimmer means that it has to rely on surprise as a method of securing its prey. When its unsuspecting prey swims by, the snapper launches itself and begins a vicious and unrelenting attack.

CROWN OF THORNS

Latin name: *Acanthaster planci*

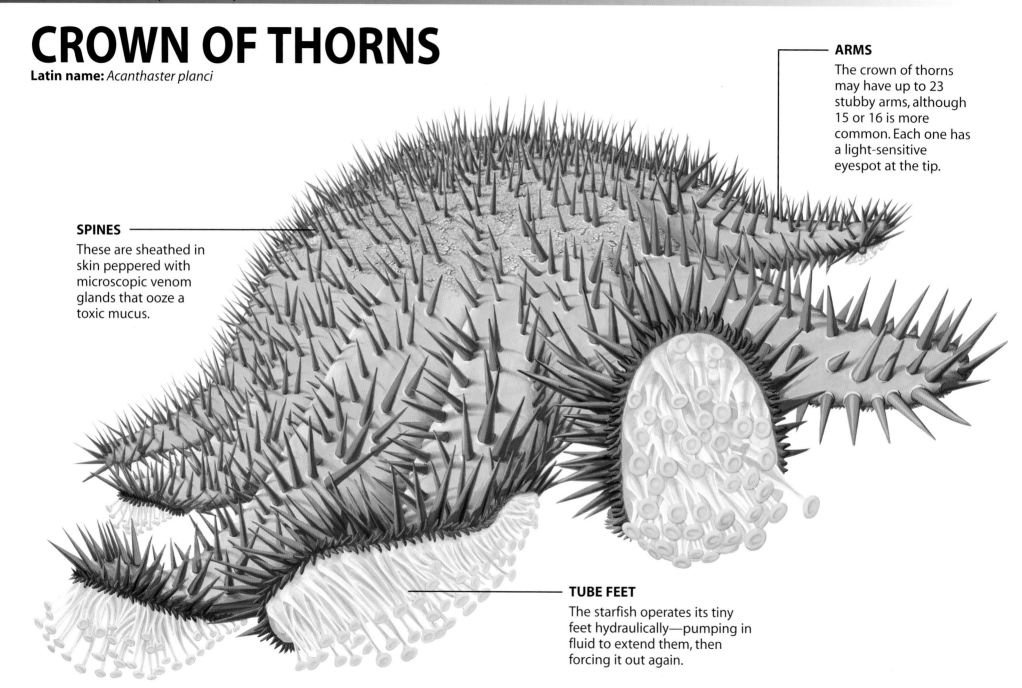

ARMS

The crown of thorns may have up to 23 stubby arms, although 15 or 16 is more common. Each one has a light-sensitive eyespot at the tip.

SPINES

These are sheathed in skin peppered with microscopic venom glands that ooze a toxic mucus.

TUBE FEET

The starfish operates its tiny feet hydraulically—pumping in fluid to extend them, then forcing it out again.

Many starfish are slender creatures that graze on algae—but not the crown of thorns. This spiky heavyweight is a killer: it clamps itself to living corals, then turns its stomach inside-out and swamps its prey with deadly digestive fluids. The crown of thorns bristles with spines, each up to 2in (5cm) long and oozing toxic mucus. They pierce human skin at the slightest touch—the shock can drown a careless diver.

Size

KEY DATA

WIDTH	Up to 30in (75cm)
PREY	Mainly coral, and other encrusting or slow-moving reef organisms
DEFENSES	Venom-charged spines
BREEDING	Female releases up to 60 million eggs each summer

The crown of thorns lives on coral reefs throughout the Indian and Pacific oceans, but seems to be most numerous on the Great Barrier Reef of northeastern Australia.

1 Mesmerized by the beauty of the coral and the glittering shoals of fish, a diver is making her way along a reef when a vividly colored starfish catches her eye.

2 Without thinking, she reaches out to touch the peculiar creature, brushing against its spines—and a sudden burst of pain jolts through her hand. Soon, she is almost immobilized by the agonizing wound, and as a wave of nausea overwhelms her she struggles not to lose control.

Did You Know?

● Like most starfish, the crown of thorns has a saclike body filled with fluid, but its central disk is bulkier to accommodate its massive stomach.

● Sometimes the crown of thorns is driven from its feeding grounds by tiny crabs, which live among the coral polyps and nip at its tubular feet until it moves elsewhere.

● One of the few known predators of the crown of thorns is the giant triton: a huge sea snail that holds the starfish down with its muscular foot, then slits it open with its rasping tongue and sucks out its juices.

● One shrimp, *Hymenocera picta*, attacks a small crown of thorns by flipping it on its back to expose its poorly defended underside and nibbling into its soft center.

● If the crown of thorns sheds an arm to escape a predator, it regrows in about six months. Other starfish can even survive being cut in half.

AMERICAN ALLIGATOR

Latin name: *Alligator mississippiensis*

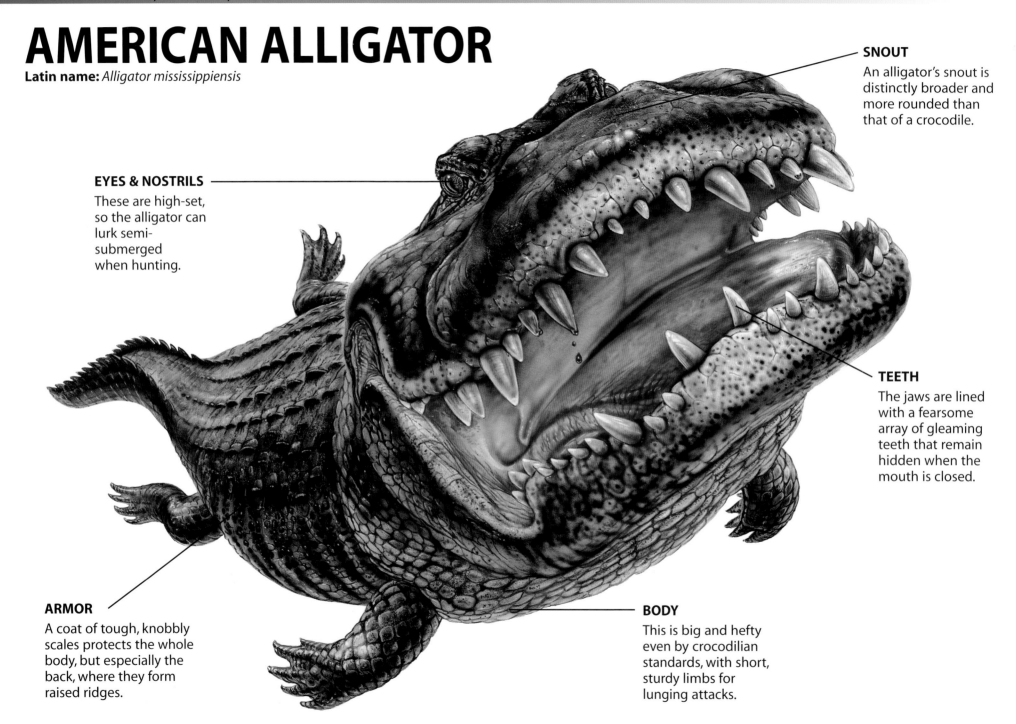

SNOUT

An alligator's snout is distinctly broader and more rounded than that of a crocodile.

EYES & NOSTRILS

These are high-set, so the alligator can lurk semi-submerged when hunting.

TEETH

The jaws are lined with a fearsome array of gleaming teeth that remain hidden when the mouth is closed.

ARMOR

A coat of tough, knobbly scales protects the whole body, but especially the back, where they form raised ridges.

BODY

This is big and hefty even by crocodilian standards, with short, sturdy limbs for lunging attacks.

It seems hard to believe that a reptile as mighty as the American alligator could hide itself away in a mirror-calm swampy backwater. It's a good idea to remember that the "floating log" just breaking the weedy surface could be staring right back at you! To a big hungry 'gator, any animal that strays close to its watery home is fair game. Even a horse isn't too large for a fully grown alligator to tackle—though the reptile prefers handy bite-size meals…

Size

KEY DATA

LENGTH	Male up to 12ft (3.6m), female up to 7 1/2ft (2.3m)	The American alligator inhabits mainly protected wetland sites in the southeastern USA, mostly in the states of South Carolina, Georgia, Florida, Alabama, Mississippi, Louisiana, and Texas. The largest populations are in the Louisiana bayous (creeks), in the Florida Everglades, and on the Mississippi River.
WEIGHT	Up to 496lb (225kg)	
PREY	Fish, amphibians, reptiles, birds, and mammals, including domestic animals	
LIFESPAN	Up to 50 years in captivity	

1 A man takes the family dog for a walk along the river. It's a lovely day, and while he enjoys a stroll in the fresh air, the dog frisks excitedly on the end of its lead, splashing in the shallow margins and nosing at clumps of reeds.

2 Suddenly, an enormous alligator bursts out of its hiding place in the weeds and seizes the dog in its jaws. Instinctively, the man holds on to the lead—which snaps like cotton as the 'gator crashes back into the water.

3 The man watches helplessly as the 'gator swims off, leaving a bloody trail in its wake. While it finds a secluded spot to gulp down its prize, the man staggers home in a state of shock—heartbroken by his loss, yet realizing he has had a lucky escape himself.

Did You Know?

● In cooler regions, the American alligator becomes inactive in winter. It digs a cosy den under a bank, or a 'gator hole in muddy shallows, and stays there for up to four months, moving little and seldom eating. Sometimes the alligator gets frozen in its 'gator hole, but as long as there is a breathing hole it can survive until the ice thaws.

● The male alligator's roar carries for 492ft (150m). He often mistakes loud noises for the calls of rivals, hissing or bellowing at sounds such as those made by horns, jet engines, jack hammers, and pneumatic drills.

● It is often said the American alligator uses its powerful tail to sweep animals off riverbanks and into the water, but there is no firm evidence for this belief.

● Some female American 'gators are fiercely protective mothers and guard their young—mainly from other alligators—for several years.

MATAMATA

Latin name: *Chelus fimbriatus*

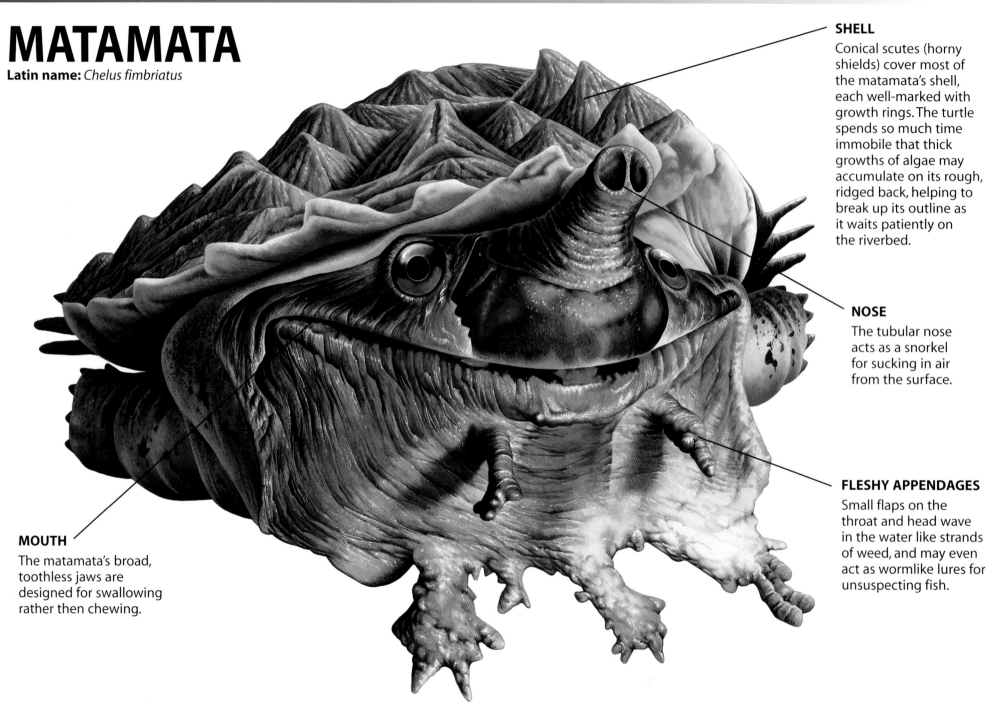

SHELL

Conical scutes (horny shields) cover most of the matamata's shell, each well-marked with growth rings. The turtle spends so much time immobile that thick growths of algae may accumulate on its rough, ridged back, helping to break up its outline as it waits patiently on the riverbed.

NOSE

The tubular nose acts as a snorkel for sucking in air from the surface.

FLESHY APPENDAGES

Small flaps on the throat and head wave in the water like strands of weed, and may even act as wormlike lures for unsuspecting fish.

MOUTH

The matamata's broad, toothless jaws are designed for swallowing rather then chewing.

The curious matamata might be the biggest of the freshwater turtles, but it's not much of a swimmer. Instead, it whiles away the hours just sitting underwater, cultivating a covering of fine weed and sucking up small fish and other creatures. The matamata is chiefly a "sit-and-suck" predator, but it occasionally "trawls" for prey by sweeping its long neck from side-to-side. It may even stir itself and plod along the bottom to corral small fish in the shallows.

Size

KEY DATA

LENGTH	Shell up to 18in (45cm)
WEIGHT	Up to 5 1/2lb (2.5kg)
PREY	Fish, other water creatures, and small birds and mammals
WEAPONS	Wide, suctioning mouth
LIFESPAN	Up to 30 years in captivity

Widely found in northern South America, especially the Orinoco and Amazon Rivers, it is most common in Venezuela and Brazil. Also occurs in northern Bolivia and eastern Peru, Ecuador, Colombia, the Guianas, and Trinidad.

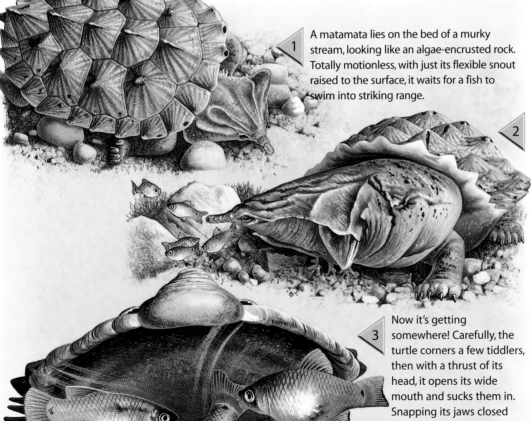

1 A matamata lies on the bed of a murky stream, looking like an algae-encrusted rock. Totally motionless, with just its flexible snout raised to the surface, it waits for a fish to swim into striking range.

2 But time passes and nothing palatable comes near, forcing the hungry turtle to change tactics. Slowly, it begins to walk across the streambed, herding some little fish toward a bank.

3 Now it's getting somewhere! Carefully, the turtle corners a few tiddlers, then with a thrust of its head, it opens its wide mouth and sucks them in. Snapping its jaws closed again, it expels the water through its lips and gulps its food down whole.

Did You Know?

● Matamata is a South American Indian term, meaning "I kill." In Latin, the turtle's name, *Chelus fimbriatus,* translates as "fringed turtle."

● The matamata is a side-neck: one of a group of turtles that are unable to retract their heads into their shells if threatened. Instead, a side-neck moves its head sideways under the overhang at the front of its shell, leaving parts of its head and neck still vulnerable to attack.

● The matamata's neck is almost as long as its back. If humans were built the same way, the average person would have a neck almost 3ft (90cm) long!

● Only a few turtles breathe air like the matamata. Others obtain their oxygen from the water, holding it in their mouths or their cloacal chambers (their reproductive and waste opening) while oxygen passes into the network of blood vessels inside. Soft-shelled turtles can also absorb oxygen through their shells.

SNAPPING TURTLE

Latin name: *Chelydra serpentina*

CARAPACE

The carapace has three knobbly keels that become smoother as the turtle grows older. Thick and hard, it protects the turtle's back against predators. And being a muddy color it provides camouflage when the turtle skulks in the bottom silt.

PLASTRON

This part of the shell protects the turtle's underside from attack by enemies such as big birds of prey.

FEET

These are large, webbed paddles, with nasty, sickle-like claws.

BEAK

A sharp hook made of plates of horn, this crushes and tears apart prey like a cross between scissors and a pair of pliers.

With its dismembering beak, disemboweling claws, and almost indestructible armor, the snapping turtle is a voracious and deadly freshwater predator. Out of the water, too, its hostile attitude makes it a real menace. A brutal end is in store for many of the creatures living in snapper-infested waters. One moment, they're swimming along unawares—the next, they're struggling desperately to escape the vicelike hold of a vicious beak.

Size

KEY DATA

LENGTH	Up to 3ft (1m) or more from beak to tip of tail, including 14–16in (35–40cm) shell		The snapping turtle is the most widespread turtle in North America. It occurs as far north as the southern regions of the Canadian border states, and is common throughout the USA east of the Rocky Mountains. Its range extends south through Mexico and Central America, as far as Ecuador in South America.
WEIGHT	Up to 35lb (16kg) or more		
DIET	Almost any creature smaller than itself, plus carrion		
LIFESPAN	At least 47 years		

At the bottom of a pond, a snapping turtle waits in the weed for the chance of a meal. A slow swimmer, it relies on surprise to secure its prey—such as the moorhen that eventually paddles overhead. Instantly, the snapper launches itself skyward and seizes a dangling leg in its jaws, then drags its frantically flapping victim beneath the surface. Even as the moorhen starts to drown and its struggles subside, the snapper begins ripping it apart and devouring it.

Did You Know?

● When disturbed, the snapping turtle often releases a powerful musky scent. The older the turtle, the stronger the odor.

● The female snapper can store sperm inside her body for several years after mating before using it to fertilize her eggs.

● Although snapping turtles usually hibernate in mud in winter, they've been seen walking on frozen waters and swimming under the ice.

● A police force once used the snapping turtle's fondness for carrion in a bizarre exercise when a large specimen attached to a long line successfully discovered the underwater whereabouts of several murder victims.

● The snapper may have evolved its aggressive nature and sharp beak as a defensive measure, because the bottom part of its shell is too small to cover its head, legs, and tail.

SEA URCHIN
Latin name: Class *Echinoidea*

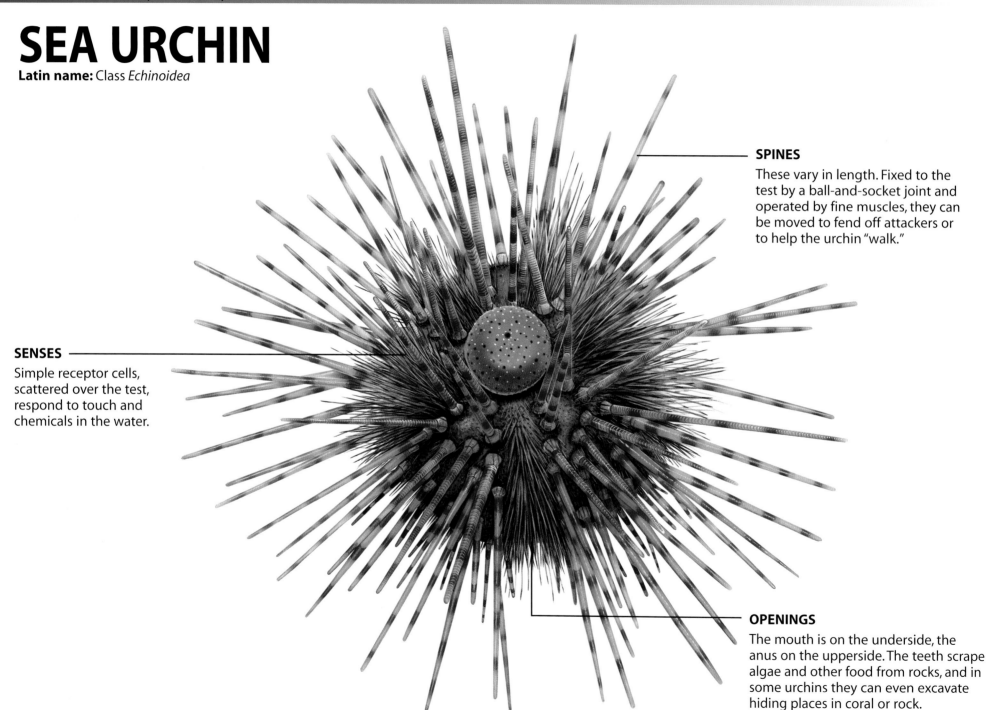

SPINES

These vary in length. Fixed to the test by a ball-and-socket joint and operated by fine muscles, they can be moved to fend off attackers or to help the urchin "walk."

SENSES

Simple receptor cells, scattered over the test, respond to touch and chemicals in the water.

OPENINGS

The mouth is on the underside, the anus on the upperside. The teeth scrape algae and other food from rocks, and in some urchins they can even excavate hiding places in coral or rock.

A sea urchin is one of the oddest and prettiest animals of the seas Almost jewel-like in its glowing colors and filigree attachments, the sea urchin bristles with armory—a pincushion primed to injure any creature unlucky or foolhardy enough to make contact with its spines or tiny "jaws." It's not fun stepping on the spines of a venomous sea urchin. The spines stab into flesh and then snap off, swamping the wound with toxins that cause hours of agony, plus a host of other ill effects.

Size

1 A holiday-maker paddling on a warm tropical beach accidentally treads on a sea urchin. He yelps with pain as several spines penetrate his foot. As he limps to the shore, an intense burning sensation throbs around the wound area.

2 A friend tries to remove the long spines with a pair of pliers, but the backward-pointing barbs on the spines make them almost impossible to withdraw. They simply break, leaving the tips of the spines embedded deep in the foot. Although the terrible pain ebbs after about six hours, it is several days before the victim can walk comfortably again.

KEY DATA

SIZE	Most species are about 3½in (8cm) in diameter	
DIET	Typically plant matter, such as algae, or organic debris	Sea urchins live in all the world's seas and oceans, from coastal shallows to the ocean depths. The most venomous species occur in tropical and subtropical areas of the Indo-Pacific.
DEFENCES	Sharp spines and tiny, snapping stalk-mounted "jaws" called pedicellariae, both of which can be toxic	

Did You Know?

● The world's largest sea urchin is *Sperosoma giganteum*. Found in deep waters off Japan, its test ("shell") is up to 12½in (32cm) across. The smallest is *Echinocyamus scaber*, found off New South Wales, Australia, with a test little more than ¼in (5mm) in diameter.

● Although the venom of sea urchins is rarely lethal to humans, it can cause the death of swimmers by incapacitating them. A Japanese pearl diver became unconscious after brushing against a sea urchin and then drowned.

● The urchin *Strongylocentrotus purpuratus* of the US Pacific coast is known to excavate holes in steel pillars underwater.

● The spines of Diadema sea urchins may be up to 12in (30cm) long. When an urchin detects an intruder, the movable spines can be swung rapidly across and clustered, presenting the intruder with a mass of venom-primed, needle-like tips.

SEA CUCUMBER

Latin name: *Class Holothuroidea*

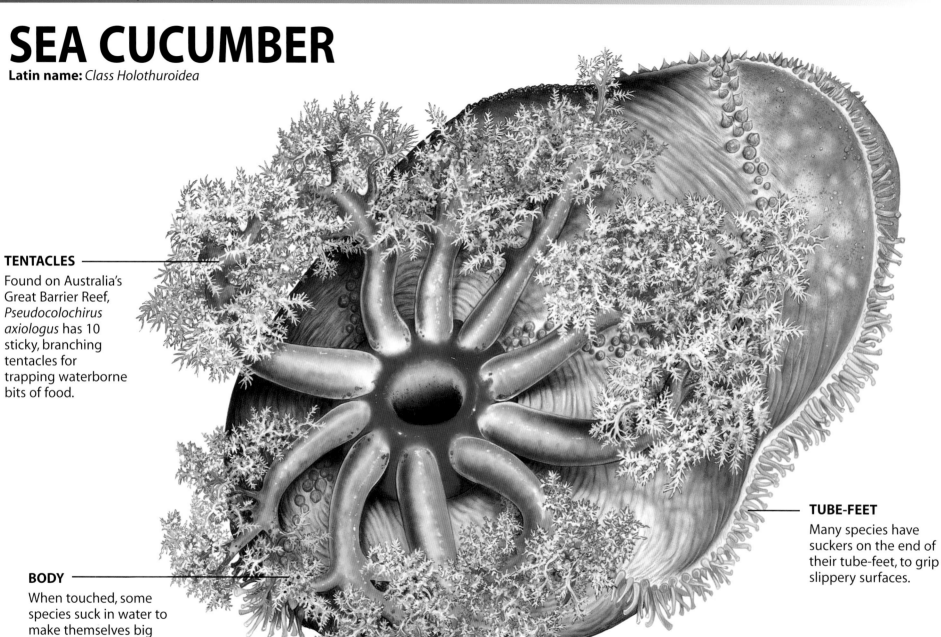

TENTACLES

Found on Australia's Great Barrier Reef, *Pseudocolochirus axiologus* has 10 sticky, branching tentacles for trapping waterborne bits of food.

TUBE-FEET

Many species have suckers on the end of their tube-feet, to grip slippery surfaces.

BODY

When touched, some species suck in water to make themselves big and floppy, while others blow out water to shrink and harden.

Sea cucumbers are close cousins of sea urchins and starfish, and many hundreds of species are known. They vary widely in color and size, but all share the same body plan: one that's bizarre, but ideally suited to a sluggish way of life on ocean floors and seabeds. When attacked, some sea cucumbers respond by firing threadlike organs called Cuvierian tubules from their anus. This doesn't hurt the sea cucumber, for the tubules grow back, but it's no joke if they hit you.

Size

KEY DATA

LENGTH	3/4in–16ft (2cm–5m); most are under 3ft (1m)
DIET	Mainly waste organic matter and plankton
DEFENSES	Holothurin toxins in the skin, flesh, and organs
LIFESPAN	Unknown

Sea cucumbers live in all the world's seas and oceans. They are most abundant in shallow waters, particularly around coral reefs, but some live 2 miles (3km) down.

1 A holiday-maker is snorkeling over the Great Barrier Reef and marveling at its wealth of colorful creatures, when he spots a plump leopard fish sea cucumber quietly minding its own business. Thinking it couldn't possibly do him any harm, he can't resist picking up the extraordinary animal for a closer look…

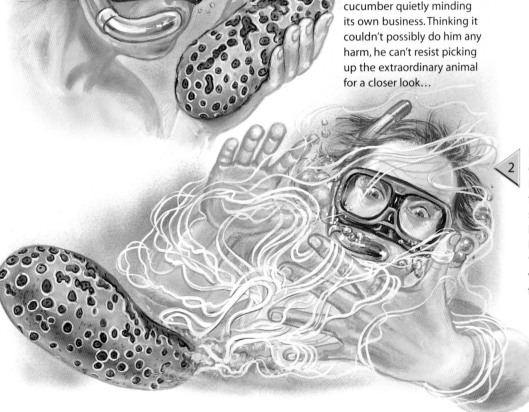

2 Instantly the sea cucumber shoots out its tubules, which coat the man's hands with sticky, stinging, holothurin toxins. He quickly drops the "cuke," but his hands will be red and sore for days.

Did You Know?

● Many sea cucumbers ooze toxins from their skin, and some Pacific islanders use particularly toxic ones to poison fish by filling reef pools with them.

● Pacific islanders also use the Cuvierian tubules of sea cucumbers to "sterilize" coral cuts and grazes.

● If you cut some species of sea cucumber in two, each half grows into a new sea cucumber.

● Many species look the same, but each has uniquely shaped ossicles in its skin. In prehistoric species, these formed a solid outer skeleton.

● Several species of pearlfish (family *Carapidae*) live inside sea cucumbers. Small and slender, a pearlfish enters a sea cucumber's anus tail-first and uses it as a safe hidey-hole. The fish darts out to grab tidbits but also nibbles on its host's insides. These grow back, so the sea cucumber isn't harmed.

SALTWATER CROCODILE

Latin name: *Crocodylus porosus*

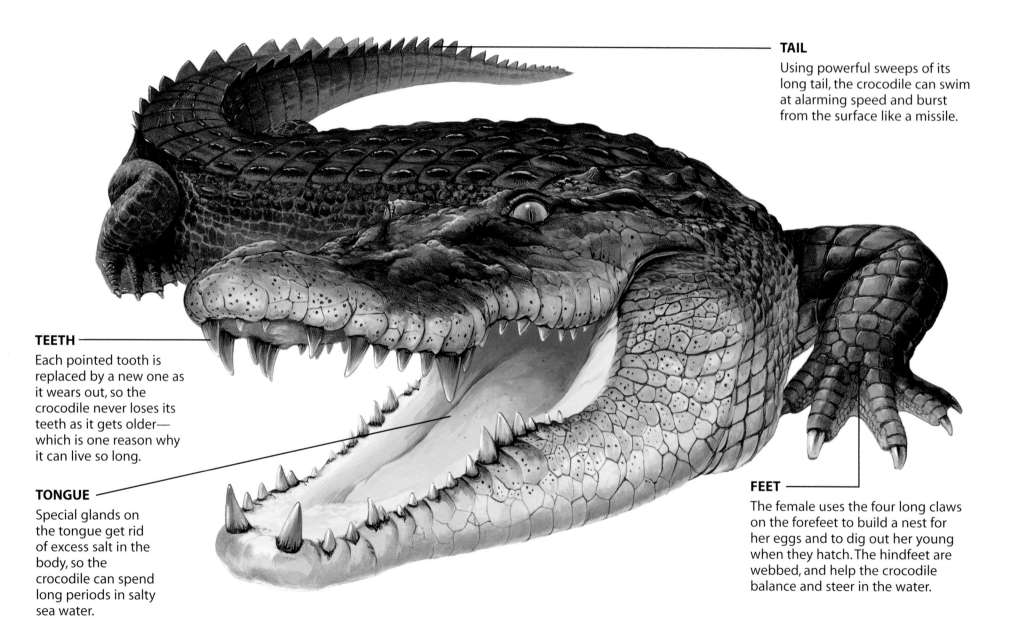

TAIL

Using powerful sweeps of its long tail, the crocodile can swim at alarming speed and burst from the surface like a missile.

TEETH

Each pointed tooth is replaced by a new one as it wears out, so the crocodile never loses its teeth as it gets older—which is one reason why it can live so long.

TONGUE

Special glands on the tongue get rid of excess salt in the body, so the crocodile can spend long periods in salty sea water.

FEET

The female uses the four long claws on the forefeet to build a nest for her eggs and to dig out her young when they hatch. The hindfeet are webbed, and help the crocodile balance and steer in the water.

This leathery monster is the world's biggest living reptile and also one of the most dangerous. Its gnarled, ancient features awaken a primeval fear in humans—mainly because of its rightful reputation as a man-eater. Any intruder on its lair is fair game for the saltwater crocodile. For such a heavy beast, it can launch an attack with terrifying speed, grabbing a victim and wrestling it into a watery grave.

Size

KEY DATA

LENGTH	Average 15ft (4.5m), but monsters of 23ft (7m) have been seen
WEIGHT	Average 1102lb (500kg); up to 2200lb (1000kg)
TEETH	64–68 sharp spikes, continually renewed
DIET	Fish, birds, pigs, deer, buffalo, monkeys, and people; also carrion
METHOD OF ATTACK	Ambush and drowning
LIFESPAN	Up to 100 years and possibly longer

The saltwater crocodile lives in rivers, estuaries, and coastal waters in tropical parts of the Indo-Pacific: from India, through Sumatra, Borneo, the Philippines, and New Guinea, to northern Australia and Fiji.

1 ▷ A water buffalo visits a cool river in rural Malaysia to slake its thirst. It neither sees nor hears the crocodile that glides, low in the water, to within striking distance. Suddenly, the reptilian killer hurls its mighty body from the water and slams its jaws shut around the buffalo's neck.

2 The crocodile hauls the buffalo out into midwater, its jaws holding the helpless, bellowing mammal in a vicelike grip. With a single flip of its broad tail, the crocodile drags the buffalo's head below water to drown the victim.

3 The crocodile cannot chew, and must reduce the size of its meal by violently shaking the carcass to pieces. Sometimes it sinks its spiked teeth into the body and whirls around, ripping away great chunks of hide, flesh, and bone.

Did You Know?

● Some stories tell of saltwater crocodiles 33ft (10m) long. The crocodile continues growing all its life, so such tales could well be true.

● A crocodile often swallows stones to grind up the food in its stomach. Similar stones have been found with dinosaur fossils.

● On one night in 1945, saltwater crocodiles were reported to have killed more than 500 Japanese soldiers trying to escape from a swampy island near Burma.

● So terrifying is the saltwater crocodile that it is often shot on sight. It is becoming rare, and is now protected in some countries.

GHARIAL
Latin name: *Gavialis gangeticus*

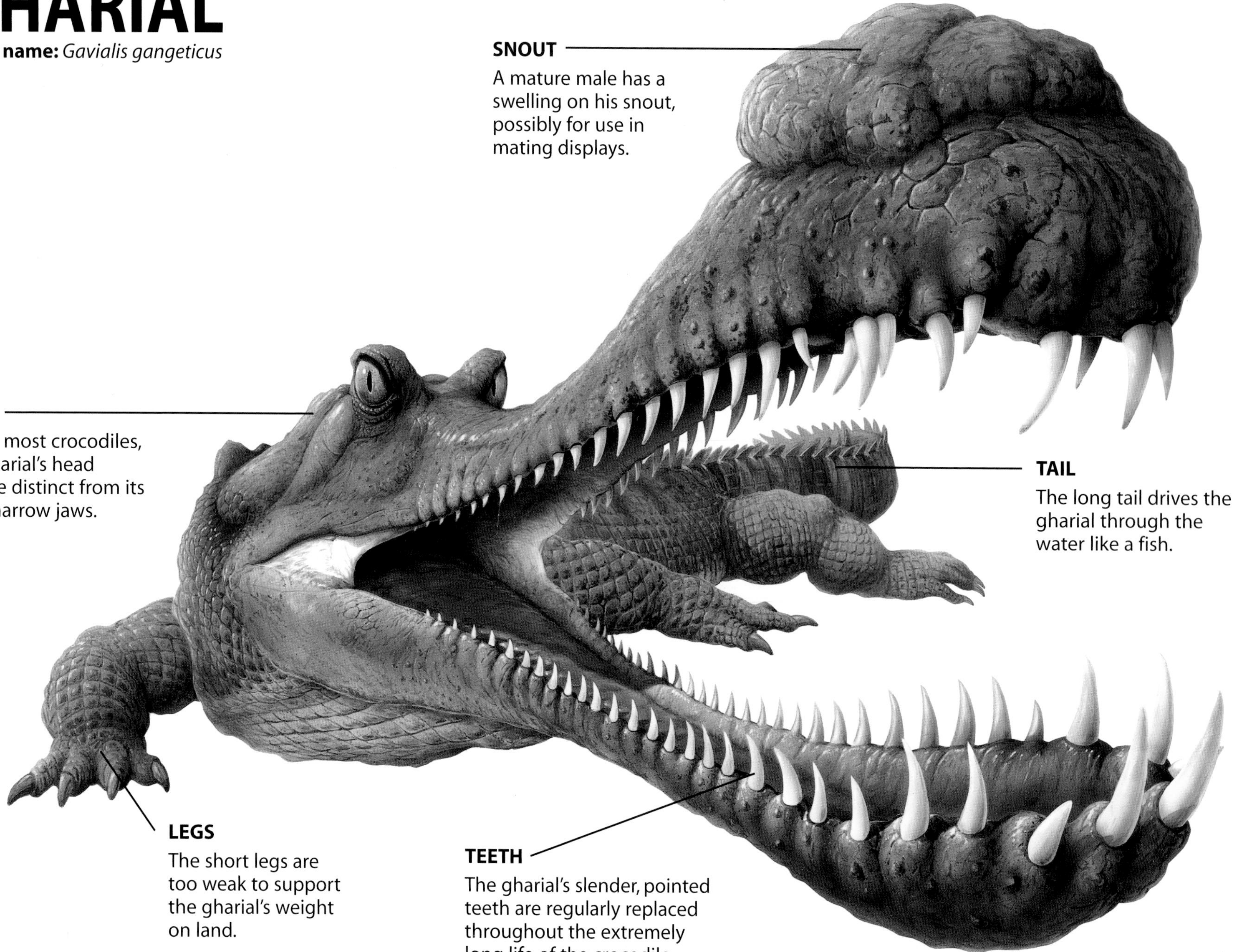

SNOUT
A mature male has a
swelling on his snout,
possibly for use in
mating displays.

HEAD
Unlike most crocodiles,
the gharial's head
is quite distinct from its
long, narrow jaws.

TAIL
The long tail drives the
gharial through the
water like a fish.

LEGS
The short legs are
too weak to support
the gharial's weight
on land.

TEETH
The gharial's slender, pointed
teeth are regularly replaced
throughout the extremely
long life of the crocodile.

A gharial's extremely long, slim snout is lined with rows of horribly sharp teeth—perfect for snatching a big, juicy catfish from the river. Armed with long, powerful jaws and more than 100 viciously sharp teeth, this colossal crocodile from Asia can do serious damage to anyone who gets in its way. A gharial loves a big catfish and gobbles one up as soon as it swims into range. Unfortunately, if someone fishing hooks a catfish on a line and its violent struggles attract a gharial, the beast won't hesitate to launch a nightmare attack.

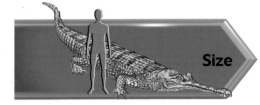
Size

KEY DATA

LENGTH	Up to 23ft (7m)	
WEIGHT	Up to 551lb (250kg)	
PREY	Mainly fish	The gharial lives in the rivers of Pakistan, Nepal, northern India, Bhutan, Bangladesh, and Burma (Myanmar), but is now scarce in most countries. Its favored habitats are the calmer stretches of fast-moving rivers and estuaries.
WEAPONS	Powerful jaws lined with rows of sharp teeth	
LIFESPAN	Possibly up to 100 years	

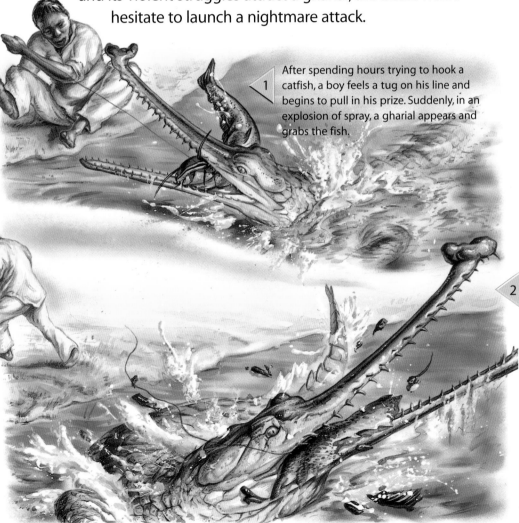

1 After spending hours trying to hook a catfish, a boy feels a tug on his line and begins to pull in his prize. Suddenly, in an explosion of spray, a gharial appears and grabs the fish.

2 With a jerk of its head, the beast snaps the line like a thread. The fish clamped between its jaws is too big to swallow whole, so the reptile thrashes its prey from side to side to break the meal into bite-size chunks. Meanwhile, the boy races to safety, grateful to escape with his life.

Did You Know?

● The gharial was once widespread throughout northern India and central Asia, but has been wiped out in many areas by human activity.

● The gharial is now rare and endangered in many regions, but in India its numbers are slowly growing thanks to captive breeding and conservation programs.

● A female lays an average of 40 eggs, but a clutch of 97 was once found. Many gharials die young, though, and only one in a hundred survives to breeding age.

● The "potlike" swelling on the male's snout surrounds the nostrils, and so may work as a resonator to amplify the loud whistles and hisses that the crocodile uses to attract a female during the breeding season. The female responds with similar calls, but they are much softer and quieter, perhaps because she lacks the male's amplifying equipment.

AQUATIC LEECH

Latin name: *Hirudinidae* family

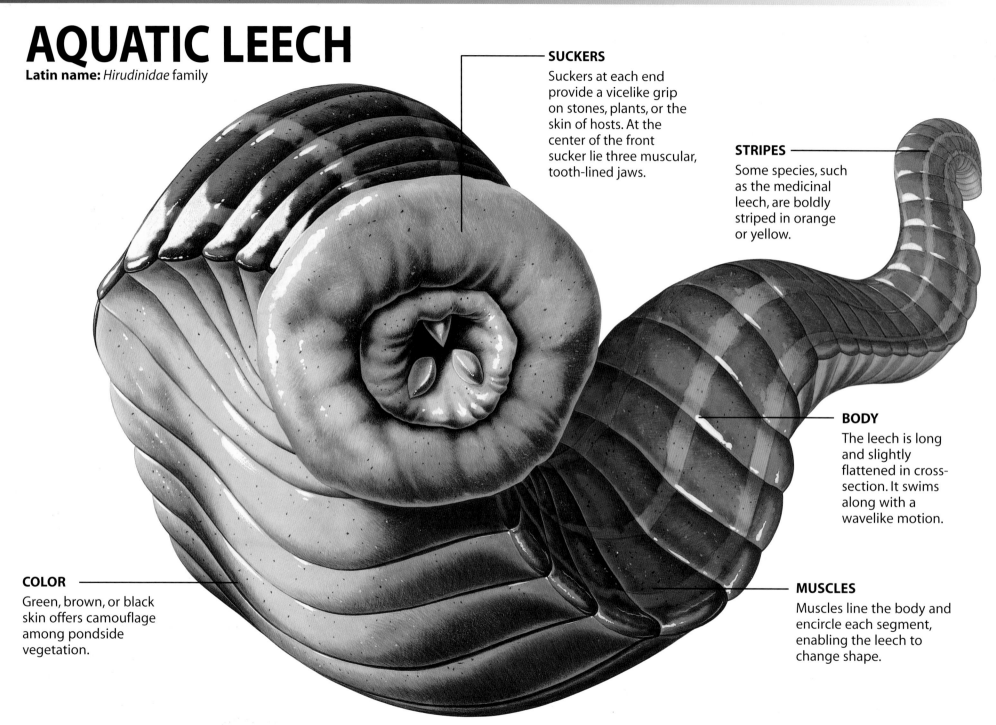

SUCKERS
Suckers at each end provide a vicelike grip on stones, plants, or the skin of hosts. At the center of the front sucker lie three muscular, tooth-lined jaws.

STRIPES
Some species, such as the medicinal leech, are boldly striped in orange or yellow.

BODY
The leech is long and slightly flattened in cross-section. It swims along with a wavelike motion.

COLOR
Green, brown, or black skin offers camouflage among pondside vegetation.

MUSCLES
Muscles line the body and encircle each segment, enabling the leech to change shape.

Of all the nightmare creatures in nature, few are more hated than the parasitic leeches. With their slithery sluglike body, savage jaws, and grisly thirst for blood—even our own—they are guaranteed to make anyone's flesh crawl. For a horse taking a cool drink of water, there's only one thing worse than walking away with a leech stuck fast to a leg. Some small leeches can swim in to the mouth or squirm in through a nostril—and the result can be deadly.

1 Keen to slake its thirst on a summer's day, a horse lowers its head to drink from a shallow pool. But it doesn't know the pond is the home of Limnatis leeches. As the horse draws in water, a leech slips inside its mouth unnoticed. It uses the powerful suckers at each end of its body to grip the throat lining and avoid being washed down. As it happens, this proves an ideal picnic site.

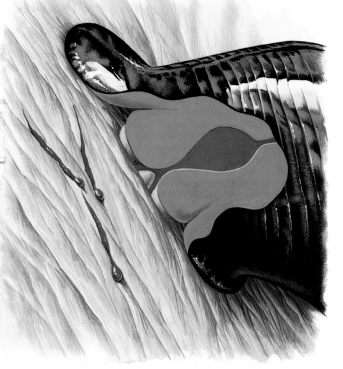

2 The throat lining is richly supplied with blood vessels. Using its three jaws, the leech cuts three slits in the thin skin. Then it drinks. It may stay in place for days or even weeks, growing ever fatter. If lots of leeches enter at one time and attack the respiratory passages, the body tissues can swell up so much that an animal dies from suffocation.

actual Size

KEY DATA

LENGTH	Usually ¾–1½in (2–4cm); some reach over 6in (15cm) at full stretch
DIET	Fresh blood of vertebrates
FEEDING METHOD	Cuts skin with triple jaws; sucks up free-flowing blood
LIFESPAN	Up to 20 years

Freshwater leeches range throughout the world, occurring almost wherever there is still or slow-flowing water. They're absent north of the Arctic Circle, and from a few lands in the extreme south.

Did You Know?

● Some water-dwelling leeches such as the European horse leech have abandoned the blood-sucking habit. They have only weak jaws, and live instead by sucking up whole molluscs, worms, and insect larvae.

● There are also leeches that live on land; they lurk in moist habitats such as tropical forests and drop on to passing animals or people. The only European land leech, *Xerobdella lecontei*, lives in the meadows of the Alps, where it sucks the blood of an amphibian, the Alpine salamander.

● Another group of leeches that dwell both in fresh water and in the seas specialize in sucking fish blood.

● Adults pass on stocks of helpful gut bacteria to their young, by secreting the microbes into the protective cocoon that holds their developing eggs. When the young leeches hatch, they eat some of the bacteria and are soon ready to digest their first blood meal.

SEA SNAKE
Latin name: Subfamily *Hydrophiinae*

SCALES

In some species, the scales overlap, like roof tiles; in others, they butt up to one another.

TAIL

Beating its flattened tail from side to side, the sea snake drives itself through the water.

NOSTRILS

When the sea snake dives, valvelike flaps close off the nostrils on top of its snout.

TONGUE

Glands under the tongue produce a salty brine that's secreted into the tongue sheath. So by sticking out its tongue, the snake passes excess salt from its body back into the sea.

BODY

The body contains a specially adapted lung that stretches almost to the tip of the tail. This long reservoir of air enables the snake to stay submerged for more than three hours at a time.

Perfectly adapted for hunting underwater, a sea snake glides elegantly through rocks and weeds. Its two pairs of fangs are erect and primed with the strongest venom known in snakes, ready to kill in an instant. A slinky, twisting death-dealer, the blue-banded sea snake slips easily through a coral reef. Its head and neck fit into the narrowest crevices to rout out prey, while it curls its burly body to cut off any escape route.

Size

1 Alerted by the sea snake's shadow, an eel flits into a tiny gap in the coral. But the snake simply eases its narrow head in behind, blocking the entrance.

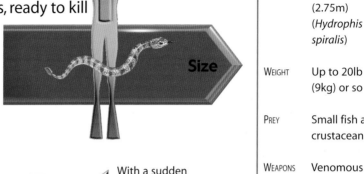

2 With a sudden lunge, the snake plunges its fangs into the eel's plump body, injecting a dose of numbing venom as the eel wriggles in vain.

3 The venom courses rapidly through the eel's body, affecting its nervous system and stopping its heart with brutal efficiency. Soon the eel's struggles are over, and its limp form floats free of the crevice. The sea snake feasts, gradually forcing the meaty meal head-first down its throat.

KEY DATA

LENGTH	Up to 9ft (2.75m) (*Hydrophis spiralis*)
WEIGHT	Up to 20lb (9kg) or so
PREY	Small fish and crustaceans
WEAPONS	Venomous fangs
SPEED	12–36in/second (30–90cm/second)

Most sea snakes live along the coasts of Australia and southeast Asia, especially Indonesia, Sumatra, and Japan. The yellow-bellied sea snake reaches western America and eastern Africa.

Did You Know?

● A sea snake usually sheds its skin every couple of weeks to get rid of the growth of small underwater organisms. Tying itself in knots, it pulls its body through the loops to leave the discarded skin behind.

● A witness on a passing ship in the Malacca Straits off Malaysia once saw a solid line, 10ft (3m) wide and 56 miles (90km) long, of Stoke's sea snakes. It wasn't clear whether they were migrating, breeding, hunting, or simply caught in the cross-current.

● The sea snake *Emydocephalus annulatus* feeds mainly on fish eggs, diving head first into the sand to find them. It never needs to subdue its "prey," so has almost completely lost its fangs and venom glands.

● The most venomous sea snake in the world is *Hydrophis belcheri*, which is found off the coast of northwest Australia. Its venom is five times more toxic than that of any land snake.

LEOPARD SEAL

Latin name: *Hydrurga leptonyx*

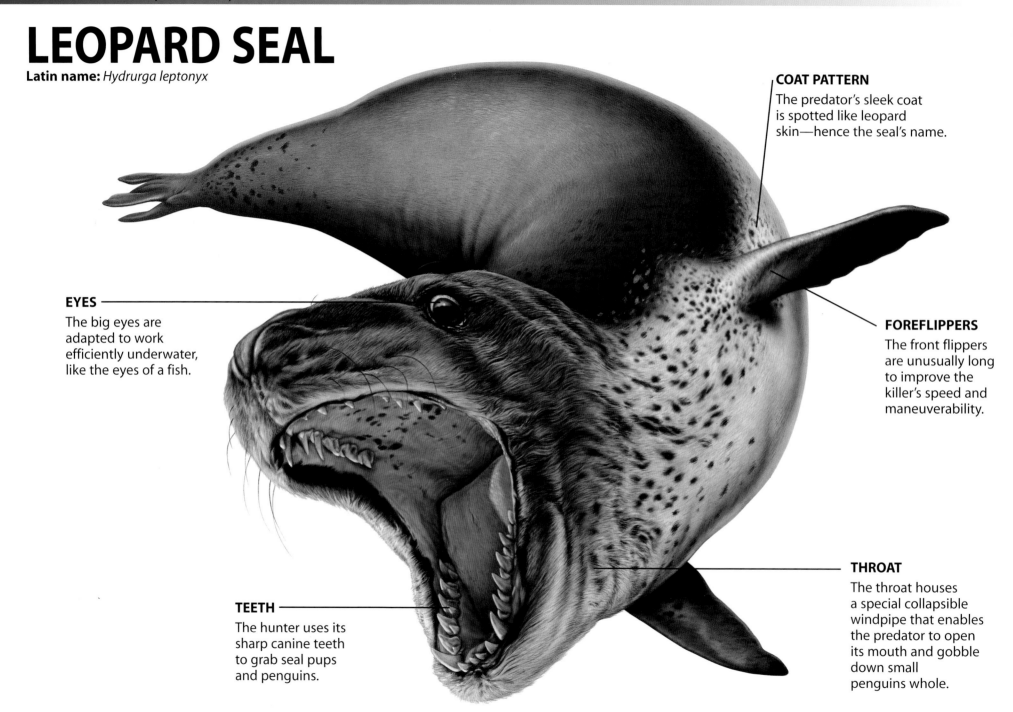

COAT PATTERN
The predator's sleek coat is spotted like leopard skin—hence the seal's name.

EYES
The big eyes are adapted to work efficiently underwater, like the eyes of a fish.

FOREFLIPPERS
The front flippers are unusually long to improve the killer's speed and maneuverability.

TEETH
The hunter uses its sharp canine teeth to grab seal pups and penguins.

THROAT
The throat houses a special collapsible windpipe that enables the predator to open its mouth and gobble down small penguins whole.

A leopard seal is a brutal but inefficient killer. Lurking in ambush beneath an Antarctic ice pack, it launches murderous attacks on seal pups and penguins—yet leaves many of its victims bruised, scarred, bloodied but alive. With its huge gape and long teeth, the leopard seal makes a dangerous enemy and Antarctic workers have learned to treat it with respect.

Size

KEY DATA

LENGTH	Up to 11ft (3.6m)	
WEIGHT	Up to 1322lb (600kg)	
PREY	Penguins, small seals, fish, squid, and krill	
WEAPONS	Long teeth; powerful jaws	
LIFESPAN	25 years or more	

The leopard seal is common among the floating pack ice surrounding Antarctica, and the animal often ventures farther north to subantarctic islands such as South Georgia. Some leopard seals even reach as far north as Australia, South America, and southern Africa.

1 Three Antarctic researchers are inspecting a gap in the pack ice. Without warning, an angry leopard seal bursts from the water and grabs one of the men by the leg.

2 As the seal tears at the victim's flesh with its teeth, one of his colleagues lashes out at the animal's head with the spikes of his crampons. His kicks force the animal to let go.

3 The uninjured men start to carry their wounded friend back to camp, leaving a long trail of blood. But the leopard seal is not so easily put off, and it surges out of the water again, with a last defiant roar.

Did You Know?

● When a leopard seal is searching for prey, it often rears up out of the water to check the pack ice for possible victims, then sinks below the surface to wait in ambush.

● When it attacks another seal, the leopard seal usually eats only the skin and insulating blubber, and discards all the meat.

● Female leopard seals have never been seen to hunt penguins, so it seems to be a speciality of a few males who live near the penguin breeding colonies. No one knows why females show so little interest.

● Since leopard seals are clumsy out of the water, prey animals such as crabeater seals can safely rest on ice floes alongside them.

● The leopard seal uses its large eyes mainly to find quarry, but in murky conditions it uses its sensitive whiskers to detect slight vibrations generated in the water by victims.

SEA KRAIT

Latin name: *Laticauda* species

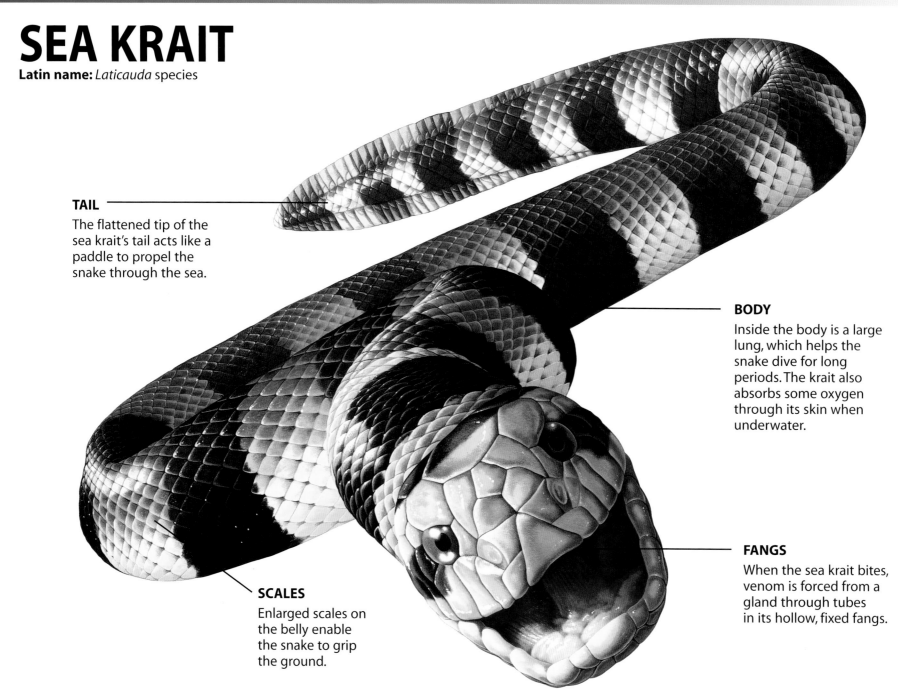

TAIL

The flattened tip of the sea krait's tail acts like a paddle to propel the snake through the sea.

BODY

Inside the body is a large lung, which helps the snake dive for long periods. The krait also absorbs some oxygen through its skin when underwater.

SCALES

Enlarged scales on the belly enable the snake to grip the ground.

FANGS

When the sea krait bites, venom is forced from a gland through tubes in its hollow, fixed fangs.

Unlike other marine snakes, the sea krait spends much time on land and is at ease both in and out of water. The highly venomous sea krait slips menacingly into the sea in the dead of night and glides along coral reefs, ready to strike at prey with its deadly fangs. The sea krait hunts in the dark, probing nooks and crannies in coral reefs for fish, particularly tasty eels. When the snake finds its prey, it loops its body to block the creature's escape route before making the fatal strike.

Size

1 ▷ A sea krait slips into the surf at dusk, just as the sun is setting low over the horizon. As the snake cruises along the coral reef, its tongue flicks in and out repeatedly, "tasting" the water for the slightest tell-tale scent of eels.

2 ▷ When it finds its prey, the sea krait bites with a lightning-fast strike and holds the eel firmly, pumping venom into the fish with its fangs. At first, the eel writhes violently in an attempt to escape, but soon its strength weakens as the venom courses through its body and paralyzes its nervous system.

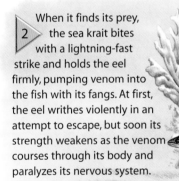

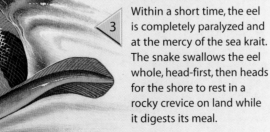

3 ▷ Within a short time, the eel is completely paralyzed and at the mercy of the sea krait. The snake swallows the eel whole, head-first, then heads for the shore to rest in a rocky crevice on land while it digests its meal.

KEY DATA

LENGTH	Up to 4 1/2ft (1.4m); females are larger
PREY	Fish, especially eels
WEAPONS	Fixed, hollow fangs inject a powerful venom that attacks the nervous system, causing paralysis and death
HABITAT	Coastal waters, reefs, atolls, rocky shores, mangrove swamps, and lagoons
NUMBER OF EGGS	Female lays up to 20 cylindrical eggs on land
LIFESPAN	Unknown

The sea krait is found in the seas and oceans around southeastern Asia, the southwestern Pacific islands, and northern Australia. Four of the five species inhabit coastal waters, but one species lives only in a land-locked, brackish lagoon on Rennell Island, one of the Solomon Islands, in the Pacific Ocean.

Did You Know?

● Many sea kraits are caught each year for their skin and meat, but the impact of this onslaught on the wild sea krait population is unknown.

● In some places, people eat the flesh of the sea krait in the belief that it acts as a "love potion."

● In winter, sea kraits gather by the thousand on sandy islets to mate. The females often lay their eggs in caves, where dripping water keeps them moist. When they hatch some four or five months later, the baby snakes make straight for the sea.

● The sea krait gets its name from the land krait of southeastern Asia, because it has similar bright bands.

ALLIGATOR SNAPPING TURTLE
Latin name: *Macroclemys temminckii*

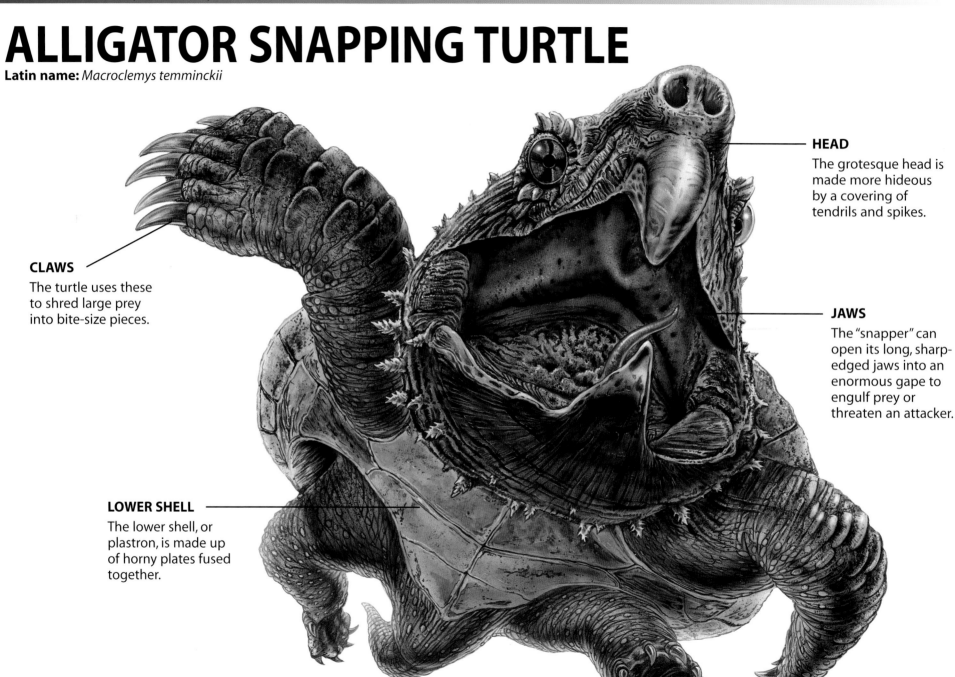

HEAD
The grotesque head is made more hideous by a covering of tendrils and spikes.

CLAWS
The turtle uses these to shred large prey into bite-size pieces.

JAWS
The "snapper" can open its long, sharp-edged jaws into an enormous gape to engulf prey or threaten an attacker.

LOWER SHELL
The lower shell, or plastron, is made up of horny plates fused together.

The alligator snapping turtle lurks in the murky depths like a demon. Its armory of horny plates, scales, and nightmare jaws and talons makes sure that the toughest turtle-hunter treats the reptile with caution and respect. This hideous reptile is undisputed ruler of its watery realm. With its pincer jaws and ripping claws, it has little to fear from bigger beasts and regards smaller creatures as lunch.

Size

KEY DATA

LENGTH	Up to 30in (80cm), with a tail as long	The alligator snapping turtle lives in waters that drain into the Gulf of Mexico in southeastern USA. It is found in all river systems from the Swanee River in Florida to eastern Texas, and from as far north as Kansas, Illinois, and Indiana down to the Gulf. The snapper likes deep, slow-running rivers, canals, lakes, swamps, and bayous.
WEIGHT	Up to 176lb (80kg)	
DIET	Fish, mollusks, snakes, frogs, reptiles, mammals, birds, carrion, and some plants	
LIFESPAN	Up to 70 years in captivity	

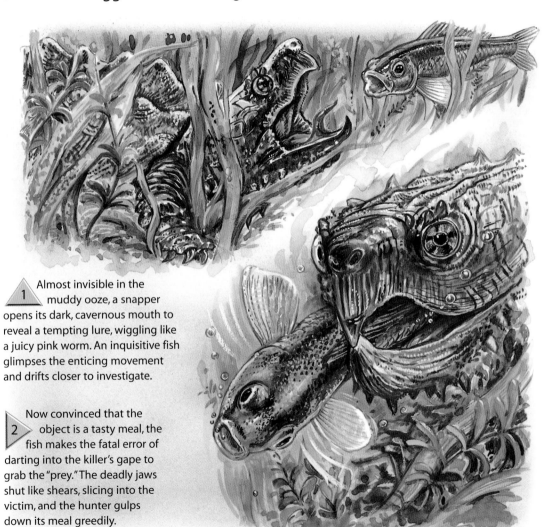

1 Almost invisible in the muddy ooze, a snapper opens its dark, cavernous mouth to reveal a tempting lure, wiggling like a juicy pink worm. An inquisitive fish glimpses the enticing movement and drifts closer to investigate.

2 Now convinced that the object is a tasty meal, the fish makes the fatal error of darting into the killer's gape to grab the "prey." The deadly jaws shut like shears, slicing into the victim, and the hunter gulps down its meal greedily.

Did You Know?

● Humans pose a double threat to the alligator snapping turtle. It is hunted for meat, and much of its marshland habitat is now being drained for farmland. The turtle is on the World Wildlife Federation's Top Ten endangered list.

● Lying motionless on the muddy bottom, the alligator snapping turtle stays submerged for 40–50 minutes before it must surface for air.

● An alligator snapping turtle bites by reflex and its jaws maintain their vicelike grip even after its head is cut off.

● The male snapping turtle never leaves its watery home willingly; the female goes on dry land only to lay her eggs, close to the water's edge.

● The sex of turtle hatchlings is governed by temperature; warm eggs at the top of a buried clutch produce females, while the cooler eggs lower down produce males.

ELEPHANT SEAL

Latin name: *Mirounga angustirostris & M. leonina*

NOSE
This reaches full size only when the male is about eight years old.

REAR FLIPPERS
Like propellers, these muscular limbs work closely together to provide the thrust to power the seal after fast-swimming prey.

NECK
The skin of the male's neck is extra-thick to absorb the blows of a rival's teeth. And as scar tissue builds up, it gets even thicker.

FRONT FLIPPERS
Important for steering when underwater, the front flippers also enable the seal to heave its huge bulk around on land.

TEETH
Long canine teeth are the male's main weapons and he uses them at every opportunity to wound and drive off rivals.

The elephant seal looks like a gigantic slug on land, but don't be fooled. Adult males are armed with nasty teeth and fight ferociously on their breeding beaches, trying to round up every female in sight. In the breeding season, an elephant seal beach is no place for the faint of heart. Every inch of sand and rock is occupied by blubber, and the burly males engage in brutal fights that end only when one seal admits defeat.

Size

KEY DATA

LENGTH	Male 13–16ft (4–5m); female 7–10ft (2–3m)	
WEIGHT	Male 6.5–8 tons (2–2.7 tonnes); female 3.2 tons (1 tonne)	The southern species of elephant seal (*M. leonina*) breeds on southern Atlantic and Pacific coasts around the world and feeds as far south as Antarctica. *M. angustirostris*, the northern species, breeds on the west coast of Baja California and feeds as far north as Alaska.
DIET	Fish and squid	
WEAPONS	Huge bulk and canine teeth	
LIFESPAN	Up to 25 years	

1 A dominant male must always be on his guard against sneaky rivals. If another male dares try to muscle in and steal his group of females, he instantly rushes over and challenges the trespasser to a no-holds-barred scrap.

2 If the challenger refuses to back down, the fight is on. The beasts rear up in fury and then stab down repeatedly with their huge canine teeth, inflicting deep and bloody gashes to the head and neck. Eventually, exhaustion usually beats the challenger, who slopes away, the bellows of the victor ringing in his ears.

Did You Know?

● When adult elephant seals are on land in the breeding season, they don't eat at all: a period of fasting that can last up to four months.

● The snarling roar of an angry male elephant seal can easily be heard up to ⅔ mile (1km) away.

● Rampaging male elephant seals squash to death up to 10 percent of all pups each breeding season.

● In the crowded conditions of the breeding beaches, enterprising pups suckle from other mothers as well as their own. Male pups that do this get an extra boost of food and often grow into big, dominant bulls.

● The oldest known seal fossils date from only 12–15 million years ago. Scientists think seals evolved from otter-like creatures.

● The southern elephant seal can reach a top speed of 16mph (25km/h) when chasing prey underwater.

NARWHAL

Latin name: *Monodon monoceros*

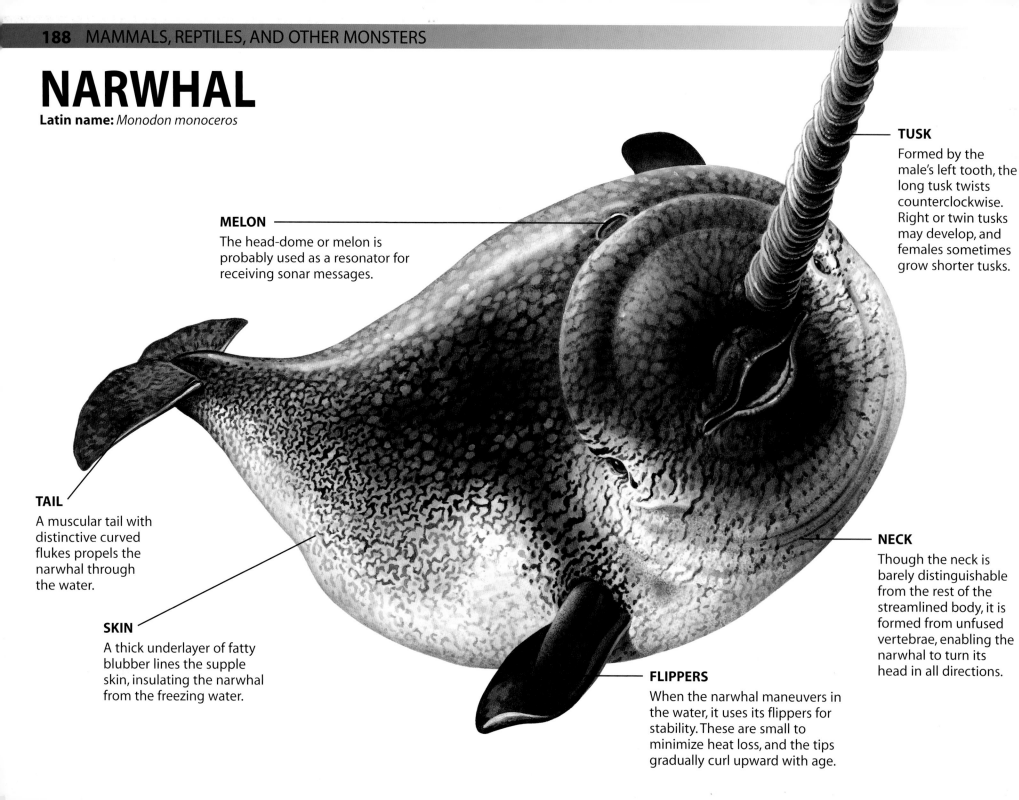

TUSK
Formed by the male's left tooth, the long tusk twists counterclockwise. Right or twin tusks may develop, and females sometimes grow shorter tusks.

MELON
The head-dome or melon is probably used as a resonator for receiving sonar messages.

TAIL
A muscular tail with distinctive curved flukes propels the narwhal through the water.

SKIN
A thick underlayer of fatty blubber lines the supple skin, insulating the narwhal from the freezing water.

NECK
Though the neck is barely distinguishable from the rest of the streamlined body, it is formed from unfused vertebrae, enabling the narwhal to turn its head in all directions.

FLIPPERS
When the narwhal maneuvers in the water, it uses its flippers for stability. These are small to minimize heat loss, and the tips gradually curl upward with age.

Male narwhals are the unicorns of the icy seas, sporting spiraling tusks that may have inspired the image of their mythical counterparts. This strange relative of the dolphin dives deep in search of fish and squid. Gulping its prey down whole, it converts the flesh into protective rolls of fat. Like rival stags, male narwhals use their tusks for status displays and jousting contests in the mating season. Youngsters engage in more light-hearted tustles, but older narwhals battle fiercely and inflict deep and lasting wounds.

Size

As a female narwhal watches from a distance, two mature males surge out of the icy water and meet head on, clashing tusks with a noisy rattle. With slashing swipes, each one tries to spear his opponent, and blood wells up from numerous gouge wounds on their flanks. These dueling matches leave permanent scars, and if the loser is unlucky, he may even end up with a broken tusk.

KEY DATA

BODY LENGTH	Male 16–19ft (5–6m); female 13–16ft (4–5m)	
TUSK	Male 7–10ft (2–3m), up to 22lb (10kg)	
WEIGHT	Male 3530–3970lb (1600–1800kg); female 1985–3970lb (900–1600kg)	The narwhal lives mainly in waters north of the Arctic Circle, its habitat extending right to the edge of the icecap. In summer, large numbers are often found in the Davis Strait, Baffin Bay, and the Greenland Sea.
PREY	Mainly squid, crabs, shrimp, and fish: flounder, halibut, salmon, Arctic cod, and char	
ENEMIES	Killer whales and humans	
LIFESPAN	50 years	

Did You Know?

● The name "narwhal" comes from the old Norse term *náhvair*, meaning "corpse-whale," due to the whale's resemblance to the bloated, floating corpse of a drowned human.

● The narwhal produces a wide range of clicks, whistles, and growls. These sounds can be heard inside the hulls of wooden ships, and may have given rise to legends of siren songs.

● A narwhal calf starts life a dark grey, but becomes lighter and more mottled as it ages. An old narwhal can be virtually white, like a beluga.

● Early theories suggested that the narwhal used its tusk to spear prey, break ice, or even to prop up its head.

GLOSSARY

AMPHIBIANS
Vertebrate animals that live in the water during their early life (breathing through gills), but usually live on land as adults (and breathe with lungs). They include frogs, toads, newts, salamanders, etc.

ANAL FINS
Paired fins near the tail end of some fish. Some sharks have an anal fin.

BARBELS
Barbels are sensory projections near the nostrils and mouth of some sharks.

CAMOUFLAGE
Natural adaptations of colour, shape or size that enable animals to blend with their surroundings.

CARNIVORE
A meat-eating creature that usually has sharp teeth and powerful jaws.

CARRION
The dead flesh of an animal. Many sharks, including the great white shark, eat carrion found floating the seas.

CARTILAGE
Sharks' skeletons are made out of cartilage, not bone.

CLASS
In classification, a class is a group of related or similar organisms. A class contains one or more orders. A group of similar classes forms a phylum.

COUNTERSHADING
A type of body coloration that sharks and some other animals have in which the top and bottom sides are colored differently, serving to camouflage the animal from different perspectives. In sharks, the top is much darker than the belly. When the shark is viewed from above, its dark top surface blends into the dark ocean depths or ocean floor; when viewed from below, the light-colored belly blends in with the light above. This helps the shark when hunting, enabling it to sneak up on prey undetected.

CRUSTACEANS
An Arthropod with a toughened outer shell covering their body and typically jaws and gills. Most are aquatic.

DORSAL FIN
One of a fish's major fins; used to control speed and direction. The dorsal fin is located on its back.

ECHOLOCATION
Whales use echolocation to sense objects. In echolocation, a high-pitched sound (usually clicks) is sent out by the whale. The sound bounces off the object and some returns to the whale. The whale interprets this returning echo to determine the object's shape, direction, distance, and texture. Bats also use echolocation.

EXOSKELETON
A tough, structural body armor made of chitin. Arthropods (insects, arachnids, trilobites, crustaceans, etc.) have exoskeletons.

FILTER FEEDER
Animals that eat by sieving through lots of sea water and straining out tiny bits of nourishment. The Whale shark, Basking shark, and Megamouth shark are filter feeders, obtaining plankton by sieving water through their gill slits.

FLIPPER
Wide, flat forelimbs that many marine animals use for swimming. Whales (and other cetaceans), pinnipeds, and many other marine animals have flippers.

FLUKE
A single lobe of a whale's tail.

GENUS
In classification, a genus is a group of related or similar organisms. A genus contains one or more species. A group of similar genera (the plural of genus) forms a family. In the scientific name of an organism, the first name is its genus (for example, people are *Homo sapiens* - our genus is *Homo*).

INVERTEBRATE
Animals that don't have a backbone.

KRILL
Tiny animals, euphasiids, that float in the oceans. They are shrimp-like crustaceans that are found in vast amounts in the cold waters of the Arctic and Antarctic Oceans. Baleen whales eat krill that they sieve through their baleen.

LATERAL LINE
A sense organ used to detect movement and vibration in the surrounding water. Lateral lines are usually visible as faint lines running lengthwise down each side of the shark.

MAMMAL
Warm-blooded animals with hair that nourish their young with milk.

ORDER
In classification, an order is a group of related or similar organisms. An order contains one or more families. A group of similar orders forms a class.

PECTORAL FIN
Generally smaller side fins on a fish.

PREY
An animal is prey when another animal hunts and kills it for food.

REPTILE
Class of cold-blooded, air breathing animals. Reptiles usually have strong, scaly outer skin and lay eggs.

SPECIES
In classification, a species is a group of closely related organisms that can reproduce. A group of similar species forms a genus. In the scientific name of an organism, the second name is its species (for example, people are *Homo sapiens* - our species is *sapiens*).

SPIRACLE
A special gill slit found in some sharks. It is located just behind the eyes and supplies oxygen directly to the eyes and brain. Tiger sharks and angelsharks have spiracles.

VERTEBRATE
Animals that have a backbone.

INDEX

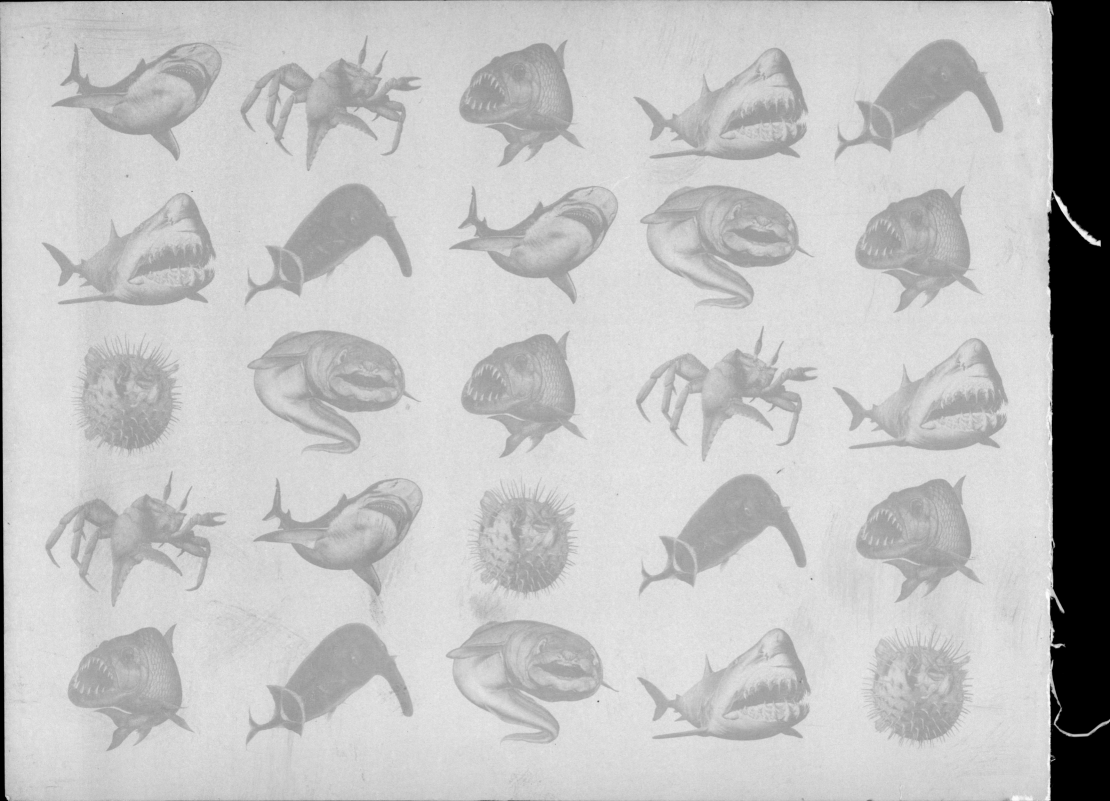